The Best Chinese Ci Poems

A Bilingual Approach to Interpretation and Appreciation

唐宋词双语析赏

The Best Chinese Ci Poems

A Bilingual Approach to Interpretation and Appreciation

唐宋词双语析赏

张畅繁译注

Translated and Annotated by

Edward C. Chang

Copyright © 2012 Edward C. Chang
All rights reserved
Printed in the United States of America

No part of this book may be reproduced or transmitted in any form or by any means, electronic, mechanical, including photocopying, recording, or by any information storage and retrieval system without the written permission of the author or publisher.

Library of Congress Cataloging-in-Publication Data

The Best Chinese Ci Poems: A Bilingual Approach to Interpretation and Appreciation / translated and annotated by Edward C. Chang, English and Chinese.

Publisher: Emnes Publishing
Fredericksburg, Virginia
www. emnespublishing.com

ISBN: 978-1469910796
1. Chinese *ci* poetry. 2. *Ci* poems. 3. Translations into English. 4. Bilingual approach. 5. Classical Chinese poetry. 6. Chinese song lyrics. 7. Chang, Edward.

Cover design by Mimi Chang

To the memory of my parents.

Contents

Preface

Part One
Introduction

    Translating Chinese Poetry: A Few Examples 3
    Factors Affecting Interpretation and Translation of Chinese Poetry 6
    Different Interpretations of Yan Jidao's Poem by Chinese Poetry Scholars 8
    How to Analyze a Poem from a Bilingual Perspective 12
    How to Analyze Yan Jidao's *Ci* Poem Written to the Tune of *Zhe Gu Tian* "Is This Reunion A Dream?" 17
    Basic Tone Patterns of *Ci* Poetry 21
    How to Remember Tones and tonal Patterns 23
    Should the Sound of the Original Poem Be a Factor in Translation? 28
    Analyzing Li Qingzhao's Poem "*Sheng Sheng Man*" 30
    Can You Create Your Own *Cipai*? 36

Part Two
The Tang and Southern Tang Period 41

Wen Tingyun   温庭筠   43

Make-up in the Morning
Tune: *"Pu Sa Man"*   44

Dreaming in Autumn
Tune: *"Pu Sa Man"*   46

When Will You Come Home?
Tune: *"Pu Sa Man"*   48

One Autumn Night
Tune: *"Geng Lou Zi"*   50

Feelings at Night
Tune: *"Geng Lou Zi"*   52

Waiting and Waiting
Tune: *"Meng Jiang Nan"*   54

So Many Regrets
Tune: "Meng Jiang Nan"   56

Wei Zhuang 韦庄   59

Grow Old in Jiangnan
Tune: *"Pu Sa Man"*   60

Dreaming in Autumn
Tune: *"Pu Sa Man"*   62

Get Intoxicated
Tune: *"Pu Sa Man"*   64

Longing
Tune: *"Wan Xi Sha"*   66

Feelings at Night
Tune: *"Qing Ping Le"*   68

On this Day Last Year
Tune: *"Nu Guan Zi"*   70

In My Dream
Tune: *"Nu Guan Zi"*   72

Feng Yan Si   冯延巳   75

Feelings of Melancholy
Tune: *"Que Ta Zhi"*   76

Spring Feelings
Tune: *"Que Ta Zhi"*   78

When Will You Come Home?
Tune: *"Que Ta Zhi"*   80

Uneasy Feelings
Tune: *"Ye Jin Men"*   82

Melancholy Mood
Tune: *"Cai Sang Zi"*   84

After the Rain
Tune: *"Qing Ping Le"*   86

Loneliness
Tune: *"Nan Xiang Zi"*   88

Li Yu   李煜   91

My Lost Kingdom

Tune: *"Yu Mei Ren"*   92

Autumn Sorrow
Tune: *"Xiang Jian Huan"*   94

Farewell Song
Tune: *"Po Zhen Zi"*   96

Raining at Night
Tune: *"Lang Tao Sha"*   98

Sad feelings
Tune: *"Lang Tao Sha"*   100

Awakening from a Dream
Tune: *"Zi Ye Ge"*   102

Flowers in the Woods
Tune: *"Wu Ye Ti"*   104

Sneaking Out
Tune: *"Pu Sa Man"*   106

Sound of Autumn
Tune: *"Wu Ye Ti"*   108

Dream
Tune: *"Wang Jiang Nan"*   110

Parting Sorrow
Tune: *"Qing Ping Le"*   112

A Fisherman's Song
Tune: *"Yu Fu Ci"*   114

Sleepless Night
Tune: *"Dao Lian Zi"*   116

Song and Music
Tune: *"Yu Lou Chun"*   118

Charming and Captivating
Tune: *"Yi Hu Zhu"*   120

Part Three
The Early and Middle Northern Song Period   123

Liu Yong 柳永   125

Parting
Tune: *"Yu Lin Ling"*   126

Melancholy in Spring
Tune: *"Feng Qi Wu"*   130

Thinking of You in Autumn
Tune: *"Ba Sheng Gan Zhou"*   132

On Failing the Civil Service Examination
Tune: *"He Chong Tian"*   136

Zhang Xian 张先   141

Thinking of My Beloved
Tune: *"Pu Sa Man"*   142

Playing the Song of Xiang River
Tune: *"Pu Sa Man"*   144

Parting of Spring
Tune: *"Tian Xian Zi"* 146

Brief Encounter
Tune: *"Su Zhong Qing"* 148

Feeling Sad at Late Spring
Tune: *"Qian Qiu Sui"* 150

Night Thought
Tune: *"Qing Men Yin"* 154

Yan Shu 晏殊 157

Last Year
Tune: *"Wan Xi Sha"* 158

Now Is the Time?
Tune: *"Wan Xi Sha"* 160

Love Sickness
Tune: *"Qing Ping Le"* 162

Where to Send My Letter?
Tune: *"Die Lian Hua"* 164

Don't Be the Only Sobering Person
Tune: *"Mu Lan Hua"* 166

Lovesickness
Tune: *"Mu Lan Hua"* 168

Ouyan Xiu 欧阳修 171

So Deep Is the Courtyard
Tune: *"Die Lian Hua"*   172

Lantern Festival
Tune: *"Sheng Cha Zi"*   174

The West Lake
Tune: *"Cai Sang Zi"*   176

The West Lake Remains Beautiful
Tune: *"Cai Sang Zi"*   178

This Year's Flowers
Tune: *"Lang Tao Sha"*   180

Parting Grief
Tune: *"Ta Suo Xing"*   182

Pretending
Tune: *"Su Zhong Qing"*   184

Waiting
Tune: *"Lin Jiang Xian"*   186

Where Are You?
Tune: *"Yu Lou Chun"*   188

Feelings of Uneasiness
Tune: *"Die Lian Hua"*   190

Sentimental Feelings
Tune: *"Yu Lou Chun"*   192

Yan Jidao   晏几道   195

Is This Reunion A Dream?

Tune: *"Zhe Gu Tian"* 196

On Hearing Cuckoo's Crying at Night
Tune: *"Zhe Gu Tian"* 198

Her Manner of Singing
Tune: *"Zhe Gu Tian"* 200

Thinking of Xiao Ping
Tune: *"Ling Jiang Xian"* 202

Part Three
The Latter Northern Song Period 205

Su Shi 苏轼   207

Mid-Autumn Moon
Tune: *"Shui Diao Ge Tou"* 208

Reflecting on the Red Cliff
Tune: *"Nian Nu Jiao"* 212

In Loving Memory of My Wife
Tune: *"Jiang Cheng Zi"* 216

Late at Night
Tune: *"Lin Jiang Xian"* 220

Separated By a Wall
Tune: *"Die Lian Hua"* 222

A Fair Lady and Pomegranate Flowers
Tune: *"He Xin Lang"* 224

Residing at Dinghui Abbey
Tune: *"Bu Suan Zi"*   228

Hunting
Tune: *"Jiang Cheng Zi"*   230

Wind and Rain
Tune: *"Ding Feng Bo"*   234

Willow Catkins
Tune: *"Shui Long Yin"*   236

Dreaming of Someone at Swallow Pavilion
Tune: *"Joy of Eternal Union"*   240

A Spring Night
Tune: *"Xi Jiang Yue"*   244

Plum Flower
Tune: *"Xi Jiang Yue"*   246

Looking Up Northward
Tune: *"Xi Jiang Yue"*   248

Another Day
Tune: *"Zhe Gu Tian"*   250

Li Zhiyi 李之仪   253

I Live By the River's Head
Tune: *"Bu Suan Zi"*   254

Seeing Each Other
Tune: *"Xie Chi Chun"*   256

Huang Tingjian 黄庭坚 261

Where Did Spring Go?
Tune: *"Qing Ping Le"* 262

Be Myself
Tune: *"Zhe Gu Tian"* 264

Seeing Plum Flowers in the South
Tune: *"Yu Mei Ren"* 266

Peach Blossom
Tune: *"Shui Diao Ge Tou"* 268

Rainy Days
Tune: *"Din Feng Bo"* 272

Qin Guan 秦观 275

One Spring Morning
Tune: *"Wan Xi Sha"* 276

Cowherd and the Weaver
Tune: *"Que Qiao Xian"* 278

At a Lonely Inn
Tune: *"Ta Suo Xing"* 280

One Spring Morning
Tune: *"Ba Liu Zi"* 282

Parting
Tune: *"Man Ting Fang"* 286

Returning to West Town
Tune: *"Jiang Cheng Zi"* 290

No Need to Ask
Tune: *"Jiag Cheng Zi"* 292

A Dream
Tune: *"Hao Shi Jin"* 294

He Zhu 贺铸 297

Mourning
Tune: *"Che Gu Tian"* 298

Enjoy the Spring at Old Age
Tune: *"Wan Xi Sha"* 300

Spring Night
Tune: *"Wan Xi Sha"* 302

Beautiful Years
Tune: *"Qing Yu An"* 304

Peach Blossom
Tune: *"Die Lian Hua"* 306

Zhou Bang Yan 周邦彦 309

Don't Go Up the Highest Stair
Tune: *"Wan Xi Sha"* 310

Where Will You Stay for the Night?
Tune: *"Shao Nian You"* 312

Part Four
The Southern Song Period 315

Li Qingzhao 李清照　　317

Answering My Question
Tune: *"Ru Meng Ling"*　318

Thinner than the Yellow Flowers
Tune: *"Zui Hua Yin"*　320

A Heavy Load of Grief
Tune: *"Wu Ling Chun"*　322

Yearning
Tune: *"Yi Jian Mei"*　324

Returning Home on a Boat
Tune: *"Ru Meng Ling"*　326

Shyness
Tune: *"Dian Jiang Chun"*　328

Looking into the Distance
Tune: *"Dian Jiang Chun"*　330

Lovesickness
Tune: *"Feng Huang Tai Shang Yi Chui Xiao"* 332

Sad Feelings
Tune: *"Sheng, Sheng Man"*　336

Yue Fei 岳飞　　341

Reflections
Tune: *"Xiao Zhong Shan"*　342

To Recover Lost Land
Tune: *"Man Jiang Hong"*   344

Lu You   陆游   349

Plum Blossom
Tune: *"Bu Suan Zi"*   350

Wishes Not Fulfilled
Tune: *"Su Zhong Qing"*   352

On Hearing Cuckoo's Crying at Night
Tune: *"Que Qiao Xian"*   354

An Ordinary Fishman
Tune: *"Que Qiao Xian"*   356

Where to Send My Letter?
Tune: *"Chai Tou Feng"*   358

Away from the World
Tune: *"Zhe Gu Tian"*   360

Getting Old
Tune: *"Zhe Gu Tian"*   362

My Home
Tune: *"Zhe Gu Tian"*   364

Looking at South Mountain
Tune: *"Qiu Bo Mei"*   366

Thinking of My Brother
Tune: *"Yu Jia Ao"*   368

Don't Leave Me Behind

Tune: *"Wan Xi Sha"*   370

Spring Feelings
Tune: *"Lin Jiang Xian"*   372

Xing Qiji   辛弃疾   375

Written on the Wall
Tune: *"Pu Sa Man"*   376

Making Up the Feelings of Sorrow
Tune: *"Cai Sang Zi"*   378

Lantern Festival
Tune: *"Qing Yu An"*   380

Walking at Night on Yellow Sand Road
Tune: *"Xi Jiang Yue"*   382

Drunkenness
Tune: *"Xi Jiang Yue"*   384

Admonition to My Son
Tune: *"Xi Jiang Yue"*   386

Seeing a Friend Off
Tune: *"Zhe Gu Tian"*   388

Parting Sorrow: Writing for Someone
Tune: *"Zhe Gu Tian"*   390

Marching on the Road
Tune: *"Zhe Gu Tian"*   392

Sorrows
Tune: *"Zhe Gu Tian"*   394

Autumn Feelings
Tune: *"Ta Suo Xing"*   396

Rural Living
Tune: *"Qing Ping Le"*   398

Reflections at Night
Tune: *"Qing Ping Le"*   400

To Chen Liang: Military Review
Tune: *"Po Zhen Zi"*   402

On Wealth and Retirement: Chiding My Son
Tune: *"Zui Gao Lou"*   404

Jiang Kui 姜夔   409

Reflections
Tune: *"Dian Jiang Chun"*   410

A Dream on the Night of Lantern Festival
Tune: *"Zhe Gu Tian"*   412

A Beauty at Tiao Brook
Tune: *"Zhe Gu Tian"*   414

Seeing You in My Dream
Tune: *"Ta Suo Xing"*   416

Nebulous Fragrance
Tune: *"An Xiang"*   418

The Plum Blossoms
Tune: *"Shu Ying"*   422

Wu Wen Ying　吴文英　　427

Feeling Sad in Late Spring
Tune: *"Wan Xi Sha"*　428

Missing You
Tune: *"Feng Ru Song"*　430

The Eve of Lantern Festival
Tune: *"Dian Jiang Chun"*　434

Parting Feelings
Tune: *"Tang Duo Ling"*　436

References　439

Preface

Let me be frank at the outset that I am neither a scholar of Chinese poetry nor a translator by profession. When it comes to *shi* and *ci* poetry, I am but a self-taught learner and late starter. However, I do have a passion for making the study of classical Chinese poetry easier and less complicated, particularly for those bilingual learners whose mother tongue is not Chinese.

The bilingual approach, as illustrated in this book, is actually the tool I used to learn the craft of writing *shi* and *ci* poems. If you are interested in writing, but you are intimidated or overwhelmed by those rigid rules and tonal patterns, you may want to try my nontraditional and unconventional approach.

Let me hasten to add that this is not intended to be a scholastic or literary work. The purpose of my book is quite simple: to offer an alternative way to read, understand, and appreciate classical Chinese poetry. It would be my thrill if, through this book, you have improved the skill you need in reading or even writing classical Chinese poetry.

Specifically, this book is useful to those readers who:

- Want to learn Chinese through poetry
- Enjoy a bilingual perspective to reading *ci* poetry
- Want an analysis of the tonal patterns and rhyme scheme for each poem included
- Want both literal and literary translations to accompany with the original poem
- Want to know how each poem would be read by the native Chinese

This book will begin with a rather lengthy introduction, focusing on the problems and issues of interpreting and translating Chinese regulated poetry. The second part of the book will cover 152 selected *ci* poems written by famous poets during the Tang and Song Dynasties. Each original poem is shown in both simplified and traditional characters, with *pinyin* transliterations, tones, and rhyme scheme. In addition to a literal translation, each poem is also provided a literary translation, which is designed to help the reader better understand the original poem.

I wish to thank all those who have given me advices, suggestions, and encouragement during all phases of this book project. I especially want to thank the following individuals for their valuable comments and encouragement: Payjuan Lin, Zhaojin Ji, Shu Fang Hisa, Yi-han Kao, and Y. Y. Hsu. Finally, this book would not have been possible without the enthusiastic support and encouragement from my wife Mimi.

— Edward C. Chang

Part One
Introduction

Subtopics

Translating Chinese Poetry: A Few Examples

Factors Affecting Interpretation of Chinese Poetry

Different Interpretations of Yan Jidao's Poem by Chinese Poetry Scholars

How to Analyze a Poem from a Bilingual Perspective

How to Analyze Yan Jidao's *Ci* Poem Written to the Tune of *Zhe Gu Tian* "Is This Reunion A Dream?"

Basic Tonal Patterns of *Ci* Poetry

How to Remember Tones and Tonal Patterns

Should the Sound and Tone of the Original Poem Be a Factor in Translation?

Analyzing Li Qingzhao's Poem "*Sheng Sheng Man*"

Can You Create Your Own *Cipai*?

Translating Chinese Poetry: A Few Examples

Robert Frost once said that "poetry is what gets lost in translation." This is especially true when it comes to translating classical Chinese poetry into any other languages, even though the target language is vernacular Chinese.

Classical Chinese poems have been widely translated into English by scholars, sinologists, bilingual poets, and translators in general. It is a known fact that, for each original poem, there could be as many different versions of translation as there are translators. Translators can differ widely from each other in their command of the Chinese language and in the way they interpret the imagery, metaphors, allusions, feelings, and tonal patterns. If a reader is exposed to the work of only one particular translator, how can he or she be sure if the translation reflects accurately the ideas, feelings, and implications in the original poem?

A review of translation literature will lead one to conclude that significant discrepancies occur in the interpretation of the original poems by different translators.

Before our discussion, I will first cite a few examples to illustrate some of the problems in the translation of ancient Chinese poetry. Let's first look at a poem written by Wang Wei, with its three different versions of translation. Although this five-character truncated verse contains only twenty Chinese characters, it has at least nineteen different translations, as pointed out by Weinberger (1987).

鹿柴 王維

空山不見人
但聞人語響
返景入深林
復照青苔上

Deer Forest Hermitage

Through the deep wood, the slanting sunlight
Casts motley patterns on the jade-green mosses.
No glimpse of man in this lonely mountain,
Yet faint voices drift on the air.
        (Tr. Chang Yin-nan & Lewis C. Walmsley, 1958)

The Deer Enclosure

On the lonely mountain
        I meet no one,
I hear only the echo
        of human voices.
At an angle the sun's rays
        enter the depths of the wood,
And shine
        upon the green moss.
        (Tr. C.J. Chen & Michael Bullock, 1960)

Deep in the Mountain Wilderness

Deep in the mountain wilderness
Where nobody ever comes
Only once in a great while
Something like the sound of a far-off voice.
The low rays of the sun
Slip through the dark forest,
And gleam again on the shadowy moss.
        (Tr. Kenneth Rexroth, 1970)

Let's look at another poem in the form of seven-character *jueju*, or truncated regulated verse. This poem was written originally by Du Mu, a famous poet in the Tang Dynasty. Three versions of rendition by well-known translators are shown below.

贈別 杜牧

多情卻似總無情
唯覺樽前笑不成
蠟燭有心還惜別
替人垂淚到天明

Farewell Poem
(Second of two to a girl of Yang-chou)

Passion too deep seems like none.
While we drink, nothing shows but the smile
　which will not come.
The wax candles feel, suffer at partings:
Their tears drip for us till the sky brightens.
　　　(Tr. A. C. Graham, 1977)

Parting (2) by Tu Mu

How can a deep love seem deep love,
How can it smile, at a farewell feast?
Even the candle, feeling our sadness,
Weeps, as we do, all night long.
　　　(Tr. Witter Bynner, 1987)

Poems for Parting (2)

Too much love
somehow became
no love at all

over this farewell bottle
we can't manage
even a friendly smile

only the candle
seems to be able
to generate some feeling

all night
it weeps
little wax tears.
    (Tr. David Young and Jiann I. Lin, 2007)

From the above examples, we can clearly see that not all translators interpret Wang Wei's poem the same way. The same thing can be said about Du Mu's poem. Which of these versions are most accurate in reflecting the original writers' ideas and feelings? There is probably no clear answer.

    I will give my own analyses and renditions of Wang and Du's poems later. But in the next section, we will first look at some factors that may contribute to different interpretations or misinterpretations of the same poems.

Factors Affecting Interpretation and Translation of Chinese Poetry

As the examples in the previous section show, translators don't always interpret classical Chinese poetry the same way. Poetry, of course, is not an exact science. Different renditions for the same poem are inevitable. I would not burden you here by passing my own judgment as to which of the translations is or is not accurate in reflecting the poetic messages and feelings of the original. The point to be made is that translators not only differ in interpretation of the Chinese original but also differ in the style of translation.

    With so many different versions of translation, how can readers be sure that each rendition they come across adequately represents the poetic ideas of the original writer?

    No one expects that the tonal patterns and rhyme scheme used in a Chinese *shi* (律诗) or *ci* (词) poem can be translated. But should the melodious harmony of the original poem be represented or transformed in a new way? Should a poem translated from Chinese to English differ widely in its basic messages, feelings, and poetic spirit other than the translators' style of expression? Which poetical style (free verse or metrical verse) is more appropriate in the translation of Chinese poetry? Should the so-called "three-character criteria" (信达雅, faithfulness, expressiveness, and gracefulness") proposed by Yan Fu be equally important in translation?

I believe these are legitimate questions to ask before one undertakes the task of translating classical Chinese poetry, particularly the *shi* and *ci* forms written in the Tang and Song Dynasties. Both *shi* and *ci* poetry are highly regulated with strict tonal patterns and rhyme scheme.

Why are there so many different interpretations in Chinese poetry? Following are, I think, some contributory factors:

The first one has to do with the nature of the Chinese language. I am referring here mainly to *wenyan*, the classical style of writing. In contrast to *baihua*, or writing in the vernacular, *wenyan* is a highly elliptic written language, making it difficult to understand and interpret, especially for those readers whose mother tongue is not Chinese. In addition, there are no articles, tenses, or cases in the Chinese language, be it *wenyan* or *baihua*. Pronouns and verbs are often omitted in the *wenyan* with which classical Chinese poems were written. An adjective may sometimes function as a verb, as in the following line: 春風又綠江南岸 (The spring wind again turns the shore of Jiangnan into green), written by Wang Anshi (1021–1086), a prime minister during the reign of Emperor Shen Zhong in the Song Dynasty.

The second problem in translating Chinese classical poetry is obviously related to the translator's own command of the Chinese language, particularly the classical style of writing. If the translator's first language is not English, then his or her writing skills in English are also relevant.

In addition, interpretation can also be influenced by the translator's knowledge of the poet's background, as well as the allusions and metaphors used in the poem. In the example of Du Mu's poem about parting, the translator would better understand what the poet alludes to if he knew that the Chinese character for the wick of a wax candle is written and pronounced the same way as the character for human heart (心). Likewise, in Wang Wei's poem, it could be interpreted in a new light if the translator knew that Wang was a devoted Buddhist and that in Buddhism the word 空 (empty or emptiness) actually carries a very positive connotation.

The translators whose work we cited in the previous examples appear to be natives from the West. But are native-born Chinese natives immune from these kinds of problems? We can find the answers from the several examples of poetry rendition by Chinese scholars or accomplished authors in both mainland and Taiwan.

In the next section, we will take a look at how Chinese poetry scholars or experts interpret Yan Jidao's poem "*Zhe Gu Tian*."

Different Interpretations of Yan Jidao's Poem by Chinese Poetry Scholars

To illustrate further the problems of interpreting Chinese poetry, let me show you a *ci* poem (which this book is all about) written by Yan Jidao (晏幾道), son of Yan Shu, prime minister and famous poet of the Song Dynasty.

鷓鴣天
晏幾道

彩袖殷勤捧玉鍾。
當年拚卻醉顏紅。
舞低楊柳樓心月，
歌盡桃花扇底風。
從別後，憶相逢。

幾回魂夢與君同。
今宵剩把銀釭照，
猶恐相逢是夢中。

We will focus only on lines three and four as they generate more disagreements in interpretation and translation.

舞低楊柳樓心月，
歌盡桃花扇底風。

Vernacular Chinese is mainly used as a teaching tool for readers who are interested in *ci* poetry. Translations from *wenyan* to vernacular Chinese are usually provided to facilitate reading and understanding the original poems. Since our primary focus is in interpretation, not their style of translation, we will only look at interpretations of those key points of interest.

> You danced and danced till the moon hung low o'er willow tree;
> You sang and sang till mid peach blossoms blushed the breeze.
> (Xu Yuan Zhong, *Golden Treasury of Chinese Lyrics*, 1990)

In Xu Yuan Zhong's English translation, Xu treats the 楊柳 (willow) as a live tree, not an adjective that modifies the building (樓). In the like manner, he translates 桃花 as peach blossoms, the live flowers, not a fan that has a picture of a peach flower on it.

與妳徹夜歌舞，直到月落柳梢頭，
無力揮舞桃花扇，方才罷休。

【丁朝陽 新解宋詞三百首】

You and I sang and danced the whole night until the moon hung below the willow tree top.

We did not stop (singing and dancing) until you could no longer wave the peach blossom fan.
(From Ding Chao Yang, *New Annotated Thee Hundred Ci Poems of the Song Dynasty*, 2006.)

To Ding, the act of singing and dancing was performed by two people: the song girl and the poet or persona. 楊柳 represents the top of the willow tree. The character 樓 is omitted in the explanation. While 楊柳 functions as a noun, not an adjective, 桃花 is used as an adjective to modify the noun fan (扇).

舞姿連月兒也引到楊柳樓中，
歌聲則透過桃花扇底，散入風裏。

【汪中 新譯宋詞三百首】

Her dancing movement draws the moon into the willow tree pavilion. The sound of her singing scatters into the wind through the bottom of the peach blossom fan.
(From Wang Zhong, *New Translation of the Three Hundred Ci Poems of the Song Dynasty*, 1977.)

Wang Zhong's translation does treat both 楊柳樓 and 桃花扇 as two proper nouns (place and an object). However, the duration and the degree of fatigue are not mentioned at all in the translation.

宴會上長久地狂舞，
直把樓心的明月催下柳陰，
歡歌一曲連著一曲，
扇底的風都被搧盡。

【沙靈娜 宋詞三百首全譯】

In the banquet, she was dancing in madness for a long time until the moonlight on the floor shifted downward below the shady willow tree.

She sang happily, one song after another, until the wind under the fan had stopped.
(From Sha Ling Na, *Complete Translation of the Three Hundred* Ci *Poems of the Song Dynasty*, 1992.)

In the above translation, Sha Ling Na interprets 楊柳樓 as two distinct entities: a tree and a building. The two characters 桃花 are omitted in the translation.

歡舞中高照樓頭的明月漸漸墜下柳梢，
歡歌後累得桃花小扇也扇不起清風。

【王筱雲 宋詞三百首】

In the midst of joyful dancing, the bright moon that shone upon the high tower gradually lowered itself to the tip of the willow tree.
After singing, she was so tired that the little peach blossom fan could no longer fan any more soothing wind.
(From Wang You Yun, *Three Hundred* Ci *Poems of the Song Dynasty*, 1992.)

In her translation, Wang You Yun has also treated 楊柳樓 as two separate entities: willow and a building. But in the case of 桃花扇, Wang has treated it as a little peach blossom fan.

It is clear from the samples illustrated that native scholars and translators in China are just as diverse as those in the West when it comes to interpreting or translating classical Chinese poetry. Of course, Yan Jidao's two lines are not truly representative of Chinese *ci* poetry as a whole. But the fact remains that Chinese writings in classical style can be subject to different interpretations.

In the next section, I will introduce an alternative approach to analyzing and interpreting regulated poetry in general and *ci* poetry in particular: a bilingual approach.

How to Analyze a Poem from a Bilingual Perspective

Different versions of translation may arguably be a good thing if the differences are merely a result of the translators' style of writing and expression. Some translators prefer free verse; others may insist on the use of rhyme scheme. Some like to make it short and precise; other stress on readability. What is debatable is whether or not a translator can freely change the original ideas in order to make it looks like a typical English verse, with or without rhyme.

Even with the best intention, no translators can be completely free from erroneous judgment or misinterpretations when it comes to translating *shi* or *ci* poetry. How can errors in translation be kept to the minimum? How can readers know if the translation adequately reflects the ideas and feelings expressed in the original language when only the target language is presented? What options can the general readers have if they want to learn about an original poem in depth?

I believe some of these problems can be alleviated by using a bilingual approach to analysis before proceeding with formal or literary translation. This way, the translator will be able to minimize his subjectivity, while the reader will understand how and why the translator reaches his interpretations.

With technical advances in language software in recent years, bilingual presentation in the same document is no longer a difficult task. Scholars or translators can now routinely supplement their translation with the word-to-word annotations.

But word-to-word translation has its own limitations as well. Following is an example of word-to-word translation of Wang Wei's poem "The Deer Enclosure."

空	山	不	見	人
empty	mountain	not	see	people
但	聞	人	語	響
but	hear	people	speech	sound

返	景	入	深	林
return	scene	enter	deep	woods

復	照	青	苔	上
again /repeat	shine	green	moss	above/on

If we do a word-for-word annotation for Du Mu's poem illustrated earlier, we can produce one like what is shown below.

多	情	卻	似	總	無	情
much	passion	but	seem	after all	no	passion

唯	覺	樽	前	笑	不	成
only	feel	wine cup	before	smile/laugh	not	succeed

蠟	燭	有	心	還	惜	別
wax	candles	have	heart	still	cherish	parting

替	人	垂	淚	到	天	明
for	people	let fall	tears	till	sky	bright

Word-for-word dictionary annotation can be done in a straightforward manner. Regardless of who does the job, the outcome should be less variable from person to person. Though it may be of some value to those who are studying the Chinese language, it can also mislead the readers into believing this is the way Chinese natives read their *shi* poetry.

Although each Chinese character is a one-syllable word that has its own meaning, it often takes a compound word to denote a noun, a verb, or an adjective. Separating compound words into separate elements only serves to change their meanings and their natural rhythm. For instance, 青苔 (green moss), 多情 (full of affection), 蠟燭 (wax candle), 惜別 (reluctant to part), 垂淚 (shedding tears), and 天明 (daybreak) are compound words that should not be read separately.

Another disadvantage of the word-for-word rendition alone is that it does not show the readers the natural way of reading the line or sentence, not to mention that it does not indicate the tonal pattern and rhyme, which is an integral part of Chinese poetry.

I believe a model of bilingual analysis will be of great help to those readers who want to know how the original poem would be read by the Chinese natives even though the readers know very little about the Chinese language.

Let me prove my points by reorganizing Wang and Du's poems into a bilingual format. As shown, more information is included for reading and understanding each poem in the analysis.

Bilingual Analysis of Wang Wei's Poem "Deer Enclosure"

空○山○[1]
kōng shān
empty mountain

不△見△人○
bù jiàn rén
no one is seen

但△聞○
dàn wén
but hear

人○語△響▲
rén yǔ xiǎng
human voice echoing

返△景△[2]
fǎn jǐng
returning light

入△深○林○
rù shēn lín
enters deep wood

復△照△
fù zhào
shines also

青○苔○上▲
qīng tái shàng
on the green moss

[1] The word "empty" here implies a sense of serenity and tranquility as in Buddhism.
[2] The time of the day when the sun shines from the west.

Bilingual Analysis of Du Mu's Poem "Parting" (2)

多○情○
duō qíng
full of love

卻△似△
què sì
yet look like

總△無○情●
zǒng wú qíng
without affection

唯○覺△
樽○前○
笑△不△成●

14

wéi jué just feel	*zūn qián* before wine cups	*xiǎo bù chéng* unable to smile/laugh
蠟△燭△ *là zhú* wax candles	有△心○[1] *yǒu xīn* to have wicks	還○惜△別△ *hái xī bié* feel reluctant to part
替△人○ *tì rén* for others	垂○淚△[2] *chuí lèi* shedding tears	到△天○明● *dào tiān míng* until dawn

[1] The character for the wick of a candle in Chinese is written and pronounced the same as the character for human heart (心).
[2] The melted wax of the candle is often compared to tears.

As can be seen from the above analyses, we now have the basic information we need to understand each poem in depth.

1. The correct way of reading the poem
2. The meaning of each keyword or phrase
3. The *pinyin* transliteration of each character in Mandarin
4. The tonal mark for each character is indicated by these symbols: ○ (*ping* or level tone); △ (*ze* or deflected tone); ● (rhyme in *ping* or level tone); ▲ (rhyme in *ze* or deflected tone).

It should be noted that the above two poems were written in the Tang Dynasty. The *pinyin* transliteration is based on Mandarin pronunciation as spoken today. Some deflected tones in the past are now pronounced as level tones in Mandarin. Even so, the modulation in tone is still largely maintained by reading the poem in modern-day Mandarin. By reading just the literal translation of the compound words or phrases, a reader who knows little or no Chinese may be able to understand generally what the poet intends to convey even though he or she (as do the Chinese natives) must mentally fill in some missing words such as certain pronouns, verbs, or adjectives.

Of course, different translators may still have different interpretations about certain words. But major discrepancies are expected to be significantly reduced. If a translator goes through this kind of bilingual analyses before actually translating the poem, accuracy in translation should be significantly improved. Following are my translations of the two poems in question as a result of my bilingual analyses. **Let me hasten to add that my translations are intended as learning aids, not "stand-alone" English poems.** By which I mean they should be accompanied by the original text.

The Deer Enclosure

Wang Wei

In the empty mountain, no one is seen.
Yet human voices can be heard echoing.
The afternoon ray enters the deep wood;
it sheds light on the green moss too.

Parting (2)

Du Mu

Full of passion, but act as though without affection.
In front of the wine cups, it is so hard to laugh!
A wax candle that has a heart is reluctant to part.
It's tears keep falling down for others until it is dawn.

The above two examples were written in the form of *shi*, or regulated verse. The tonal pattern of *shi* is the basis for *ci* poetry, which we will get into later in this book. In the next section, we will analyze the *ci* poem written by Yan Jidao, whose poem we discussed in part earlier.

How to Analyze Yan Jidao's *Ci* Poem Written to the Tune of *Zhe Gu Tian* "Is This Reunion A Dream?"

Now, let's first use the bilingual approach to analyze Yan Jidao's poem. Then we will discuss why line three and line four can be subject to different interpretations.

彩△袖△
cǎi xiù
colorful sleeves

當○年○
dāng nián
in those days

舞△低○
wǔ dī
danced; (until moon) let droop

歌○盡△
gē jìn
sang; (until wind) exhausted

從○
cóng
since

憶△
yì
remembered

幾△回○
jǐ huí
several times

今○宵○
jīn xiāo
tonight

猶○恐△

殷○勤○
yīn qín
very courteous

拚△卻△
pàn què
went all out

楊○柳△
yáng liǔ
willow tree (tower)

桃○花○
táo huā
peach blossom (fan)

別△後△
bié hòu
we bade farewell

相○逢●
xiāng féng
how we met

魂○夢△
hún mèng
my dreams

剩△把△
shèng bǎ
to make sure

相○逢○

捧△玉△鍾●
pěng yù zhōng
hold a wine cup in both hands

醉△顏○紅●
zuì yán hóng
to drink, resulting in a flushed face

樓○心○月△
lóu xīn yuè
moon on the tower's floor

扇△底△風●
shàn dǐ fēng
wind under fan

與△君○同●
yǔ jūn tóng
were with you; were like yours

銀○釭○照△
yín gōng zhào
the lamp is well lighted

是△夢△中●

17

yóu kǒng	xiāng féng	shì mèng zhōng
for fear that	our meeting	is in the dream

As it was pointed out earlier, the third and fourth lines (in bold) in Yan's poem to the tune of *Zhe Gu Tian* were interpreted quite differently by translators. One of the reasons for such diverse opinions in the interpretation of Yan's lines may have to do with the structure of the two sentences, which is rather ambiguous to say the least. As difficult to interpret as they are, scholars in general agree that these two lines are elegantly written. The problem lies in the fact that the sentence structure is not well-defined and obvious. For example, it is not clear as to which represents the subject and which represents the verb.

Let's take another look at these two sentences in the original:

舞低楊柳樓心月，
歌盡桃花扇底風。

A careful comparison of these two lines will lead one to detect that it is a couplet constructed on the basis of parallelism. Although parallelism is not normally required in *ci* poems, individual poets can use parallel lines if they so choose. Parallelism is quite common in poems written to the tune of *Zhe Gu Tian*.

If translators recognize that the two lines are parallel in structure, they will be able to determine the function of each word in the sentence. For instance, if we know that 楊柳樓 is a proper noun in line three, we can logically assume that both 楊柳 and 桃花 function as adjectives that modify their nouns, 樓 and 扇, respectively. If the second character on line one denotes an act, then the character at the same position on line two will also function as a verb.

We can see more clearly by separating the seven characters from each other in terms of their relative function in the sentence.

舞　低　楊柳樓　心 月，
歌　盡　桃花扇　底 風。

From the above arrangement, we can reasonably assume that the verbs in the two sentences appear to be 低 and 盡. If so, are 舞 and 歌 the subjects of these two verbs, respectively? My short answer is no.

A bilingual analysis leads me to believe that these two lines actually consist of two subjects and two verbs. We can see its grammatical relationship more clearly if we rearrange these words as follows:

> 舞；月　低　　楊柳樓　心，
> 歌；風　盡　　桃花扇　底。

By moving 月 and 風 from the last position to the second position, we can tell that the subject of the verb 低 is 月, not 舞. By the same token, 風 should be the subject of 盡, not 歌. Then what is the grammatical function for 舞 and 歌, respectively? In my opinion, each of these two characters represents the verb of its own subject in an elliptical construction. The omitted subject in both case should be song girl or the pronoun "she."

If you are wondering why the characters 月 and 風 are placed at the end of the line in the first place, the reason is that the character 風 rhymes with the other rhyming words in the poem.

From the bilingual perspective, each seven-character line, using the terminology of English grammar, actually represents two independent clauses. Literally, we can translate these two lines as follows:

> She kept dancing; the moon was lower than the "heart" of the Willow Tree Tower.
>
> She continued to sing; the wind stopped at the bottom of the peach blossom fan.

If we use the conjunction "until" to link the two independent clauses, the meanings will be even clear.

> She kept dancing until the moon hung lower than the floor of the Willow Tree Tower.

She continued to sing until the wind
ceased at the bottom of the peach blossom
fan.

Of course, my own analysis and interpretation are not necessarily what the poet had in mind. But by using a bilingual approach to analysis, we can at least identify where the problems lie. The readers can draw their own conclusions by examining the information provided. Perhaps they can even produce, if they like, their own version of translation with the help of the information.

Following is my own rendition, which was done after a bilingual analysis.

Is This Reunion a Dream?

Tune: *Zhe Gu Tian*

Yan Jidao

Her sleeves looked colorful and bright;
she politely handed me a cup of wine.
I went all out to drink in those days
for a flushed and red face.
She kept dancing until the moon shone
upon the floor of the Willow Tree Tower.
She quitted singing only after she was too tired
to create a wind with her peach-blossom fan.
Since we parted, I never forget our first encounter.
Time and again, I dream of us being together.
Tonight, I just want to make sure that the lamp is bright.
I am so afraid that we are reunited in dream,
not in the real life.

Basic Tonal Patterns of *Ci* Poetry

Yan Jidao's poem, just like all 152 poems included in this book, was written in the *ci* style. In contrast to *shi* poetry, which may take the form of *lushi* (regulated verse) or *jueju* (truncated verse) with equal length in each line, *ci* poetry can follow any one of the established tune patterns called *cipai* or *cipu*. There are more than eight hundred tune patterns from which a poet can choose for composing his or her poem. The tune of Yan Jidao's *ci* poem we analyzed earlier is called *Zhe Gu Tian*, which literally means "Partridge Sky." Unlike *shi* poetry, *ci* lyric can contain lines of irregular length.

Ci is sometime called song lyric poetry because the lyric was initially based on songs composed for entertainment purposes. *Ci* originated during the Tang period, but it did not become more popular and widespread until the Song Dynasty. In the beginning, lyrics were written as part of the melody composition, often done by musicians themselves. In time, more and more poets began to write lyrics for the *cipai* after the original melody had been lost. In its place, tone and rhyme pattern, as well as the number of words, were set for that particular *cipai*. So what began as a lyric for a song had gradually evolved into a popular poetic genre.

Today, *cipai,* such as *Zhe Gu Tian* (鷓鴣天), actually bears no resemblance to its original tune or melody. In this book I will not translate the tune title so as to spare the readers from associating with something no longer used.

Although there are more than eight hundred titles of such *cipai*, they all share something in common with *shi* poetry in terms of tonal patterns and lyrical harmony. Yan Jidao's *ci* poem is a case in point. If you compare Yan's poem with Du Mu's *jueju*, you will notice that the tonal patterns of seven-character lines are very similar. The number of *cipai* may be large, but the *ping-ze* (flat or deflected tone) patterns, though with some exceptions, are comparable from *cipai* to *cipai*.

Common Tonal Patterns for Lines of the Same Length

So what are the most common *ci* tonal patterns for lines of the same length? In *ci*, the number of characters in each line usually falls with the range of two to seven. As you read through each of the 152 poems in this book, you will notice that the tonal patterns in terms of *ping-ze* arrangement are quite similar. Following are the basic patterns, as grouped by the number of Chinese characters:

Two- character line:
- (a) ○○
- (b) △△
- (c) ○△
- (d) △○

Three-character line:
- (a) ○○○
- (b) ○○△
- (c) △○○
- (d) ○△△
- (e) △△○
- (f) △△△

Four-character line:
- (a) ○○△△
- (b) △△○○
- (c) △○○△
- (d) ○△△○

Five-character line:
- (a) ○○△△△
- (b) △△△○○
- (c) △△○○△
- (d) ○○△△○

Six-character line:
- (a) ○○△△○○
- (b) △△○○△△
- (c) △○○△△△
- (d) ○△○○○△
- (e) △○○△○○

Seven-character line:
(a) ○○△△○○△
(b) △△○○△△○
(c) △△○○○△△
(d) ○○△△△○○
(e) △○○△○○△
(f) ○△△○○△○

How to Remember Tones and Tonal Patterns?

The Four Tones in Chinese Poetry

Let's face it, even native Chinese find it challenging to master the tones and tonal patterns used in ancient Chinese poetry.

This section will not make you an instant expert on tones and tonal patterns, but I hope you will have the working knowledge you need to fully enjoy reading *ci* poetry. Further familiarity with the Pinyin system of Romanization will be beneficial, too.

Chinese is a tonal language in which the same set of sounds can have different meanings depending on the voice pitch or tone. Tones are used to tell whether the voice pitch is high, medium, or low. They also suggest whether the pitch is level, falling, or rising. A clearly defined voice pitch is the basis for determining the meaning of a Chinese spoken word.

First, let me briefly mention about the four tones used in modern Mandarin Chinese, namely, the first, second, third and fourth tones.

Take a look at these four characters below: 媽 (mother), 麻 (hemp), 馬 (horse), or 罵 (to scold). The Pinyin transliterations for the above words, in the exact order, are the following: *mā, má, mǎ,* and *mà*.

As you can tell from the above example, characters that have the same sound (*ma*) can have different tones with different meanings.

To study *shi* and *ci* poetry, we need to understand the four tones in ancient Chinese poetry: *ping* (平), *shang* (上), *qu* (去), and *ru* (入).

ping (平) is the level tone which includes the first and second tone in modern standard Chinese pronunciation. Examples: 媽 (mā), 麻 (má), 平 (píng) 東 (dōng), 山 (shān), 川 (chuān).

shang (上) is the falling-rising tone (the third tone in modern standard Chinese pronunciation). Examples: 馬 (mǎ), 好 (hǎo), 我 (wǒ), 水 (shuǐ), 古 (gǔ), 口 (kǒu).

qu (去) is the falling tone (the fourth tone in modern standard Chinese pronunciation). Examples: 地 (dì), 未 (wèi), 路 (lù), 外 (wài), 大 (dà), 下 (xià).

ru (入) is the "entering" tone which is pronounced in a short and abrupt manner. Examples: 玉 (yù), 日 (rì), 月 (yuè), 仄 (zè) 葉 (yè), 力 (lì).

It should be pointed out that in Mandarin Chinese today, there is no *ru or* "entering" tone. Those characters classified as "*ru*" tone in classical Chinese now can fall under any one of the four tones in Mandarin pronunciation. For example, the following "*ru-sheng*" words (入聲字) are now pronounced in either the first, second, or third tone: 出 (chū), 菊 (jú), 白 (bái), 學 (xué), 國 (guó), 敵 (dí), 雪 (xuě). However, the *ru* tone is still retained in some southern dialects such as Cantonese. In classical Chinese poetry, *shang*, *qu*, and *ru* are all considered *ze* or deflected tones.

Some Helpful Tips

You may find the following mnemonics helpful for differentiating and remembering these tones:

A *ping* tone comes very close to the "actual" sound of the pronunciation of the syllable. It is represented by a macron accent which suggests that the word is pronounced with a constant high but flat pitch. You will get a good idea about its general characteristic by saying the following English words aloud: an, ban, fan, pan, song, sun, tan, you. Incidentally, these syllables would be called *ping* tone if the Chinese characters they represent are as follows: 安 (ān), 斑 (bān), 番 (fān), 攀 (pān), 鬆 (sōng), 孫 (sūn), 灘 (tān), and 幽 (yōu).

We can tell from the tonal mark that mā, pān, tān, and yāng are all in the *ping* tone. Now repeat the same sound by pretending that, instead of just saying it, you were actually asking a series of one-syllable questions, such as "mā?" "pān?" "tān?" "yāng?" When you do that, you will be inclined to change the pitch from the first to the second tone (má, pán, tán, yáng) without being conscious about it. As you can tell, the tonal mark for this tone is an acute accent which suggests that a word starting in a relative high pitch continues to rise even higher.

The *shang* (上) tone could be the most tricky one for native English speakers because, to my knowledge, there is no equivalent (one syllable) sound in the English language. To say a word in the *shang* tone, you will most likely go through these three steps in rapid succession: start a sound in low pitch, lower the pitch further, and then raise the pitch higher than its starting point. We can also represent the pitch variation of the *shang* tone by following the sequence of these three numbers: 2-1-4, where 1 represents the lowest pitch and 5 represents the highest pitch.

You may get the picture intuitively if you try to mimic Santa's voice when he utters "ho ho ho." However, instead of saying it in three syllables, try to pronounce "ho" in the 2-1-4 pitch pattern.

The *qu* (去) tone, the fourth tone in Mandarin Chinese, is represented by a grave accent. The tonal mark implies that the tone starts high in pitch and then falls rapidly below its initial pitch. You may get a better "feel" if you pretend that you are yelling at somebody as you are pronouncing this tone.

The *ru* (入) tone tends to fall rapidly and come to an immediate halt. The quality of its sound somewhat resembles the short-vowel words in the English language such as "dug, luck, cut, rig, dig, fit, and dog." Pretend that you are very "impatient" and "upset" as you pronounce the *ru-sheng* words.

Tonal Patterns

In *ci* poetry, the tones of *ping* and *ze* must be taken into account when one chooses his or her verse line. A verse line is defined by the tonal pattern which is basically the assignment of tones in a specific order so as to produce a harmonious effect.

If you find it difficult to differentiate *ping* (平) from *ze* (仄), as well as to remember the common tonal patterns, try to imagine that you are beating a drum. When you beat at the center of the drum, you will hear a sound that appears to be leveling and lingering. When you beat at the edge or the side of a drum, you will hear a sound that seems abruptly stopped or cut short. The leveling and lingering sound is close to the *ping* tone, while the cut-short tone resembles the *ze* tone.

Of course, we don't talk about *ping* and *ze* in the English language. In English metrical verse, stressed and unstressed syllables are used to harmonize the rhythmical effect of a line. But the long and short vowels may be more analogous to the *ping-ze* modulation. In our drum-beating analogy, the "doom" sound, which involves a long vowel, can be considered a *ping*. On the other hand, the short vowel "dug" is equivalent to a *ze* sound. In the Chinese phonetic system, words in *ping* tone such as 陽 (yang), 年 (nián), and 山 (shān) can be elongated in speech, but words in *ze* tone such as 淚 (lèi), 月 (yuè), and 歲 (suì) will have to come to an immediate stop soon after the words are uttered.

The tonal pattern of △△ ○○ △△ would be like first beating the side of a drum twice (dug, dug), followed by a short pause, then two beats at the center (doom, doom), short pause, two beats again from the side (dug, dug). For pattern (a) of the seven-character line (○○△△○○△), the tone will sound like this:

doom doom, dug dug, doom doom, dug

Let's go back and take another look at the tonal patterns of Yan Jidao's *ci* poem: Zhe Gu Tian.

彩△袖△　　　殷〇勤〇　　　捧△玉△鍾●
當〇年〇　　　拚△卻△　　　醉△顏△紅●
舞△低〇　　　楊〇柳△　　　樓〇心〇月△
歌〇盡△　　　桃〇花〇　　　扇△底△風●

從〇　　　　　別△後△
憶△　　　　　相〇逢●
幾△回〇　　　魂〇夢△　　　與△君〇同●
今〇宵〇　　　剩△把△　　　銀〇釭〇照△
猶〇恐△　　　相〇逢〇　　　是△夢△中●

If you don't know how to read the Chinese characters in Mandarin, you may still get a feel on the tonal patterns of *Zhe Gu Tian* by humming the following sounds or by beating the drum yourself:

<u>dug</u> dug	doom doom	<u>dug</u> ___	dug **doom**
<u>doom</u> doom	<u>dug</u> dug	dug ___	doom **doom**
<u>dug</u> doom	<u>dug</u> dug	doom doom	dug ___
<u>doom</u> dug	doom doom	<u>dug</u> dug	**doom** ___
doom	dug dug		
dug	doom **doom**		
<u>dug</u> doom	<u>doom</u> dug	dug ___	doom **doom**
<u>doom</u> doom	<u>dug</u> dug	doom doom	dug ___
<u>doom</u> dug	doom doom	<u>dug</u> ___	dug **doom**

In the tonal patterns of the *cipai Zhe Gu Tian* shown above, the underlined tones indicate that they can be switched to a different tone if you like. The tone denoted in bold face is the rhyme tone. In this case, *ping*-tone characters must be used as rhyme.

Please be reminded that in *shi* poetry, the character corresponding to the first, third, and fifth position in a seven-character line can be changed to a word with a different tone, provided that certain conditions are met. The same rule applies to *ci* except that it is made even more flexible. For example, in the seventh line of Yan's poem, the tone pattern of "<u>dug</u> doom <u>doom</u> dug dug doom

doom" is actually a variation of the tone pattern of "*doom doom dug dug dug doom doom.*"

Although there are more than eight hundred names of *cipai* used in *ci* poetry, the tone variations in each line are actually quite limited. For the tune of *Zhe Gu Tian*, the basic tonal patterns line by line, as discussed above, can be summarized as follows: 7b, 7d, 7a, 7b, 3d, 3c, 7a, and 7b. You may notice that the above tonal patterns are very close to that of Du Mu's *shi* poem: 7d, 7b, 7c, and 7d.

The similarity between Du's *jueju* and Yan's *ci* is expected since most, if not all, names of *cipai* are derived from the set tonal patterns of *shi* poetry. Although there are exceptions, the basic principles are quite similar in tonal modulation. This is why poets who used to write *shi* poems can usually master the genre of *ci* poetry with ease.

Later, we will look at another *cipai* that employs some unusual tonal pattern in an attempt to intensify the effect of strong emotions. The poem was written by Li Qingzhao, who has been universally acknowledged as the best female poet in the Song Dynasty. The poem to the tune of *Sheng Sheng Man* was written after her husband died and she was in a state of financial distress and loneliness. This *cipai* may also be rhymed in the *ping* tone.

Should the Sound and Tone of the Original Poem be a Factor in Translation?

Questions can be raised whether or not the phonetic elements of a *cipai* should be considered a factor in translation. For example, should tones be completely ignored because Chinese phonetic system is not transferable to the English language? Should poetic ideas and feelings, as expressed in the original poem with special tonal emphasis, be clearly conveyed in whatever poetic form the translator chooses to take?

An informal review of translations of traditional Chinese poetry suggests that most, if not all, translations take the form of either free verse or rhymed verse with a strict metric order. Most Western translators seem to be in favor of the free verse, while Chinese natives tend to prefer the rhymed approach. Obviously, culture and tradition can influence the translator's own decisions.

Translating a Chinese *shi* or *ci* poem as a free verse has its advantages as well as drawbacks. On the plus side, the translation may look more like an English verse in form and appearance; it can also be made more accurate in reflecting poetic ideas since it does not have to alter the meanings to fit meters and rhymes. On the minus side, translators who like this form may find it necessary to ignore the tones and rhymes in the original.

Some translators, particularly the native Chinese, feel the need to maintain meter and rhyme as exemplified by the Victorian form. To accomplish this, they often have to modify the ideas of the original, which means that the sequence and wordings must be rearranged. Such renditions may actually sound unnatural or even awkward, making it even more deviated from the spirit and feeling tone of the Chinese original.

A balanced approach in translation may involve paying more attention to the sound of the Chinese original while translating it as a free verse. Such an approach avoids the tendency to omit words or modify the content to fit the rhyming and metric scheme. The musical quality in a Chinese poem can be maintained to a certain degree without adhering to a rigid pattern.

In this regard, I am encouraged to learn that well-known translators such as Tony Barnstone have called for the need to pay attention to the sound element when it comes to translating classical Chinese poetry. In the preface of *The Anchor Book of Chinese Poetry: From Ancient to Contemporary, The Full 3000-Year Tradition*, Barnstone (2005) has these to say:

> I don't recommend a return to the practice of translating Chinese poems into rhyming iambics (generally, this overwhelms the Chinese poem). But I do think that as much attention should be given to the way the Chinese poem triggers sound as to how it triggers sight, and that translators should use the whole poetic arsenal—syllabics, sprung rhythm, off rhyme, half rhyme, internal rhyme, assonance, consonance, and so forth—to try to give the English version of the poem a deeply resonant life.

In my translation of Li Qingzhao's "Sad Feelings (*Sheng Sheng Man*)," I have tried to incorporate the sound element in the translation loosely and naturally. I use the kind of English words that in some way resemble a *ze* sound in Chinese, such as: chill, still, up, dark, dusk, drop, drip, enough. These short-vowel words all sound like, though not exactly, *ze* words to the Chinese ears.

Analyzing Li Qingzhao's Poem "*Sheng Sheng Man*"

李清照

聲聲慢

尋尋覓覓，冷冷清清，凄凄慘慘戚戚。乍暖還寒時候，最難將息。三杯兩盞淡酒，怎敵他、晚來風急。 雁過也，正傷心、卻是舊時相識。 滿地黃花堆積。憔悴損，如今有誰堪摘。守著窗兒， 獨自怎生得黑。梧桐更兼細雨，到黃昏、點點滴滴。這者次第，怎一個、愁字了得。

It was pointed out that the character at a certain position can be either in *ping* tone or in *ze* tone, depending on the number of characters that comprise the line. On a six-character line, characters corresponding to the first, third, and fifth position are usually replaceable. On the other hand, characters associated with the second, fourth, and sixth positions are not as flexible because they occupy a more important tonal position. In the case of 卻是舊時相識, the tonal pattern is: △△△○○△. It is actually derived from the normal pattern of △△○○△△ by swapping the two tones that correspond to the third and fifth positions. Similarly, it is acceptable to replace a *ze* tone with a *ping* tone at the fifth position in the following line: 滿地黃花堆積.

As can be seen by the ▲ indicator, the rhyming scheme involved in "*Sheng Sheng Man*" is the *ze* sound. The *ze* rhyme is especially appropriate for conveying strong emotions, such as feeling depressed or indignation. But reading this poem in Mandarin may not be as intense as reading it in some southern dialects such as Cantonese. The reason is that those *ru*-sound (入聲) characters used as rhyming words in Li's poem are now pronounced as *ping sheng* (平聲) in Mandarin. A *ru*-sound character is characterized by a sound that tends to be short and cut off.

Thus, if you speak both Mandarin and Cantonese, you will be able to tell the difference in its tonal effect. The reason is that in Cantonese, the *ru*-sound characters are still retained, whereas in Mandarin, all former *ru*-sound characters are now pronounced in either *ping* or *qu sheng* (去聲). *Qu sheng*, a *ze*, is the fourth tone in modern Chinese phonetics.

Let's take a look at the rhyming characters used in Li's poem "*Sheng Sheng Man*" and see how they sound in Mandarin and Cantonese.

Pronunciation of the Rhyming Words in Mandarin and Cantonese

戚	息	急	識	積
qī	xī	jí	shí	jī
chìk	sìk	gàp	sìk	jìk

摘	黑	滴	得
zhāi	hēi	dī	dé
jaahk	hàk	dìhk	dàk

As we can see, the rhyming characters in Li's *ci* poem differ a lot in pronunciation, depending on which Chinese dialect we use to read the poem. In Mandarin, we can say each of these characters (the first row) in long duration, but the sound will inevitably come to a quick stop when we say the same words (the second row) in Cantonese. The reason is that in Mandarin these Chinese characters are now pronounced in the level tone. Since in this *cipai* the rhyming characters must be in *ze* tone, reading this poem in Cantonese will more easily feel the actual feelings as conveyed by the writer.

The same thing can be said when we read Yue Fei's famous *ci* (written to the tune of *Man Jiang Hong*) aloud. In this poem, Yue used a series of *ze*-sound words to express his strong emotion of indignation and agitation. These strong and agitated feelings can best be appreciated by reading the poem in Cantonese in which 入聲 (*ru*-sound), the fourth tone in traditional Chinese phonetics, is still retained. Yue Fei's poem can be found on page 343.

Let's break-up Li's poem into sections according to its rhyming scheme. Try to pay attention to the tonal pattern of each line and reconstruct what the poet was trying to convey by mentally filling the missing elements. I will give my version of interpretation and translation below for your comparison. If you like, you can also write up your own version of translation.

尋〇尋〇
xún xún
search and search

覓△覓▲
mì mì
seek and seek

冷△冷△
lěng lěng
so cold

清〇清〇
qīng qīng
so dreary

凄〇凄〇
qī qī
so miserable

慘△慘△
cǎn cǎn
so woeful

戚△戚▲
qī qī
so sorrowful

For what am I looking?
For what am I seeking?
So chilly, so dreary;
so miserable, so woeful, and so sorrowful.

In her poem, Li Qingzhao repeated the first seven characters in a row to convey her inner feelings: the feelings of loneliness and hopelessness. In 尋尋覓覓, she describes succinctly her pattern of behavior. That is, searching and seeking for something intangible without consciously knowing exactly what she wanted. Presumably these were the things that were lost after the death of her beloved husband. In 冷冷清清, she told us of the condition in which she lived: desolate and dreary both inside and outside the house. These words suggest that she was alone and that the time of the year could be late autumn. Her depressed feelings were strongly revealed in these words: so miserable (凄凄), so woeful (慘慘), and so sorrowful (戚戚).

乍△暖△	還〇寒〇	時〇候△
zhà nuǎn	huán hán	shí hòu
suddenly warm	and suddenly cold	at such a time

最△難〇	將〇息▲	
zuì nán	jiāng xī	
most difficult	to rest; calm down (the mind)	

At a time of sudden warmth and sudden chill,
it is hard to keep my mind still.

The phrase 乍暖還寒 suggests that it was the time of the year at which temperature could fluctuate from warm to cold on the same day. Most likely, it was late fall when imagery associated with autumn feelings could make it hard for the mind to be at peace.

三〇杯〇	兩△盞△	淡△酒△
sān bēi	liǎng zhǎn	dàn jiǔ
three cups	two small cups	light /weak wine

怎△敵△他〇	晚△來〇	風〇急▲
zěn dí tā	wǎn ái	fēng jí
how can it resist	arriving in the evening	hurried wind

Two or three cups of light wine
hardly can quiet the gust wind at night.

The fact that Li enjoyed wine drinking is not at issue here. But scholars are divided on the phrase *wan lai* (晚來). Some argue that it should have been *xiao lai* (曉來) on the assumption that the writer was to describe what she actually saw and experienced in the order of occurrence on that particular day. But a different assumption is just as valid: she was to relate what she did, felt, and experienced as a general pattern, not a reflection of any particular day and in a particular order. It is also a bit far-fetched to construe that she would start drinking at the early morning hour. To me, *wan lai* (晚來) is more consistent with the spirit of the poem as a whole. After all, poetry writing is different from events reporting.

雁△過△也△　　　正△傷○心○
yàn guò yě　　　 zhèng shāng xīn
swan geese passing　just break my heart
by

卻△是△　　　　舊△時○　　　　相○識▲
què shì　　　　 jiù shí　　　　 xiāng shí
turn out to be　 old time　　　　acquaintances

    Seeing a flock of geese passing by
    only breaks my heart.
    For they once were my old acquaintances from afar.

    In traditional Chinese poetry, "swan goose" was often used as a metaphor for a message delivered from a distance far away. It was a sight of hope and comfort. Seeing a flock of geese after the death of her husband could only bring back old memories and pain.

滿△地△　　　　黃○花○　　　　堆○積▲
mǎn dì　　　　 huáng huā　　　 duī jī
everywhere　　 yellow flowers　 pile up

憔○悴△　　　　損△
qiáo cuì　　　　sǔn
withered　　　 damaged

如○今○　　　　有△誰○　　　　堪○摘▲
rú jīn　　　　　yǒu shéi　　　　kān zhāi
now　　　　　 who will　　　　bear to pluck

    The ground is piled up with yellow flowers,
    so pallid, hurt, and withered.
    Who now cares to pick them up?

    Yellow flowers most likely were chrysanthemums, which also renders support to the idea that the background of the poem was in late fall when chrysanthemums start to wither and fall. The fact that Li, who used to love and care for yellow flowers, would let them pile up on the ground unattended further tells something about the mood and state of her mind: preoccupied, helpless, and despondent.

守△著△　　　　窗○兒○
shǒu zhāo　　　chuāng ér
watching by　　 window

獨△自△
dú zì
alone

怎△生○
zěn shēng
how to wait

得△黑▲
de hēi
until dark

> Alone by the window, how long must I
> wait until it gets dark?

In the above lines, the writer tells us that she was sitting (or standing) by the window alone. Obviously, it was still hours until nightfall, from the tune of the language. The time, to her, seemed moving very slowly as nothing exciting could divert her attention away from her sorrowful feelings. To her, life at that moment was but a dread, with nothing promising to look forward to.

梧○桐○
wú ong
parasol tree

更△兼○
gèng jiān
with also

細△雨△
xì yǔ
drizzle

到△黃○昏○
dào huáng hūn
when dusk sets in

點△點△
diǎn diǎn
drip by drip

滴△滴▲
dī dī
drop after drop

> Drizzling rain drifts
> from the parasol tree at dusk,
> drip by drip, drop by drop.

In these few lines, Li used the imageries of Chinese parasol tree, drizzling rain, and dusk to convey her inner feelings, which were intensified by the sound of the dripping rain. The use of four *ze* sounds in a row was an effective way to convey strong emotions. To give the reader a feel of the *ze* sound in the Chinese original, I also try to use, in my translation, some key words that are pronounced in short vowels such as drizzle, dusk, set, drip, and drop.

這△次△第△
zhě cì dì
at such a moment

怎△一△個△   愁○字△   了△得▲
zěn yī gè   chóu zì   liǎo dé
how can one   word of "sorrow" be enough

    To sum up my feelings at this very moment,
    how can one single word of "sorrow" be enough!

    In the last two lines, Li used all but one *ze*-sound characters to depict her feelings of loneliness, helplessness, and sadness.
    Such a tonal pattern is rare in Chinese poetry, but it is an effective way, if used sparingly, to convey feelings of sorrow and despair. If you read them aloud, you would probably feel the sound resonant in her (or your) mind.

Can You Create Your Own *Cipai*?

As mentioned earlier, there are more than eight hundred tunes of *cipai* that can be used as models for composing *ci* poems. Actually the number would be significantly reduced if those tunes that are infrequently used are excluded. The poems selected in this book were written by the masters of *ci* poetry. The tunes to which they wrote their poems are among the more popular ones.
    Although there are so many established tunes, the basic principles under which tunes were composed are actually quite similar, if not the same. If ancient musicians or poets could create their tonal patterns, why can't modern people do the same by applying the sample principles? As pointed out earlier, the tonal patterns for each poetic line, usually ranging from two to seven characters, are rather limited. To refresh our memory, let us list those basic line patterns below:

    (2a)○○ (2b)△△ (2c)△○ (2d)○△

    (3a)○○○ (3b)○○△ (3c)△○○ (3d)○△△ (3e)△△○ (3f)△△△

    (4a)○○△△ (4b)△△○○ (4c)△○○△ (4d)○△△○ (4e)○○○△

    (4f)△△△○

(5a)○○△△△ (5b)△△△○○ (5c)△△○○△ (5d) ○○△△○
(5e)○○○△△
(6a)○○△△○○ (6b)△△○○△△ (6c) △○○△△△ (6d) ○△○○○△
(6e)△○○△○○
(7a)○○△△○○△ (7b)△△○○△△○ (7c)△△○○○△△
(7d)○○△△△○○ (7e)△○○△○○△ (7f) ○△△○○△○

 As you read through this book, you will notice that most tunes used to compose those great *ci* poems are quite similar in terms of their basic line patterns. If you happen to be interested in writing *ci* poetry, there is no reason why you cannot create your own *cipai* by arranging the above line patterns that sound pleasant to your ears. Of course, if you find it more convenient to write your *ci* poems based on the established tunes, you certainly can do that too.

 Let me conclude my discussion by citing two poems that I wrote as examples for writing *ci* poems without the established *cipai*. These "*cipai-less*" poems may be called "simplified *ci* poetry" so as to distinguish them from those written on the basis of set patterns.

 Allow me to add that I did not construct a set tune before I started composing the poem. Rather, whichever line pattern came next was dictated by the pace of my thought and emotion. In other words, I chose words that are consistent with line patterns, not the other way around.

 My poems of course are in no way near the quality of those great poets whose works are included in this book. But the quality of the two examples is not at issue here. I just want to demonstrate that you can write your own *ci* poems if you don't want to be confined with certain established patterns.

 In my first poem, I use the *ping*-tone characters to set up my rhyme scheme. Notice that the *ping-ze* arrangement in each line is enclosed in the parenthesis. The line number is also given for easy reference.

重陽

林木改新妝。（○△△○●） 5b

綠葉變紅黃。（△△△○●）5b
又是秋涼。（△△○●）4b
又是重陽。（△△○●）4b
年年今日，（○○△△）4a
矚目神傷。（△△○●）4a
萬里孤墳誰去掃？（△△○○○△△）6b
誰人化紙共燒香？（○○△△△○●）7d
慈母淚，（○△△）3d
游子恨，（○△△）3d
最難忘。（△○●）3c
流光數十載，（○○△△△）5a
歲歲斷人腸。（△△△○●）5b

The Double Nine Festival

Trees in the woods have put on new dresses.
Green leaves have transformed their colors
to yellow and red.
Once again the cool autumn has arrived.
It is the Double Nine Festival Day.
Every year on this day, I feel especially sad.
Who will sweep the site of a lonely grave
that is ten thousand miles away?
Who will burn joss money and joss sticks
in front of her burial place?
How can one forget a mother's tears,
and a wandering son's regret?
Suddenly many years have already passed.
Each year, there is always one day
to especially remind me of her face.

   In the next poem, I tried a different approach: alternating a *ze*-tone rhyme with a *ping*-tone rhyme to generate some contrasting effect. As you can see, the line patterns chosen are the most typical ones in traditional poetry.

冰河

高峰聳立陰明滅。（○○△△○○▲）7a
冰河埋積千秋雪。（○○△△○○▲）7a
碧水映藍天，（△△△○●）5b
雪山十里延。（△○△△●）5d
飛瀑雲中裂。（○△○○▲）5c
流泉聲不絕。（○○○△▲）5e
冰塊訣冰川，（○△△○●）5b
玲瓏清澈，（○○○△）4e
彷若小冰船。（△△△○●）5b
蒼坡湖壑接。（○○○△▲）5e
孤鳥高飛悅。（○△○○▲）5c
滄桑靜變萬千年，（○○△△△○●）7d
四時景物憑誰說。（△○△△○○▲）7e）

The Glaciers

Standing tall are the mountain peaks.
They are shining bright at times,
if not gloomy or in the mist.
For thousands of years, the glacier
is the burial ground of accumulated snow.
The blue sky is reflected on
the emerald water below.
Snowcapped mountains
extend over ten miles.
From behind the clouds,
cascades of water come out to fly.
Streams never cease flowing over the rocks.
Breaking away from the glacier are the
crystal boat-like icebergs.
The green slope is joined by
the lake and valley.
A lone bird is flying high happily.
Slow and imperceptible changes take place

over thousands of years.
How can one accurately describe the scenery at a particular time of the year?

If one of your reasons for studying this book is, among other things, to improve your skill of composing *ci* poetry in traditional format, you need to master the rules of tonal patterns. The following activities may be helpful to you:

1. Recite your favorite poems until you can remember them with ease.
2. Study the line patterns in each poem by paying attention to both the tonal symbols and *pinyin* transliteration.
3. Without looking at the tonal symbols, mentally translate each line into its *ping-ze* sequence.
4. Compare your translation with the tonal symbols shown in this book.
5. Compare poems written to the same tune in terms of their similarities and differences.
6. Compose your *ci* poems by selecting those tunes that are relatively short and easy to remember.
7. Avoid using words and phrases that are obscure and difficult to understand.
8. Try to recall the tone patterns from the well-rehearsed lines, not a *cipai* book.

Part Two

The Tang and Southern Tang Period (618–975)

Wen Ting Yun (812–870?)

温庭筠

Wen Ting Yun, also known as Wen Feiqing, was a famous poet in the Tang Dynasty. He was born in present-day Qi county in Shanxi Province in the year 812.

Wen was a descendant of a prime minister in the early Tang period. But the family, once wealthy and influential, suffered a big fall financially long before Wen was born. In fact, Wen often had a hard time making ends meet for a significant part of his life.

Wen was widely known in and around his home town for his literary talent while he was still growing up. He was also talented and knowledgeable in phonology, music, and rhyme scheme. He could even play music with his favorite string instruments. As talented and gifted as he was, he failed repeatedly in civil examinations. From all indications, he was physically unattractive. His behavior was always unconventional and unbridled. The time he spent with song girls in the brothels might have enriched his experience in the development of the *ci* form of poetry.

In his time, he was often associated with the famous poet Li Shang Yin as they were not only friends but they also were alike in poetical style. While Li excelled in *shi* form, Wen is better known for his *ci*, or lyric poetry. In fact, Wen was often considered the founder of the movement of *ci* called *huajianpai* (among flowers), which tended to emphasize the delicate expression of human emotion with elegant and beautiful diction. Not surprisingly, the themes of his lyric poems tend to have something to do with love, parting, and flowers.

温庭筠

菩萨蛮

小山重叠金明灭，鬓云欲度香腮雪。懒起画蛾眉，弄妆梳洗迟。　照花前后镜。花面交相映，新贴绣罗襦，双双金鹧鸪。

Wen Tingyun

Tune: "Pu Sa Man"

Make-up in the Morning

Her eyebrows look like superimposed hills
viewed in distance at twilight.
Her cloud-like hair drifts over her fragrant
cheeks that look snowy and bright.
Getting up idly, she starts to pencil her brows.
To comb her hair and dolls up, she takes her time.

In the mirror, she repeatedly looks at the
flowery hairpin from front and behind.
She is pleased that both her face
and the hairpin make each other look nice.
Newly sewn golden partridges in pairs
can be seen on the silken coat she wears.

溫庭筠　　**wēn tíng yún**
菩薩蠻　　**pú sà mán**

○ = 平声 (*ping* or flat tone)
△ = 仄声 (*ze* or deflected tone)
● = 平声韵 (rhymed in *ping* or flat tone)
▲ = 仄声韵 (rhymed in *ze* or deflected tone)

小△山○ *xiǎo shān* little hills	重○疊△ *chóng dié* superimpose	金○明○滅▲ *jīn míng miè* golden, bright, gloomy
鬢△雲○ *bìn yún* cloud-like hair	欲△度△ *yù dù* want to pass	香○腮○雪▲ *xiāng sāi xuě* snowy and fragrant cheeks
懶△起△ *lǎn qǐ* idly get up	畫△ *huà* to pencil	蛾○眉● *é méi* long, slender eyebrows
弄△妝○ *nòng zhuāng* to makeup	梳○洗△ *shū xǐ* wash and comb hair	遲● *chí* late
照△花○ *zhào huā* see flower in	前○後△ *qián hòu* front and back	鏡▲ *jìng* a mirror
花○面△ *huā miàn* flower and face	交○相○ *jiāo xiāng* reciprocally	映▲ *yìng* to shine
新○貼△ *xīn tiē* newly attached	繡△羅○襦● *xiù luó rú* embroidered silk coat	
雙○雙○ *shuāng shuāng* pairs of	金○ *jīn* golden	鷓△鴣● *zhè gū* partridges

温庭筠

菩萨蛮

水精帘里颇黎枕，暖香惹梦鸳鸯锦。江上柳如烟，雁飞残月天。 藕丝秋色浅，人胜参差剪。双鬓隔香红，玉钗头上风。

Wen Tingyun

Tune: "Pu Sa Man"

Dreaming in Autumn

Glass-like pillows are behind
the crystal screen.
A double-size gilt warmed by
incense can induce a sweet dream.
Mist veils willows by the riverside.
Wild geese fly in the moon-waning sky.
The pink silken dress fits autumn's light color.
Shown also are all kinds of paper-cut flowers.
In between two temples reveals the blossom's red.
A breeze bathes her jade hairpin on her head.

溫庭筠　　**wēn tíng yún**
菩薩蠻　　**pú sà mán**

○ = 平声 (*ping* or flat tone)
△ = 仄声 (*ze* or deflected tone)
● = 平声韵 (rhymed in *ping* or flat tone)
▲ = 仄声韵 (rhymed in *ze* or deflected tone)

水△精○簾○
shuǐ jīng lián
crystal screen

裏△
lǐ
inside

頗○黎○枕▲
pō lí zhěn
glasslike pillows

暖△香○
nuǎn xiāng
warm incense

惹△夢△
rě mèng
dream-inducing

鴛○鴦○錦▲
yuān yāng jǐn
embroidered gilt for married couple

江○上△
jiāng shàng
riverside

柳△
liǔ
willows

如○煙●
rú yān
like mist

雁△飛○
yàn fēi
wild geese fly

殘○月△
cán yuè
waning moon

天●
tiān
sky

藕△絲○
ǒu sī
lotus (pink) silk

秋○色△
qiū sè
autumn color

淺▲
qiǎn
light

人○勝△
rén shèng
paper flowers

參○差○
cēn cī
irregular in size

剪▲
jiǎn
cut

雙○鬢△
shuāng bìn
both temples

隔△
gé
separated by

香○紅●
xiāng hóng
fragrant red (face)

玉△釵○
yù chāi
jade hairpin

頭○上△
tóu shàng
on the head

風●
fēng
wind

47

温庭筠

菩萨蛮

玉楼明月长相忆，柳丝袅娜春无力。门外草萋萋，送君闻马嘶。画罗金翡翠，香烛消成泪。花落子规啼，绿窗残梦迷。

Wen Tingyun

Tune: "Pu Sa Man"

When Will You Come Home?

The bright moon over the elegant
house will be long remembered.
Fine willow branches wave tenderly;
spring appears to lose its vitality.
The grass looks so luxuriant outside.
I heard the horse neigh as we say good-bye.
On the painted gauze screen,
the picture of kingfishers can be seen.
Incense sticks and candles are burned into tears.
Flowers have fallen; cuckoos cry.
By the green window, I remain fascinated
by the dream of last night.

溫庭筠　**wēn tíng yún**
菩薩蠻　**pú sà mán**

玉△樓〇
yù lóu
jade chamber

明〇月△
míng yuè
bright moon

長〇相〇憶▲
zhǎng xiāng yì
long be remembered

柳△絲〇
liǔ sī
willow fine branches

裊△娜△
niǎo nuó
slender and graceful; willowy

春〇無〇力▲
chūn wú lì
spring lacks strength

門〇外△
mén wài
outside

草△
cǎo
grass

萋〇萋●
qī qī
luxuriant.

送△君〇
sòng jūn
seeing you off

聞〇
wén
hear

馬△嘶●
mǎ sī
horse neigh

畫△羅〇
huà luó
painted gauze curtain

金〇
jīn
golden

翡△翠▲
fěi cuì
kingfisher

香〇燭△
xiāng zhú
joss sticks and candles

消〇成〇
xiāo chéng
dissolve into

淚▲
lèi
tears

花〇落△
huā luò
flowers fall

子△規〇
zi guī
cuckoo

啼●
tí
cry

綠△窗〇
lǜ chuāng
green window

殘〇夢△
cán mèng
unfinished dream

迷●
mí
to fascinate

温庭筠

更漏子

玉炉香，红蜡泪，偏照画堂秋思。眉翠薄，鬓云残， 夜长衾枕寒。 梧桐树，三更雨， 不道离情正苦。一叶叶，一声声， 空阶滴到明。

Wen Tingyun

Tune: "Geng Lou Zi"

One Autumn Night

Scent from the censer spreads.
A red candle sheds tears.
Its light in the painted hall
shines purposely on someone who is
preoccupied with the fall.
Her eyebrows' colors tarnished;
her temples hair looks disheveled.
The gilt and pillow are not warm
enough for the long night.

A parasol tree;
a rain continues after midnight.
Not knowing the pain of parting grief,
the leaves one by one start to fall.
The rain drifts drop by drop.
It falls on the vacant steps
until daybreak without pause.

溫庭筠
更漏子

**wēn tíng yún
gèng lòu zi**

玉△爐○香○
yù lú xiāng
scent of censer

紅○蠟△淚▲
hóng là lèi
red candle tears

偏○照△
piān zhào
shine sideward;
shine on purpose

畫△堂○
huà táng
painted hall

秋○思▲
qiū sī
(one who) is
occupied with
autumn

眉○翠△薄△
méi cuì bó
eyebrow color
becomes lighter

鬢△雲○殘●
bìn yún cán
temple hair looks
disheveled

夜△長△
yè cháng
night is long

衾○枕△寒●
qīn zhěn hán
gilt and pillow cold

梧○桐○樹▲
wú tóng shù
parasol tree

三○更○雨▲
sān gèng yǔ
after midnight rain

不△道△
bù dào
not knowing

離○情○
lí qíng
parting feelings

正△苦▲
zhèng kǔ
hard to bear right
now

一△葉△葉△
yī yè yè
leaf by leaf

一△聲○聲●
yī shēng shēng
sound after sound

空○階○
kōng jiē
vacant steps

滴△到△
dī dào
dropping until

明●
míng
daybreak

51

温庭筠

更漏子

柳丝长，春雨细，花外漏声迢递。惊塞雁，起城乌，画屏金鹧鸪。香雾薄，透帘幕，惆怅谢家池阁。红烛背，绣帘垂，梦长君不知。

Wen Tingyun

Tune: "Geng Lou Zi"

Feelings at Night

Long are the willow osiers;
So light are the spring drizzles.
Beyond flowers the water clock drifts all night.
The migrated wild geese are startled;
the crows start to fly.
Golden partridges on the painted screen
seem ready to try.

Fragrant mist spreads thin;
It seeps through the curtain, filling
the gloomy air over the pool and pavilion.
Red candle burning will soon be over.
The brocaded curtains hang low.
The dream is too long for you to know.

温庭筠　**wēn tíng yún**
更漏子　**gèng lòu zi**

柳△絲○長○
liǔ sī cháng
willow osiers long

春○雨△細▲
chūn yǔ xì
spring rain light

花○外△
huā wài
beyond flowers

漏△聲○
lòu shēng
sound of water clock

迢○遞▲
tiáo dì
from afar

驚○塞△雁△
jīng sāi yàn
startle wild geese from frontier

起△城○烏●
qǐ chéng wū
crows fly away

畫△屏○
huà píng
painted screen

金○鷓△鴣●
jīn zhè gū
golden partridges

香○霧△薄▲
xiāng wù bó
fragrant mist thin

透△簾○幕▲
tòu lián mù
seep through curtain

惆○悵△
chóu chàng
melancholy

謝△家○
xiè jiā
our house

池○閣▲
chí gé
pool and pavilion

紅○燭○背△
hóng zhú bèi
red candle near the end

繡△簾○垂●
xiù lián chuí
brocaded screens hang low

夢△長○
mèng cháng
long dream

君○
jūn
you

不△知●
bù zhī
don't know

温庭筠

梦江南

梳洗罢,独倚望江楼。过尽千帆皆不是,斜晖脉脉水悠悠。肠断白萍洲。

Wen Tingyun

Tune: "Meng Jiang Nan"

Waiting and Waiting

After combing my hair and dressing up,
I climb the tower by the riverside.
Alone I lean on the railing and look afar.
His boat is not among the thousand sails
that have passed.
The slanting sun lingers affectionately;
the water flows unhurriedly.
Seeing the white duckweed on the
islet breaks my heart.

温庭筠 **wēn tíng yún**
梦江南 **mèng jiāng nán**

梳〇洗△
shū xǐ
wash and dress

罢△
bà
done

独△倚△
dú yǐ
lean alone

望△江〇
wàng jiāng
river facing

楼●
lóu
tower

过△尽△
guò jìn
all pass through

千〇帆〇
qiān fān
a thousand sails

皆〇不△是△
jiē bú shì
none of them is (his)

斜〇晖〇
xié huī
slanting sun

脉△脉△
mài mài
lovingly

水△悠〇悠●
shuǐ yōu yōu
water unhurried

肠〇断△
cháng duàn
heart breaks

白△苹〇
bái píng
white duckweed

洲●
zhōu
islet

温庭筠

梦江南

千万恨,恨极在天涯。山月不知心里事,水风空落眼前花。摇曳碧云斜。

Wen Tingyun

Tune: "Meng Jiang Nan"

So Many Regrets

Thousands and thousands of regrets.
The most painful one stays in the remote corner.
Mountain and moon know nothing
about what is on my mind.
Rain and wind blow down flowers
in front of my eyes.
The emerald clouds sway slantwise in the sky.

溫庭筠　**wēn tíng yún**
夢江南　**mèng jiāng nán**

千〇萬△
qiān wàn
thousands of

恨△
hèn
regrets

恨△極△
hèn jí
most serious regret

在△
zài
is in

天〇涯●
tiān yá
remote corner

山〇月△
shān yuè
mountain and moon

不△知〇
bù zhī
know not

心〇裏△事△
xīn lǐ shì
what's on my heart

水△風〇
shuǐ fēng
rain with wind

空〇落△
kōng luò
fall in vain

眼△前〇花●
yǎn qián huā
flowers in front of the eyes

搖〇曳△
yáo yì
sway

碧△雲〇
bì yún
emerald clouds

斜●
xié
slantwise

山月不知心里事，
水风空落眼前花。

Mountain and moon know nothing
about what is on my mind.
Rain and wind blow down flowers
in front of my eyes.

— Wen Tingyun

Wei Zhuang (836–910)

韦庄

Like Wen Tingyun, Wei Zhuang was a descendant of a powerful and wealthy family. Wei's ancestor Wei Dai Jia was Empress Wu's prime minister during the early Tang period. He was also the great-grandson of the famous Tang poet Wei Ying Wu. His father died when he was still young. He had to work hard to support his family in his early years.

At the age of forty five, Wei went to the capital Chang'an for the imperial examination. He failed the examination and was forced to stay in Chang'an for three years because of the Huang Chao rebellion. Later, he left the capital for Luoyang. While he was there, he wrote his famous long poem "The Song of a Qin Woman." In this poem, Wei describes the miseries of the war through the character of a woman. When Luoyang was in turmoil, Wei moved his family to Jiangnan, south of the Yangtze River.

At the age of nearly sixty, Wei finally passed the examination. Wei Zhuang and Wen Ting Yun were often mentioned and described together as they both were the most influential figures in the early development of *ci* poetry. Although he wrote good *shi* poems, Wei was better known for his *ci* poems, particularly his five poems to the tune of *Pu Sa Man*.

Like Wen Tingyun, Wei's *ci* poems are almost exclusively about love and women. In contrast to Wen Tingyun, however, Wei was more explicit and personal in articulating his feelings. Influenced by the great poet Bai Ju Yi, Wei wrote his poems in plain language so ordinary people can understand.

Wei Zhuang died at the age of seventy-five in Cheng Du, where Du Fu used to live.

韦庄

菩萨蛮

人人尽说江南好。游人只合江南老。春水碧于天。画船听雨眠。垆边人似月。皓腕凝霜雪。未老莫还乡。还乡须断肠。

Wei Zhuang

Tune: "Pu Sa Man"

Grow Old in Jiangnan

Everyone talks about the beautiful scenery
in Jiangnan all the time.
It is only fitting for tourists to stay
there before they retire.
The spring water there is as bluish as the sky.
One can lie on a pleasure boat, listening to the rain.
The person by the wine stand looks like
the moon beam.
Her wrist is as bright as frost and snow.
Don't return to your native home before you are old.
It will break your heart when you must do so.

韋庄　　**wéi zhuāng**
菩薩蠻　　**pú sà mán**

○ = 平声 (*ping* or flat tone)

△ = 仄声 (*ze* or deflected tone)

● = 平声韵 (rhymed in *ping* or flat tone)

▲ = 仄声韵 (rhymed in *ze* or deflected tone)

人○人○
rén rén
everybody

游○人○
yóu rén
tourists

春○水△
chūn shuǐ
spring water

画△船○
huà chuan
pleasure boat

鑪○边○
lú biān
earthen stand for wine jars

皓△腕△
hào wàn
bright wrist

未△老△
wèi lǎo
not yet old

還○鄉○
huán xiāng
returning to native land

盡△說△
jìn shuō
says all the time

只△合△
zhī hé
only fit

碧△
bì
bluish green

聽△
tīng
listen to

人○似△
rén sì
person looks like

凝○
níng
formed by

莫△
mò
don't

須△
xū
must

江○南○好▲
jiāng nán hǎo
Jiang Nan (River South) is so good

江○南○老▲
jiāng nán lǎo
to grow old in Jiang Nan

於○天●
yú tiān
than the sky

雨△眠●
yǔ mián
rain while sleeping

月▲
yuè
a moon

霜○雪▲
shuāng xuě
frost and snow

還○鄉●
huán xiāng
return to native land

斷△腸●
duàn cháng
break the heart

韦庄

菩萨蛮

红楼别夜堪惆怅。香灯半卷流苏帐。残月出门时。美人和泪辞。琵琶金翠羽。弦上黄莺语。劝我早归家。绿窗人似花。

Wei Zhuang

Tune: "Pu Sa Man"

Dreaming in Autumn

How can one not be sad in a red
chamber on parting night?
The tasseled canopy was half
closed in scented lamplight.
The waning moon was still hanging when I left home.
With tears in her eyes, she said good-bye.
She played the *pipa* decorated with
a golden-green feather.
She plucked the strings in oriole language
for me to decipher.
She advised me to return home soon.
For the person by the green window
would be like a flower in bloom.

韋庄 **wéi zhuāng**
菩薩蠻 **pú sà mán**

○ = 平声 (*ping* or flat tone)
△ = 仄声 (*ze* or deflected tone)
● = 平声韵 (rhymed in *ping* or flat tone)
▲ = 仄声韵 (rhymed in *ze* or deflected tone)

紅○樓○
hóng lóu
red chamber

香○燈○
xiāng dēng
scented lamp

殘○月△
cán yuè
waning moon

美△人○
měi rén
fair lady

琵○琶○
pí pá
pipa

弦○上△
xián shàng
over the string

勸△我△
quàn wǒ
advise me

綠△窗○
lǜ chuāng
green window

別△夜△
bié yè
parting night

半△捲△
bàn juǎn
half-rolled

出△門○
chū mén
leaving home

和○淚△
hé lèi
in tears

金○翠△
jīn cuì
kingfisher

黃○鶯○
huáng yīng
oriole

早△
zǎo
early

人○似△
rén sì
person looks like

堪○惆○悵▲
kān chóu chàng
can make one sad

流○蘇○帳▲
liú sū zhàng
tassel curtain

時●
shí
time of

辭●
cí
bid farewell

羽▲
yǔ
feathers

語▲
yǔ
spoken words

歸○家●
guī jiā
to return home

花●
huā
flower

63

韦庄

菩萨蛮

劝君今夜须沉醉。尊前莫话明朝事。珍重主人心。酒深情亦深。 须愁春漏短。莫诉金杯满。遇酒且呵呵。人生能几何？

Wei Zhuang

Tune: "Pu Sa Man"

Get Intoxicated

Get drunk tonight to drive away sorrow.
Facing a wine jar, talk not about tomorrow.
Your goodwill should be taken to heart.
Your wine jar is deep, but your hospitality deeper.

Be aware of the short duration of spring.
Don't complain of a golden wine cup filled to the brim.
Laugh out loud whenever you are offered wine.
How many times can it be repeated in life?

韋庄　　**wéi zhuāng**
菩薩蠻　　**pú sà mán**

勸△君〇
quàn jūn
advise you

今〇夜△
jīn yè
tonight

須〇沉〇醉▲
xū chén zuì
must become intoxicated

樽〇前〇
zūn qián
in front of a wine jar

莫△話△
mò huà
don't talk about

明〇朝〇事▲
míng zhāo shì
tomorrow's matters

珍〇重△
zhēn zhòng
appreciate

主△人〇
zhǔ rén
host

心●
xīn
good will

酒△深〇
jiǔ shēn
wine cup is deep

情〇
qíng
affection

亦△深●
yì shēn
also deep

須〇愁〇
xū chóu
beware of

春〇漏△
chūn lòu
spring water clock

短▲
duǎn
short/brief

莫△訴△
mò sù
don't complain

金〇杯〇
jīn bēi
golden cup

滿▲
mǎn
is full

遇〇酒△
yù jiǔ
encountering wine

且△
qiě
let it be

呵〇呵●
hē hē
guffaw

人〇生〇
rén shēng
in life

能〇
néng
can

幾△何●
jǐ hé
how many times like this

65

韦庄

浣溪沙

夜夜相思更漏残。伤心明月凭栏杆。想君思我锦衾寒。咫尺画堂深似海，忆来唯把旧书看。几时携手入长安。

Wei Zhuang

Tune: "Wan Xi Sha"

Longing

Pining for you until the water clock
fades, night after night.
Leaning on the railing in sadness,
I look at the moon so bright.
Your quilt would be turning cold
if you were thinking of me now.
The painted hall is so close to me,
yet it is as deep as the sea.
I read the old letter to get rid of
the thought from my mind.
When will we be able to walk hand
in hand into Chang'an?

韋庄　　**wéi zhuāng**
浣溪沙　**wǎn xī shā**

夜△夜△
yè yè
night after night

傷○心○
shāng xīn
heartbroken

想△君○
xiǎng jūn
I assume you

咫△尺△
zhǐ chǐ
so near

憶△來○
yì lái
thinking about it

幾△時○
jǐ shí
when

相○思○
xiāng sī
longing

明○月△
míng yuè
bright moon

思○我△
sī wǒ
thinking of me

畫△堂○
huà táng
pained hall

唯○把△
wéi bǎ
can only

攜○手△
xié shǒu
hand in hand

更△漏△殘●
gèng lòu cán
water clock fades

憑○欄○杆●
píng lán gān
lean on railing

錦△衾○寒●
jǐn qīn hán
brocaded quilt turns cold

深○似△海△
shēn sì hǎi
as deep as sea

舊△書○看●
jiù shū kàn
read old letters

入△長○安●
rù cháng ān
enter Chang'an

67

韦庄

清平乐

莺啼残月。绣阁香灯灭。门外马嘶郎欲别。正是落花时节。妆成不画蛾眉。含愁独倚金扉。去路香尘莫扫，扫即郎去归迟。

Wei Zhuang

Tune: "Qing Ping Le"

Feelings at Night

Orioles cry under the waning moon.
The scented lamp goes out in the embroiled room.
The horse neighs outside;
my man is about to say goodbye.
This happens to be the flowers-falling time.

I have done my makeup, but my
brows are not penciled.
With sadness, I alone lean on the golden gate.
Don't sweep the fragrant dust on the walk.
Lest he will leave sooner and return late.

韋庄 **wéi zhuāng**
清平樂 **qīng píng lè**

鶯○啼○ *yīng tí* orioles cry	殘○月▲ *cán yuè* waning moon	
繡△閣△ *xiù gé* embroidered boudoir	香○燈○ *xiāng dēng* scented lamp	滅▲ *miè* extinguished
門○外△ *mén wài* outside	馬△嘶○ *mǎ sī* horse neighs	郎○欲△別▲ *láng yù bié* my man about to leave
正△是△ *zhèng shì* just happen to be	落△花○ *luò huā* flowers-falling	時○節▲ *shí jié* season
妝○成○ *zhuāng chéng* makeup done	不△畫△ *bù huà* not to pencil	蛾○眉● *é méi* slender eyebrows
含○愁○ *hán chóu* showing sorrow	獨△倚△ *dú yǐ* alone lean on	金○扉● *jīn fēi* golden gate
去△路△ *qù lù* walking path	香○塵○ *xiāng chén* fragrant dust	莫△掃△ *mò sǎo* don't sweep
掃△即△ *sǎo jí* if swept	郎○去△ *láng qù* he will leave (now)	歸○遲● *guī chí* return late

韦庄

女冠子

四月十七,正是去年今日,别君时。忍泪佯低面,含羞半敛眉。不知魂已断,空有梦相随。除却天边月,没人知。

Wei Zhuang

Tune: "Nu Guan Zi"

On this Day Last Year

Last year this day
was the seventeenth of May.
It was the parting day.
Holding back my tears,
I pretended to lower my face.
With shyness, my brows
moved a little closer in space.

Not knowing that my spirit
had gone astray,
my dream still followed you
in vain all the way.
No one knew what's on my mind,
except the moon at the edge of the sky.

韋庄　**wéi zhuāng**
女冠子　**nǚ guān zi**

四△月△
sì yuè
fourth month

十△七▲
shí qī
seventeen

正△是△
zhèng shì
happens to be

去△年〇
qù nián
last year

今〇日▲
jīn rì
today

別△君〇
bié jūn
parting with you

時●
shí
at that time

忍△淚△
rěn lèi
hold back my tears

佯〇
yáng
to pretend

低〇面▲
dī miàn
lower the face

含〇羞〇
hán xiū
with shyness

半△
bàn
half

斂△眉●
liàn méi
draw together eyebrows

不△知〇
bù zhī
don't know

魂〇
hún
soul

已△斷△
yǐ duàn
has broken

空〇有△
kōng yǒu
only there is

夢△
mèng
dream

相〇隨●
xiāng suí
to follow

除〇卻△
chú què
except

天〇邊〇
tiān biān
edge of sky

月△
yuè
moon

沒△人〇
méi rén
no one

知●
zhī
knows

71

韦庄

女冠子

昨夜夜半，枕上分明梦见。语多时。依旧桃花面，
频低柳叶眉。半羞还半喜，欲去又依依。
觉来知是梦，不胜悲。

Wei Zhuang

Tune: "Nu Guan Zi"

In My Dream

At midnight last night,
I vividly dreamed of you
on the pillow lying.
You kept talking and talking.
Your face still looked like a peach flower.
Your slender eyebrows often appeared lower.

Half shy, half joyful.
It was time for you to leave now,
but you were so reluctant to go.
Awaken, I found out to be a dream.
I felt so sadly overwhelmed.

韋庄　　**wéi zhuāng**
女冠子　　**nǚ guān zi**

昨△夜△
zuó yè
last night

夜△半▲
yè bàn
midnight

枕△上△
zhěn shàng
on the pillow

分〇明〇
fēn míng
obviously

夢△見▲
mèng jiàn
dream of seeing you

語△多〇
yǔ duō
talking and talking

時●
shí
at that time

依〇舊△
yī jiù
still the same

桃〇花〇
táo huā
peach blossom

面▲
miàn
face

頻〇低〇
pín dī
repeatedly lower

柳△葉△
liǔ yè
willow-leaf

眉●
méi
eyebrows

半△羞〇
bàn xiū
half shy

還〇
huán
though

半△喜△
bàn xǐ
half happy

欲△去△
yù qù
wishing to go

又△
yòu
but then

依〇依●
yī yī
reluctant to leave

覺△來〇
jué lái
awaken

知〇是△
zhī shì
knowing it is

夢△
mèng
a dream

不△勝△
bù shèng
extremely

悲●
bēi
sad

73

遇酒且呵呵。人生能几何？

Laugh out loud whenever
you are offered wine.
How many times can it be repeated in life?

— Wei Zhuang

Feng Yan Si (903–960)

冯延巳

Feng Yan Si, who was brought up in Guangling (present-day Yang Zhou, Jiansu Province), was a scholar, a poet, and a politician in the Southern Tang period. Southern Tang was one of the ten states during the Five Dynasties, which lasted from 937 to 975.

Feng served as a prime minister for Li Jing, the monarch of Southern Tang and father of the great poet Li Yu. Feng knew not only how to write beautiful poetry, but also how to play the game of politics to his advantage. In spite of instances of mishandling governmental affairs, he was able to whether the storm repeatedly. Feng was not well-liked by his colleagues because he could go to extremes for personal gain. He died at the age of fifty-eight. Over one hundred of his poems have survived.

Feng was strongly influenced by Wen Tingyun and Wei Zhuang in his style of writing. Like Wen and Wei, the themes of his poems tend to be around romantic love, flowers, and parting. However, he was more creative in poetic conception.

His poems also show greater depth as indicated by his poetic expression of free-floating anxiety and pop-up feelings.

Ruler Li Jing, who himself was also a poet, loved to read Feng's poems. He once teased Feng by asking him why did "a pool of spring water ruffled by the wind" become his problem?（吹皱一池春水，干卿底事）The first part of the quotation has since become a common expression for the idea "None of your business."

Feng's poetry exerted strong influence on other poets in the Song Dynasty, notably An Shu and Ouyang Xiu.

冯延巳

鹊踏枝

谁道闲情抛弃久。每到春来，惆怅还依旧。日日花前常病酒。不辞镜里朱颜瘦。　河畔青芜堤上柳。为问新愁，何事年年有。独立小桥风满袖。平林新月人归后。

Feng Yan Si

Tune: "Que Ta Zhi"

Feelings of Melancholy

Who says that pop-up feelings
can be discarded for long?
When spring comes, my
melancholy remains strong.
I often drown myself with wine
In front of the flowers every day.
I care little that the image in the
mirror shows a thinner face.

So green is the grass by the riverside.
Willows on the bank look so nice.
Why then year after year,
new sorrow always comes along?
Standing alone by the little bridge,
I feel as though the wind fills my sleeves.
After everybody has gone home,
I see over the wooded plain the crescent moon.

馮延巳　**féng yán sì**
鵲踏枝　**què tà zhī**

- ○ = 平声 (*ping* or flat tone)
- △ = 仄声 (*ze* or deflected tone)
- ● = 平声韵 (rhymed in *ping* or flat tone)
- ▲ = 仄声韵 (rhymed in *ze* or deflected tone)

誰○道△
shéi dào
who says

每△到△
měi dào
whenever

惆○悵△
chóu chàng
melancholy

日△日△
rì rì
every day

不△辭○
bù cí
care not

河○畔△
hé pàn
riverside

為○問△
wéi wèn
to ask why

何○事△
hé shì
for what reason

獨△立△
dú lì
standing alone

平○林○
píng lín
plain grove

閒○情○
xián qíng
pop-up feelings

春○來○
chūn lái
spring comes

還○
hái
remains

花○前○
huā qián
before flowers

鏡△裏△
jìng lǐ
in the mirror

青○蕪○
qīng wú
green glass

新○愁○
xīn chóu
new sorrow

年○年○
nián nián
every year

小△橋○
xiǎo qiáo
little bridge

新○月△
xīn yuè
new moon

拋○棄△久▲
pāo qì jiǔ
long abandoned

依○舊▲
yī jiù
as ever

常○病△酒▲
cháng bìng jiǔ
often drink excessively

朱○顏○瘦▲
zhū yán shòu
face to become thin

堤○上△柳▲
dī shàng liǔ
willows on bank

有▲
yǒu
it is here

風○滿△袖▲
fēng mǎn xiù
sleeves filled with wind

人○歸○後▲
rén guī hòu
after one has returned

冯延巳

鹊踏枝

六曲阑干偎碧树。杨柳风轻，展尽黄金缕。谁把钿筝移玉柱。穿帘海燕又飞去。 满眼游丝兼落絮。红杏开时，一霎清明雨。浓睡觉来莺乱语。惊残好梦无寻处。

Feng Yan Si

Tune: "Que Ta Zhi"

Spring Feelings

By the winding balustrade,
I leaned on a green tree.
The willow was gently brushed by the breeze.
The golden threads swing from side to side.
Who moved the fingers on the filigreed zither?
A petrel flew away again through the blind.

The drifting branches and
fallen catkins catch my eyes.
When the red apricot flowers bloom,
a sudden rain fall on this day of Sweeping Tomb.
Awaken after a sound sleep, I hear the orioles tweet.
Where can I find my broken dream that was so sweet?

馮延巳　**féng yán sì**
鵲踏枝　**què tà zhī**

六△曲△ liù qū a winding	欄○杆○ lán gān railings; balustrade	偎○碧△樹▲ wēi bì shù lean on green trees
楊○柳△ yáng liǔ willows	風○輕○ fēng qīng in gentle breeze	
展△盡△ zhǎn jìn display all	黃○金○ huáng jīn golden	縷▲ lǚ threads
誰○把△ shéi bǎ who holds	鈿○箏○ tián zhēng filigreed zither	移○玉△柱▲ yí yù zhù move the jade pin
穿○簾○ chuān lián through curtain	海△燕△ hǎi yàn petrels	又△飛○去▲ yòu fēi qù again fly away
滿△眼△ mǎn yǎn in full view	游○絲○ yóu sī drifting branches	兼○落△絮▲ jiān luò xù and fallen catkins
紅○杏△ hóng xìng red apricot	開○時○ kāi shí in blossom	
一△霎△ yī shà in a moment	清○明○ qīng míng Tomb-Sweeping	雨▲ yǔ rain
濃○睡△ nóng shuì sound sleep	覺△來○ jiào lái awaken	鶯○亂△語▲ yīng luàn yǔ orioles chirping disorderly
驚○殘○ jīng cán afraid of remaining	好△夢△ hǎo mèng sweet dream	無○尋○處▲ wú xún chù nowhere to be found

冯延巳

鹊踏枝

几日行云何处去。忘却归来，不道春将暮。百草千花寒食路。香车系在谁家树。　泪眼倚楼频独语。双燕来时，陌上相逢否。撩乱春愁如柳絮。悠悠梦里无寻处。

Feng Yan Si

Tune: "Que Ta Zhi"

When Will You Come Home?

Last several days, floating cloud,
where did you go?
You have forgotten to return home.
Don't you know spring is about to grow old?
By the time when food is eaten cold,
all glasses and flowers by the roadside grow.
Around whose tree is your scented
carriage encircled?

As I lean on the tower, I repeatedly
whisper to myself in tearful eyes.
On your way here, did you happen
to meet a pair of swallows?
My stirred spring sorrows are like
catkins falling randomly from the willows.
Where can I go to find you in my dream?
It is so far and indistinct!

馮延巳 **féng yán sì**
鵲踏枝 **què tà zhī**

幾△日△
jǐ rì
several days

忘△卻△
wàng què
forget

不△道△
bù dào
not knowing

百△草△
bǎi cǎo
hundred glasses

香○車○
xiāng chē
fragrant carriage

淚△眼△
lèi yǎn
tearful eyes

雙○燕△
shuāng yàn
a pair of swallows

陌△上△
mò shàng
on a road

撩○亂△
liáo luàn
stirred

悠○悠○
yōu yōu
indistinct

行○雲○
xíng yún
floating cloud

歸○來○
guī lái
to return

春○
chūn
spring

千○花○
qiān huā
thousand flowers

繫△在○
xì zài
ties to

倚△樓○
yǐ lóu
leaning on tower

來○時○
lái shí
come

相○逢○
xiàng féng
(did you) meet

春○愁○
chūn chóu
spring sorrows

夢△里△
mèng lǐ
in the dream

何○處△去▲
hé chǔ qù
where to go

將○暮▲
jiāng mù
will soon be over

寒△食△路▲
hán shí lù
road on Cold Food Day

誰○家○樹▲
shéi jiā shù
whose tree

頻○獨△語▲
pín dú yǔ
whisper repeatedly

否▲
fǒu
or not

如○柳○絮▲
rú liǔ xù
like willow catkins

無○尋○處▲
wú xún chǔ
no place to find

冯延巳

谒金门

风乍起。吹皱一池春水。闲引鸳鸯香径里。手挼红杏蕊。斗鸭阑干独倚。碧玉搔头斜坠。终日望君君不至。举头闻鹊喜。

Feng Yan Si

Tune: "Ye Jin Men"

Uneasy Feelings

The wind suddenly blows.
A pool of spring water is ruffled with wrinkles.
On a fragrant pathway, I play
with the mandarin ducks.
I gently rub in my hand a red apricot bud.
Alone, I watch ducks fighting
by leaning on the railing.
My emerald jade hairpin is half falling.
I wait for your return the whole day,
but I have not yet seen your face.
Raising my head, I listen to what
the magpies have to say.

馮延巳　**féng yán sì**
謁金門　**yè jīn mén**

風○ *fēng* wind	乍△起▲ *zhà qǐ* suddenly blows	
吹○皺△ *chuī zhòu* ruffle	一△池○ *yī chí* a pool of	春○水▲ *chūn shuǐ* spring water
閒○引△ *xián yǐn* to play for fun	鴛○鴦○ *yuān yāng* mandarin ducks	香○徑△裏▲ *xiāng jìng lǐ* in a fragrant path
手△挼△ *shǒu lè* rub with palms	紅○杏△ *hóng xìng* pink apricot	蕊▲ *ruǐ* bud
鬥△鴨△ *dòu yā* duck fighting	欄○杆○ *lán gān* railing	獨△倚▲ *dú yǐ* lean alone
碧△玉△ *bì yù* jade green	搔○頭○ *sāo tóu* hairpin	斜○墜▲ *xié zhuì* drop slantwise
終○日△ *zhōng rì* all day	望△君○ *wàng jūn* wait for you	君○不△至▲ *jūn bù zhì* you have not arrived
舉△頭○ *jǔ tóu* lifting up head	聞○ *wén* hear	鵲△喜▲ *què xǐ* magpies

冯延巳

采桑子

花前失却游春侣，独自寻芳。满目悲凉。纵有笙歌亦断肠。林间戏蝶帘间燕，各自双双。忍更思量。绿树青苔半夕阳。

Feng Yan Si

Tune: "Cai Sang Zi"

Melancholy Mood

I stand before the flowers without my
mate during spring outings.
I am out alone trying to have a good time.
Everything seems sad in my eyes.
I still feel very sad even with music and song.
In the glove two merry butterflies play around.
Two swallows fly through the blind.
They are together or in pairs.
I can't get you out from my mind
no matter how hard I try.
I see the green trees and mosses
under the slanting sunlight.

馮延巳　**féng yán sì**
采桑子　**cǎi sāng zi**

花○前○
huā qián
in front of flowers

獨△自△
dú zì
alone

滿△目△
mǎn mù
in full view

縱△有△
zòng yǒu
even there is

林○間○
lín jiān
in the woods

各△自△
gè zì
each

忍△更△
rěn gèng
more to bear

綠△樹△
lǜ shù
green trees

失△卻△
shī què
to have lost

尋○芳●
xún fāng
go see flowers

悲○涼●
bēi liáng
sadness

笙○歌○
shēng gē
music and song

戲△蝶△
xì dié
playing butterflies

雙○雙●
shuāng shuāng
in pair

思○量●
sī liàng
more to think

青○苔○
qīng tái
green mosses

遊○春○侶△
yóu chūn lǚ
spring-tour companion

亦△斷△腸●
yì duàn cháng
can only break the heart

簾○間○燕△
lián jiān yàn
swallows in curtain

半△夕△陽●
bàn xī yáng
half sunset

冯延巳

清平乐

雨晴烟晚。绿水新池满。双燕飞来垂柳院。小阁画帘高卷。黄昏独倚朱阑，西南新月眉弯。砌下落花风起，罗衣特地春寒。

Feng Yan Si

Tune: "Qing Ping Le"

After the Rain

Clear sky after the rain;
mist pervades toward evening.
Green water fills up the new pool.
A pair of swallows fly over to the
courtyard grown with weeping willows.
In the small attic, she rolls up high
the painted screen.
Leaning on the red railing alone at twilight,
she looks at the new crescent moon
over the southwestern sky.
The wind blows the fallen flowers
below the steps.
She feels a spring chill in her silken dress.

馮延巳　　**féng yán sì**
清平樂　　**qīng píng lè**

雨△晴〇
yǔ qíng
rain is clear

煙〇晚▲
yān wǎn
mist at dusk

綠△水△
lǜ shuǐ
green water

新〇池〇
xīn chí
new pool

滿▲
mǎn
is full

雙△燕△
shuāng yàn
a pair of swallows

飛〇來〇
fēi lái
fly here

垂〇柳△院▲
chuí liǔ yuàn
willow-dropping courtyard

小△閣△
xiǎo gé
small attic

畫△簾〇
huà lián
paint screen

高〇捲▲
gāo juǎn
rolled up high

黃〇昏〇
huáng hūn
at dusk

獨△倚△
dú yǐ
lean alone

朱〇欄●
zhū lán
red railing

西〇南〇
xī nán
southewst

新〇月△
xīn yuè
new moon

眉〇彎●
méi wān
curved like eyebrow

砌△下△
qì xià
steps below

落△花〇
luò huā
fallen flowers

風〇起△
fēng qǐ
wind blows

羅〇衣〇
luó yī
thin-silk dress

特△地△
tè dì
especially feel

春〇寒●
chūn hán
spring chill

87

冯延巳

南乡子

细雨湿流光。芳草年年与恨长。烟锁凤楼无限事，茫茫。鸾镜鸳衾两断肠。 魂梦任悠扬。睡起杨花满绣床。薄幸不来门半掩，斜阳。负你残春泪几行。

Feng Yan Si

Tune: "Nan Xiang Zi"

Loneliness

A fine rain moistens the flow of time.
Year after year my sorrow is
as long as the fragrant grass.
In my boudoir that is shrouded in mist,
I simply have too much to remember.
So endless!
It breaks my heart when both mirror
and quilt now look much larger.

Let me in the dreams freely drift higher or lower.
Awaken and up, I notice that my
embroidered bed is full of willow flowers.
I still leave the door half open even though
my fickle lover will not come.
In slanting sunlight.
Seeing spring off, I find several streams
of tears in my eyes.

馮延巳　**féng yán sì**
南鄉子　**nán xiāng zi**

細〇雨△
xì yǔ
fine rain

芳〇草△
fāng cǎo
fragrant grass

煙〇鎖△
yān suǒ
mist shrouds

茫〇茫●
máng máng
indistinct

鸞△鏡△
luán jìng
a couple's mirror

魂〇夢△
hún mèng
dream

睡△起△
shuì qǐ
get up from bed

薄△倖△
bó xìng
fickle lover

斜〇陽●
xié yáng
slanting sun

負△你△
fù nǐ
to owe you

濕△
shī
moistens

年〇年〇
nián nián
year after year

鳳〇樓〇
fèng lóu
phoenix tower

鴛〇衾〇
yuān qīn
a couple's quilt

任△
rèn
to let

楊〇花〇
yáng huā
catkins

不△來〇
bù lái
not come

殘〇春〇
cán chūn
waning spring

流〇光●
liú guāng
time

與△恨△長●
yǔ hèn cháng
as long as sorrows

無〇限△事△
wú xiàn shì
so many things

兩△斷△腸●
liǎng duàn cháng
both break heart

悠〇揚●
yōu yáng
flow high or low

滿△繡△床●
mǎn xiù chuáng
all over embroidered bed

門〇半△掩△
mén bàn yǎn
door half closed

淚△幾△行●
lèi jǐ háng
several strings of tears

风乍起。吹皱一池春水。

The wind suddenly blows.
A pool of spring water is ruffled with wrinkles.

— Feng Yansi

Li Yu (937–978)

李煜

Li Yu, popularly known as Li Houzi (last ruler), was the third and last ruler of the Southern Tang (937–975) period. His poetry was influenced by Feng Yansi, who also served as the prime minister for Li's father.

Li Yu was Li Jing's sixth son. Normally he was not in line for the throne, but the death of his elder brothers for various reasons unexpectedly altered his fortune. When Li emerged as Southern Tang's third ruler, his country had already become a vassal state of the Song Empire.

Li demonstrated exceptional talents not only in literature, but also in art and calligraphy. Although he was recognized as one of the best poets in *ci* form, he was by all indications a failed and inept ruler. His incompetence and lack of interest in national affairs played an important part in the loss of his reign. Three years after he was captured, he was poisoned to death, presumably for the poem (to the tune of *Yu Mei Ren*) in which he lamented the loss of his kingdom. The Song emperor was said to be especially upset at the following line: 故国不堪回首月明中 (It was so unbearable to think of my lost kingdom in bright moonlight.) At the time of his death, he was only forty-one years old.

The number of Li's poems surviving today is only about thirty-two. However, most of them are recognized as poems that are highly resonant. His writing style also plays an important part in his continued popularity as a *ci* poet after his death. His ideas and language are natural, clear, and genuine in expression. His failure as a ruler was definitely a momentous accomplishment in the world of poetry.

李煜

虞美人

春花秋月何时了，往事知多少。小楼昨夜又东风，故国不堪回首月明中。　雕阑玉砌应犹在，只是朱颜改。问君能有几多愁，恰似一江春水向东流。

Li Yu

Tune: "Yu Mei Ren"

My Lost Kingdom

Spring flowers and autumn moon:
When will this cycle be over?
So many past events to remember!
East wind again pierced through
the small tower last night.
It was so unbearable to think of my
lost kingdom in bright moonlight.
Carved railings and jade steps
should still be there.
Beautiful faces can no longer be as fair.
Ask me how much sorrow can I bear?
It is like a river full of spring water,
flowing to the east forever!

李煜 **lǐ yù**
虞美人 **yú měi rén**

○ = 平声 (*ping* or flat tone)
△ = 仄声 (*ze* or deflected tone)
● = 平声韵 (rhymed in *ping* or flat tone)
▲ = 仄声韵 (rhymed in *ze* or deflected tone)

春○花○
chūn huā
spring flower

往△事△
wǎng shì
past events

小△楼○
xiǎo lóu
little storied building

故△国△
gù guó
native land

月△明○中●
yuè míng zhōng
in moonlight

雕○栏○
diāo lán
carved railings

只△是△
zhī shì
only

问△君○
wèn jūn
ask me (you)

恰△似△
qià sì
just like

向△东○流●
xiàng dōng liú
flowing to the east

秋○月△
qiū yuè
autumn moon

知○
zhī
know

昨△夜△
zuó yè
last night

不△堪○
bù kān
can't bear

玉△砌△
yù qì
jade steps

朱○颜○
zhū yán
beautiful faces

能○有△
néng yǒu
can have

一△江○
yī jiāng
a river (of)

何○时○了▲
hé shí liǎo
when will it be over?

多○少▲
duō shǎo
how many

又△东○风●
yòu dōng fēng
east wind again

回○首△
huí shǒu
to look back

应○犹○在▲
yìng yóu zài
should still be there

改▲
gǎi
have altered

几△多○愁●
jǐ duō chóu
how much sorrow

春○水△
chūn shuǐ
spring water

93

李煜

相见欢

无言独上西楼。月如钩。寂寞梧桐深院锁清秋。
剪不断，理还乱，是离愁。别有一番滋味在心头。

Li Yu

Tune: "Xiang Jian Huan"

Autumn Sorrow

Silently I ascend the western tower alone.
The moon is like a hook.
With a lonely parasol tree,
the deep courtyard has captured
the clear autumn tune.
Cut it, it is unbreakable.
Straighten it, it remains entangled.
Is this a feeling of sadness to part?
It feels like a strange taste in my heart.

李煜　**lǐ yù**
相見歡　**xiāng jiàn huān**

無○言○
wú yán
without a word

獨△上△
dú shàng
alone go up to

西○樓●
xī lóu
west tower

月△
yuè
moon

如○
rú
is like

鉤●
gōu
a hook

寂△寞△
jì mò
lonely

梧○桐○
wú tóng
parasol tree

深○院△
shēn yuàn
deep courtyard

鎖△
suǒ
has locked

清○秋●
qīng qiū
clear autumn

剪△
jiǎn
to cut (it)

不△斷△
bù duàn
unbreakable

理△
lǐ
to manage (it)

還○亂△
huán luàn
still disarranged

是△
shì
(it) is

離○愁●
lí chóu
parting sorrow

別△有△
bié yǒu
(it) has another

一△番○
yī fān
kind of

滋○味△
zī wèi
taste

在△
zài
in (my)

心○頭●
xīn tóu
heart

李煜

破阵子

四十年来家国，三千里地山河。凤阁龙楼连霄汉，玉树琼枝作烟萝。几曾识干戈？　一旦归为臣虏，沈腰潘鬓消磨。最是仓皇辞庙日，教坊犹奏别离歌。垂泪对宫娥。

Li Yu

Tune: "Po Zhen Zi"

Farewell Song

Forty years of family and reign.
Three thousand *li** of river and mountainous scenes.
Phoenix pavilions and dragon towers rose to the sky.
Deep into the mist were beautiful trees,
flowery branches, and vines.
How little I knew about weapons
and military might?

Suddenly I have become a captured prisoner.
So emaciated I now have the look of
Shen's slender waist and Pan's hoary hair.**
How could I forget the day I hurriedly
left my ancestral shrine?
The imperial musicians played farewell songs
as we said good-bye.
I faced my court ladies with tears in my eyes.

*li is a Chinese unit of length that is equivalent to about a half kilometer.
**Shen Yue (441–513) was an official and scholar of the Liang Dynasty.
Pan Yue (247–300), known for his attractive appearance, was a scholar in the Jin Dynasty.

李煜　　　　lǐ yù
破陣子　　　pò zhèn zi

四△十△年○ sì shí nián forty years	來○ lái over time	家○國△ jiā guó home and country
三○千○里△ sān qiān lǐ three thousand li	地△ dì in distance	山○河● shān hé mountains and rivers
鳳△閣△ fèng gé phoenix pavilion	龍○樓○ long lóu dragon tower	連○霄○漢△ lián xiāo hàn join the sky
玉△樹△ yù shù beautiful trees	瓊○枝○ qióng zhī decorated branches	作△煙○蘿● zuò yān luó form misty vines
幾△曾○ jǐ céng how little	識△干○戈● shí gān gē (I) know weapons of war	
一△旦△ yī dàn once	歸○為○ guī wéi (I am) included as	臣○虜△ chén lǔ captive subject
沈○腰○ shěn yāo Shen Yue's waist	潘○鬢△ pān bìn Pan Yue's temples	消○磨● xiāo mó wear and tear
最△是△ zuì shì to be especially	倉○惶○ cāng huáng flee in panic	辭○廟△日△ cí miào rì day of leaving ancestors' shrine
教△坊○ jiào fáng musical institute	猶○奏△ yóu zòu still played	別△離○歌● bié lí gē parting songs
垂○淚△ chuí lèi tears falling	對△宮○娥● duì gōng é (I) faced court ladies	

李煜

浪淘沙

帘外雨潺潺。春意阑珊。罗衾不奈五更寒。梦里不知身是客，一向贪欢。独自莫凭栏。无限江山。别时容易见时难。流水落花春去也，天上人间。

Li Yu

Tune: "Lang Tao Sha"

Raining at Night

Outside the curtain, the rain is murmuring.
Spring is on the wane.
The quilt is not warm enough
to withstand the chill just before dawn.
Forgetting being a captive in my sleep,
I indulge in a momentary joy of dreaming.

Don't lean against the railing alone.
So boundless are the rivers and mountains to roam!
Parting is the easy part,
but seeing again is so hard.
Water flows; flowers fall.
This spring will soon be over.
Gone also are my paradise and kingdom forever!

李煜　　lǐ yù
浪淘沙　làng táo shā

簾○外△
lián wài
outside the curtain

雨△
yǔ
rain

潺○潺●
chán chán
is murmuring

春○意△
chūn yì
spring about to

闌○珊●
lán shān
come to an end

羅○衾○
luó qīn
a silken quilt

不△耐△
bù nài
can't withstand

五△更○寒●
wǔ gèng hán
chill just before dawn

夢△裡△
mèng lǐ
in the dream

不△知○
bù zhī
(I) don't know

身○是△客△
shēn shì kè
I am a guest

一△晌△
yī shǎng
for a short while

貪○歡●
tān huān
(I) indulge in pleasure

獨△自△
dú zì
alone

莫△
mò
do not

憑○欄●
píng lán
lean on railing

無○限△
wú xiàn
endless

江○山●
jiāng shān
rivers and mountains

別△時○
bié shí
time of parting

容○易△
róng yì
is easy

見△時○難●
jiàn shí nán
seeing is hard

流○水△
liú shuǐ
water flows

落△花○
luò huā
flowers fall

春○去△也△
chūn qù yě
spring is gone

天○上△
tiān shàn
in heaven

人○間●
rén jiān
in the human world

99

李煜

浪淘沙

往事只堪哀。对景难排。秋风庭院藓侵阶。一任珠帘闲不卷，终日谁来。金剑已沉埋。壮气蒿莱。晚凉天净月华开。想得玉楼瑶殿影，空照秦淮。

Li Yu

Tune: "Lang Tao Sha"

Sad feelings

Past events can only evoke sad feelings.
Facing the scenery can be overwhelming.
As the autumn wind blows, the courtyard steps
are overrun with green moss.
Just let the beaded screen hanging idly and unrolled.
From morning to night, no face will show!

My golden sword was already buried deep.
My heroic spirit was lost in the weeds.
The night is cool; the moon is full and bright.
Even if I am content with seeing the shadows
of those splendid buildings and palace hall,
I still could not be there to see the moon
beaming over River Qinhuai.*

* Qinhuai River flows through present-day Nanjing City.

李煜 **lǐ yù**
浪淘沙 **làng táo shā**

往△事△
wǎng shì
past events

對△景△
duì jǐng
facing a scenery

秋○風○
qiū fēng
autumn wind

一△任△
yī rèn
just let

終○日△
zhōng rì
the whole day

金○劍△
jīn jiàn
golden sword

壯△氣△
zhuàng qì
heroic spirit

晚△涼○
wǎn liáng
evening cool

想△得△
xiǎng de
even if I can get

空○照△
kōng zhào
shines in vain upon

只△
zhī
only

難○排●
nán pái
hard to get rid of it

庭○院△
tíng yuàn
courtyard

珠○簾○
zhū lián
beaded screen

誰○來●
shéi lái
who will come

已△
yǐ
already

蒿○萊●
hāo lái
weeds; jungle

天○淨△
tiān jìng
clean sky

玉△樓○
yù lóu
jade buildings

秦○淮●
qín huái
Qinhuai River

堪○哀●
kān āi
can bring sorrow

蘚△侵○階●
xiǎn qīn jiē
steps invaded by moss

閑○不△捲△
xián bù juǎn
idly unrolled

沉○埋●
chén mái
sunk and buried

月△華○開●
yuè huá kāi
moon shines in full

瑤○殿△影△
yáo diàn yǐng
shadow of the richly decorated palace

李煜

子夜歌

人生愁恨何能免。销魂独我情何限。故国梦重归。觉来双泪垂。高楼谁与上。长记秋晴望。往事已成空。还如一梦中。

Li Yu

Tune: "Zi Ye Ge"

Awakening from a Dream

How can one avoid sorrows and regrets in life?
But I have a greater share of them that
will never subside.
I dreamt of returning to my lost land again.
Awakened, I found tears falling from my eyes.
Who would go with me to ascend the high tower?
I will remember the clear autumn scenes forever.
Past events have left me with nothing.
I feel as though I am still in a dream.

李煜　　**lǐ yù**
子夜歌　　**zi yè gē**

人○生○ *rén shēng* in life	愁○恨△ *chóu hèn* sorrows and regrets	何○能○免▲ *hé néng miǎn* can't be avoided
銷○魂○ *xiāo hún* overwhelmed with grief	獨△我△ *dú wǒ* only I am	情○何○限▲ *qíng hé xiàn* feeling so hard to bear
故△國△ *gù guó* my lost kingdom	夢△重○歸● *mèng zhòng guī* dreamt to return to	
覺△來○ *jué lái* awoke afterward	雙○淚△垂● *shuāng lèi chuí* two streams of tears fell down	
高○樓○ *gāo lóu* the high tower	誰○與△ *shéi yǔ* who with me	上▲ *shàng* will go up
長○記△ *cháng jì* (I) often remember	秋○晴○ *qiū qíng* clear autumn	望▲ *wàng* looking (into distance)
往△事△ *wǎng shì* past memories	已△成○ *yǐ chéng* are left with	空● *kōng* emptiness
還○如○ *hái rú* it is like	一△夢△中● *yī mèng zhōng* in a dream	

李煜

乌夜啼

林花谢了春红。太匆匆。无奈朝来寒雨晚来风。
胭脂泪，留人醉，几时重。自是人生长恨水长东。

Li Yu

Tune: "Wu Ye Ti"

Flowers in the Woods

Flowers in the woods have withered.
Gone also is spring's red color.
In such a hurry!
Alas, they are helplessly assaulted:
cold rain in the morning,
wind in the evening.
The rouged tears kept me stayed and intoxicated.
Could this scene be replicated?
Like the water to the east it flows,
life is full of never-ending sorrows.

李煜　　**lǐ yù**
烏夜啼　　**wū yè tí**

林〇花〇
lín huā
flowers in the woods

謝△了△
xiè le
have withered

春〇紅●
chūn hóng
spring red (has faded)

太△匆〇匆●
tài cōng cōng
in such a hurry

無〇奈△
wú nài
can't help because

朝〇來〇
cháo lái
in morning it comes

寒〇雨△
hán yǔ
cold rain

晚△來〇
wǎn lái
at night it comes

風●
fēng
wind

胭〇脂〇淚△
yān zhī lèi
rouge tears

留〇人〇醉△
liú rén zuì
kept one staying and drinking

幾△時〇重●
jī shí zhóng
when will it occur again

自△是△
zì shì
is in itself

人〇生〇
rén shēng
life

長〇恨△
zhǎng hèn
filled with sorrows

水△
shuǐ
water

長〇東●
cháng dōng
always goes east

105

李煜

菩萨蛮

花明月黯笼轻雾。今霄好向郎边去。衩袜步香阶。手提金缕鞋。画堂南畔见。一向偎人颤。奴为出来难。教君恣意怜。

Li Yu

Tune: "Pu Sa Man"

Sneaking Out

Bright flowers, thin mist, and dim moonlight.
To sneak out to his side, now is the time.
Stockings unrestrained, she tiptoes
over the fragrant steps.
Holding in her hand a pair of shoes
sewn in golden threads.
They meet on the southern side
of the painted hall.
She snuggles to his arms
as trembling as before.
It isn't easy to come out at night.
Please understand, but you can be
unscrupulous if you like.

李煜　　lǐ yù
菩薩蠻　pú sà mán

花○明○
huā míng
flowers: bright

今○宵○
jīn xiāo
tonight

衩△襪△
chà wà
stockings without bands

手△提○
shǒu tí
holding in hand

畫△堂○
huà táng
painted hall

一△向△
yī xiàng
up to now

奴○為○
nú wé
for me it is

教△君○
jiào jūn
you should

月△黯△
yuè àn
moon: dim

好△向△
hǎo xiàng
is the good time

步△
bù
walk over

金○
jīn
gold

南○畔△見▲
nán pàn jiàn
see each other at south side

偎○人○顫▲
wēi rén chàn
snuggle in arms tremblingly

出△來○難●
chū lái nán
hard to come out

恣△意△憐●
zì yì lián
feel pity and do as you please

籠○輕○霧▲
lóng qīng wù
shrouded in thin mist

郎○邊○去▲
láng biān qù
to go to my lover's side

香○階●
xiāng jiē
fragrant steps

縷△鞋●
lǚ xié
threaded shoes

107

李煜

乌夜啼

昨夜风兼雨，帘帏飒飒秋声。烛残漏滴频欹枕，起坐不能平。　世事漫随流水，算来一梦浮生。醉乡路稳宜频到，此外不堪行。

Li Yu

Tune: "Wu Ye Ti"

Sound of Autumn

Last night, it was wind and rain.
The swishing sound of autumn
came through the curtain.
Candles waned; water clock stopped.
I could not fall asleep.
I tried to get up and sit,
but my mind was restless.

World affairs end up like water flowing.
Life can be summed up as a dream.
I should often visit the land of drunkenness
as the roads there are even and steady.
Aside from that, I can't bear to walk at all.

李煜　**lǐ yù**
烏夜啼　**wū yè tí**

昨△夜△
zuó yè
last night

風○兼○雨△
fēng jiān yǔ
wind and rain

簾○幃○
lián wéi
curtain

颯△颯△
sà sà
swished

秋○聲●
qiū shēng
autumn sound

燭○殘○
zhú cán
candle on the wane

漏△滴△
lòu dī
water clock dripped

頻○欹○枕△
pín yī zhěn
(I) repeatedly leaned on pillow

起△坐△
qǐ zuò
getting up and sitting down

不△能○平●
bù néng píng
unable to calm down

世△事△
shì shì
world affairs

漫△隨○
màn suí
follow endlessly

流○水△
liú shuǐ
flowing water

算△來○
suàn lái
calculated to be

一△夢△
yī mèng
a dream

浮○生●
fú shēng
this floating life

醉△鄉○
zuì xiāng
paradise of drunkenness

路△穩△
lù wěn
road is steady

宜○頻○到△
yí pín dào
proper to visit more often

此△外△
cǐ wài
aside from this

不△堪○行●
bù kān xíng
can't bear to walk

李煜

望江南

多少恨，昨夜梦魂中。还似旧时游上苑，车如流水马如龙。花月正春风。

Li Yu

Tune: "Wang Jiang Nan"

Dream

How much regret?
In my dream last night,
the imperial garden
still looked the same.
The chariots moved
like water flowing;
the horses galloped
like dragons flying.
We enjoyed bright moonlight
and beautiful flowers in the spring wind.

李煜　　**lǐ yù**
望江南　**wàng jiāng nán**

多○少△
duō shǎo
how much

恨△
hèn
regret

昨△夜△
zuó yè
last night

夢△魂○中●
mèng hún zhōng
in the dream

還○似△
hái sì
still like

舊△時○
jiù shí
old time

游○上△苑△
yóu shàng yuàn
imperial garden

車○如○
chē rú
chariots like

流○水△
liú shuǐ
flowing water

馬△如○龍●
mǎ rú lóng
horses like dragons

花○月△
huā yuè
flowers and moon

正△
zhèng
perfect

春○風●
chūn fēng
spring wind
(pleasant)

李煜

清平乐

别来春半。触目柔肠断。砌下落梅如雪乱。拂了一身还满。雁来音信无凭。路遥归梦难成。离恨恰如春草，更行更远还生。

Li Yu

Tune: "Qing Ping Le"

Parting Sorrow

Spring is about half gone
since we parted.
Everything that touches my eyes
breaks my heart.
Fallen plum petals swirl over
the steps like snowflakes.
Soon after I have wiped them off,
they are again in full display.
The swan geese can't be counted on
to bring a message.
Too far a distance for a dream
to return to its former place.
Parting sorrow is like spring grasses.
The longer and further you go,
the more luxuriant they grow.

李煜 lǐ yù
清平樂 qīng píng lè

別△來○
bié lái
since parting

觸△目△
chù mù
to meet the eye

砌△下△
qì xià
over the steps

拂△了△
fú le
wipe off

雁△來△
yàn lái
swan geese come

路△遙○
lù yáo
road is far

離○恨△
lí hèn
parting sorrow

更△行○
gèng xíng
the more (you) walk

春○半▲
chūn bàn
half of spring

柔○腸○斷▲
róu cháng duàn
can cause heartbreak

落△梅○
luò méi
fallen plum flowers

一△身○
yī shēn
whole body

音○信△
yīn xìn
message

歸○夢△
guī mèng
returning dream

恰△如○
qià rú
just like

更△遠△
gèng yuǎn
the further away

如○雪△亂▲
rú xuě luàn
disorderly like snow

還○滿▲
hái mǎn
still full

無○憑●
wú píng
can't depend on

難○成●
nán chéng
hard to make

春○草△
chūn cǎo
spring grasses

還○生●
hái shēng
still grow

113

李煜

渔父词

浪花有意千重雪，桃李无言一队春。一壶酒，一竿纶。世上如侬有几人。　一棹春风一叶舟。一纶丝缕一轻钩。花满渚，酒满瓯。万顷波中得自由。

Li Yu

Tune: "Yu Fu Ci"

A Fisherman's Song

Sea spray breaks away to
a thousand layers of snow.
A row of peach and plum blossoms
silently shows off spring's vital growth.
A bottle of wine; a fishing rod.
Who on earth can do as what I like?

In spring breeze, with an oar on a leaf-like boat,
A rod with a light hook and silken thread.
A flower-covered islet;
a jug full of wine;
Among endless waves,
I will be free to enjoy my time.

李煜　　**lǐ yù**
漁父詞　　**yú fù cí**

浪△花〇
làng huā
sea spray

桃〇李△
táo lǐ
peach and plum

一△壺〇酒△
yī hú jiǔ
a bottle of wine

世△上△
shì shàng
on earth

一△楫△
yī jí
an oar of

一△綸〇
yī lún
a pole of

花〇滿△渚△
huā mǎn zhǔ
an islet full of flowers

萬△頃△
wàn qǐng
boundless

有△意△
yǒu yì
likes the ideas

無〇言〇
wú yán
without a word

一△竿〇綸●
yī gān lún
a fishing rod

如〇儂〇
rú nóng
like me

春〇風〇
chūn fēng
spring wind

絲〇縷△
sī lǚ
silk thread

酒△滿△甌●
jiǔ mǎn ōu
a bowl full of wine

波〇中〇
bō zhōng
waves

千〇重〇雪△
qiān zhòng xuě
(of showing) a thousand layers of snow

一△隊△春●
yī duì chūn
(display) a row of spring

有△幾△人●
yǒu jǐ rén
how many people

一△葉△舟●
yī yè zhōu
a leaf of boat

一△輕〇鉤●
yī qīng gōu
a light hook

得△自△由●
de zì yóu
(I can) get freedom

李煜

捣练子

深院静，小庭空。断续寒砧断续风。无奈夜长人不寐，数声和月到帘栊。

Li Yu

Tune: "Dao Lian Zi"

Sleepless Night

Small front yard is empty;
deep back yard is quiet.
I hear intermittently
a laundry club pounding.
I hear intermittently
the wind blowing.
So helpless is this long
and sleepless night.
I count the sound and
respond to the moonlight,
as they come through the windows,
doors, and blinds.

李煜　　lǐ yù
搗練子　dǎo liàn zi

深〇院△　　　　静△
shēn yuàn　　　jìng
deep back yard　quiet

小△庭〇　　　　空●
xiǎo tíng　　　kōng
small front yard　empty

斷△續△　　　　寒〇砧〇
duàn xù　　　　hán zhēn
intermittent　　cold wooden club

斷△續△　　　　風●
duàn xù　　　　fēng
intermittent　　wind

無〇奈△　　　　夜△長〇　　　　人〇不△寐△
wú nài　　　　　yè cháng　　　rén bù mèi
can't help it　　long night　　one can't fall asleep

數△聲〇　　　　和〇月△　　　　到△簾〇櫳●
shù shēng　　　hé yuè　　　　dào lián lóng
counting the sounds　responding to the moon　(when they) reach windows, doors and screens

李煜

玉楼春

晚妆初了明肌雪。春殿嫔娥鱼贯列。凤箫吹断水云闲，重按霓裳歌遍彻。　　临风谁更飘香屑。醉拍阑干情味切。归时休放烛花红，待踏马蹄清夜月。

Li Yu

Tune: "Yu Lou Chun"

Song and Music

After evening makeup, the skin complexion
looks snowy bright.
In Spring Palace, the court ladies line
up row after row.
The sound of flute and pipe
drifts as far as water and clouds.
The revised version of the Rainbow Tune
resonates with each mind.

Why does someone still need to burn
fragrant chips in the wind?
Beating the rails tipsily we have reached
our emotional height.
On our way of returning, don't let red candles shine.
Just enjoy the horse ride under clear moonlight.

李煜　**lǐ yù**
玉樓春　**yù lóu chūn**

晚△妝〇
wǎn zhuāng
evening toilet

春〇殿△
chūn diàn
Spring Palace

鳳△簫〇
fèng xiāo
bamboo flutes

重△按△
zhòng àn
play again

臨〇風〇
lín fēng
in the wind

醉△拍△
zuì pāi
beating tipsily

歸〇時〇
guī shí
on returning

待△踏△
dài tà
wait to tread upon

初〇了△
chū le
just done

嬪〇娥〇
pín é
court ladies

吹〇斷△
chuī duàn
blowing to reach

霓〇裳〇
ní cháng
The Rainbow Tune

誰〇更△
shéi gèng
who even bothers to

闌〇干〇
lán gān
rails

休〇放△
xiū fàng
don't display

馬△蹄〇
mǎ tí
hoofs of horse

明〇肌〇雪▲
míng jī xuě
brighten snowy skin

魚〇貫△列▲
yú guàn liè
line up in rows

水△雲〇閑〇
shuǐ yún xián
water and clouds at ease

歌〇遍△徹▲
gē biàn chè
song deeply resonates

飄〇香〇屑▲
piāo xiāng xiè
spread fragrant chips

情〇味△切▲
qíng wèi qiē
with genuine feelings

燭△花〇紅〇
zhú huā hóng
red candle light

清〇夜△月▲
qīng yè yuè
clear night under moonlight

李煜

玉楼春

晚妆初过，沉檀轻注些儿个。向人微露丁香颗，一曲清歌，暂引樱桃破。罗袖裛残殷色可，杯深旋被香醪涴。绣床斜凭娇无那，烂嚼红茸，笑向檀郎唾。

Li Yu

Tune: "Yi Hu Zhu"

Charming and Captivating

After evening makeup, she applied
a little bit of sandalwood oil to her lip.
Then she slightly revealed her lilac tongue's tip.
Before singing her song, she started to open her
mouth, as if a cherry was about to break.

Drinking in deep cup, she accidently spilled
on her silken sleeves some sweet wine.
Moistened in crimson red, they actually
looked cute and fine.
Leaning aslant on the embroidered bed,
she acted like a spoilt child.
After chewing a little red woolen yarn, she
spat at me with a smile.

李煜 **lǐ yù**
一斛珠 **yī hú zhū**

晚△妝〇 wǎn zhuāng evening toilet	初〇過▲ chū guò just done	
沉〇檀〇 chén tán sandalwood oil	輕〇注△ qīng zhù lightly touch up	些〇兒〇個▲ xiē ér gè just a little bit
向△人〇 xiàng rén toward person (me)	微〇露△ wéi lù reveal barely	丁〇香〇顆▲ dīng xiāng kē lilac tongue's tip
一△曲△ yī qū a melody of	清〇歌〇 qīng gē pure song	
暫△引△ zàn yǐn temporally induce	櫻〇桃〇 yīng táo cherry	破▲ pò to break
羅〇袖△ luó xiù silken sleeves	裛△殘〇 yì cán moisten	殷〇色△可▲ yīn sè kě in cute dark-red color
杯〇深〇 bēi shēn deep cup	旋〇被△ xuán bèi then let	香〇醪〇涴▲ xiāng láo wò stained by fragrant and sweet wine
繡△床△ xiù chuáng embroidered bed	斜〇憑〇 xié píng lean aslant on	嬌〇無〇那▲ jiāo wú nà seductive freely
爛△嚼△ làn jué chew thoroughly	紅〇茸〇 hóng róng red woolen yarn	
笑△向△ xiào xiàng smiley toward	檀〇郎〇 tán láng her lover	唾▲ tuò to spit

问君能有几多愁，恰似一江春水向东流。

Ask me how much sorrow can I bear?
It is like a river full of spring water,
flowing to the east forever!

— Li Yu

Part Three

The Early and Middle Northern Song Period

Liu Yong (987–1053)

柳永

Liu Yong was originally named Liu San Bian. San Bian means "three changes." He was also popularly known as Liu Qi (seven) as he was the seventh child in his family. Growing up in present-day Fujian, he was very talented in poetry writing as well as in song composition.

Before Liu's time, *ci* poetry was mainly written in the short form on the subject of flowers and romantic love. The arrival of Liu marked a new beginning in the development of the long form. Many of his *ci* poems were written for singing.

While Liu demonstrated his versatility in music and poetry, he did not do well in governmental service. He did not pass the civil examination until he was fifty-seven years old. He apparently did not help himself in future examinations after his sarcastic lyric to the tune of "*He Chong Tian*" (the Sky-Soaring Crane). In which, he reflects on his failing the civil service examination. It was said that the last line in the poem 忍把浮名，换了浅斟低唱 (Why not trade away an empty name for soft singing and a small cup of wine?) might have angered the Song emperor. The emperor suggested that Liu might as well do just that: composing *ci*. Afterward, Liu often sarcastically said that he was "feng zi tian ci" (ordered by the emperor to compose *ci*).

Liu was well known in the masses, especially among song girls and prostitutes in the so-called "green chamber," where he was widely admired and supported. It was said that the girls collected funds for his burial upon his death. His grave was visited frequently by his admirers.

柳永

雨霖铃

寒蝉凄切。对长亭晚，骤雨初歇。都门帐饮无绪，方留恋处、兰舟催发。执手相看泪眼，竟无语凝噎。念去去、千里烟波，暮霭沉沉楚天阔。　多情自古伤离别。更那堪、冷落清秋节。今宵酒醒何处，杨柳岸、晓风残月。此去经年，应是良辰、好景虚设。便纵有、千种风情，更与何人说。

Liu Yong

Tune: "Yu Lin Ling"

Parting

The autumn cicadas utter their sad tunes.
We face each other at the long pavilion in late afternoon.
The downpour has come to a halt.
Drinking at the city gate with no mood at all.
Just as we have become attached in our heart,
the boatman signals to soon depart.
Holding hands with tearful eyes,
we are choked up to gesture good-bye.
I am going away on a thousand-*li* journey
in misty waves over the southern sky.

柳永　**liǔ yǒng**
雨霖鈴　**yǔ lín líng**

○ = 平声 (*ping* or flat tone)
△ = 仄声 (*ze* or deflected tone)
● = 平声韵 (rhymed in *ping* or flat tone)
▲ = 仄声韵 (rhymed in *ze* or deflected tone)

寒○蟬○
hán chán
cold cicadas

對△
duì
face

驟△雨△
zòu yǔ
downpour

都○門○
dōu mén
city gate

方○
fāng
just

蘭○舟○
lán zhōu
boat (man)

執△手△
zhí shǒu
holding hands

竟△
jìng
unexpectedly

念△去△去△
niàn qù qù
the thought of parting

暮△靄△
mù ǎi
evening mist

凄○切▲
qī qiē
mournful

長○亭○
cháng tíng
long pavilion

初○歇▲
chū xiē
has just stopped

帳△飲△
zhàng yǐn
drinking in tent

留○戀△
liú liàn
can't bear to part

催△發▲
cuī fā
urges to leave

相○看○
xiāng kàn
look at each other

無○語○
wú yǔ
without words

千○里△
qiān lǐ
thousand *li*

沉○沉○
chén chén
hangs heavily on

晚△
wǎn
late (in afternoon)

無○緒△
wú xù
without the mood

處△
chù
at that point

淚△眼△
lèi yǎn
with tearful eyes

凝○噎▲
níng yē
feel congealed and choked

煙○波○
yān bō
in mist and waves

楚△天○闊▲
chǔ tiān kuò
the South's wide sky

127

Since ancient times, parting is the price
lovers must pay for giving their hearts and minds.
It is so unbearable to part in the cool autumn scene.
Where will I end up tonight after waking up from
drinking?
Could it be at the willow bank in
breeze with the moon lingering?
I will leave you for years until we meet again.
What good it is to me even
it is a bright day and a fair scene?
Even though I have a thousand things to say,
with whom can I convey my feelings?

多○情○ *duō qíng* affectionate (people)	自△古△ *zì gǔ* since ancient time	傷○离○別▲ *shāng lí bié* (must) bear parting grief
更△那△堪○ *gèng nà kān* especially at this	冷△落△ *lěng luò* desolate	清○秋○節▲ *qīng qiū jié* cool autumn season
今○宵○ *jīn xiāo* tonight	酒△醒△ *jiǔ xǐng* sobered up	何○處△ *hé chǔ* where to end up
楊○柳△岸△ *yáng liǔ àn* willows' bank	曉△風○ *xiǎo fēng* breeze at dawn	殘○月▲ *cán yuè* waning moon
此△去△ *cǐ qù* after this parting	經○年○ *jīng nián* for years	應△是△ *yìng shì* should be like
良○辰○ *liáng chén* bright day	好△景△ *hǎo jǐng* good scene	虛○設▲ *xū shè* come in vain
便△縱△有△ *biàn zòng yǒu* even there are	千○種△ *qiān zhòng* a thousand kinds of	風○情○ *fēng qíng* amorous feelings
更△與△ *gèng yǔ* with	何○人○ *hé rén* whom	說▲ *shuō* can I talk

柳永

凤栖梧

伫倚危楼风细细。望极春愁,黯黯生天际。草色烟光残照里。无言谁会凭栏意。 拟把疏狂图一醉。对酒当歌,强乐还无味。衣带渐宽终不悔。为伊消得人憔悴。

Liu Yong

Tune: "Feng Qi Wu"

Melancholy in Spring

I lean for a long while on the high
tower in gentle breeze.
Spring melancholy looms on
the horizon as far as I can see.
Over the green grass smoke rises
in the fading daylight.
No one knows why I am
leaning silently on the rails at this time.

I wish to dispel my unrestrained feelings
away with a few cups of wine.
Drinking and singing bring me
no relief but reluctant smiles.
I don't regret at all, gradually letting my
clothes and sash become loose and wide.
For her sake, I am willing to look thin,
weary, and tired.

柳永　　**liǔ yǒng**
鳳棲梧　**fèng qī wú**

佇△倚△
zhù yǐ
leaning for a long time on

望△極△
wàng jí
looking afar

黯△黯△
àn àn
dimly

草△色△
cǎo sè
color of grass

無○言○
wú yán
silently

擬△把△
nǐ bǎ
wanting to let

對△酒△
duì jiǔ
in front of wine

強○樂△
qiáng lè
forcing to enjoy

衣○帶△
yī dài
sash

為△伊○
wèi yī
for her

危○樓○
wēi lóu
high tower

春○愁○
chūn chóu
spring melancholy

生○
shēng
to grow; to rise

煙○光○
yān guāng
light of smoke

誰○會△
shéi huì
who can understand

疏○狂○
shū kuáng
unrestraint

當○歌○
dāng gē
sing song

還○
huán
still

漸△寬○
jiàn kuān
gradually is wider

消○得△
xiāo de
to wear down

風○細△細▲
fēng xì xì
wind is very fine

天○際▲
tiān jì
on the horizon

殘○照△裡▲
cán zhào lǐ
in fading sunlight

憑○欄△意▲
píng lán yì
reason for leaning on rails

圖○一△醉▲
tú yī zuì
trying to get drunk

無○味▲
wú wèi
feel tasteless

終○不△悔▲
zhōng bù huǐ
still not regretful

人○憔○悴▲
rén qiáo cuì
one is thin and pallid

柳永

八声甘州

对潇潇暮雨洒江天，一番洗清秋。渐霜风凄紧，关河冷落，残照当楼。是处红衰翠减，苒苒物华休。惟有长江水，无语东流。 不忍登高临远，望故乡渺邈，归思难收。叹年来踪迹，何事苦淹留？想佳人妆楼颙望，误几回、天际识归舟。争知我，倚阑干处，正恁凝愁。

Liu Yong

Tune: "Ba Sheng Gan Zhou"

Thinking of You in Autumn

I watch the evening rain pattering down
and sprinkling the air and river.
The clear autumn has been washed and cleaned,
Here comes the chilly and hurrying wind.
The river checkpoint looks desolate;
the waning light lingers above the tower.
As the red has faded everywhere,
the green has lost its luster.
All beautiful things have gradually subdued.
Only the Long River flows silently to the east as ever.

柳永　**liǔ yǒng**
八聲甘州　**bā shēng gān zhōu**

對△瀟○瀟○
duì xiāo xiāo
face pattering

一△番○
yī fān
one round of

漸△
jiàn
gradually

關○河○
guān hé
pass and river

殘○照△
cán zhào
waning light

是△處△
shì chù
everywhere

苒△苒△
rǎn rǎn
gradually

惟○有△
wéi yǒu
only

無○語△
wú yǔ
silently

暮△雨△
mù yǔ
rain at dusk

洗△
xǐ
washing

霜○風○
shuāng fēng
frosted (autumn) wind

冷△落△
lěng luò
desolate

當○樓●
dāng lóu
above the tower

紅○衰○
hóng shuāi
red deteriorates

物△華○
wù huá
beautiful things

長○江○
cháng jiāng
Long River

東○流○
dōng liú
flows to the east

灑△江○天○
sǎ jiāng tiān
sprinkle river and sky

清○秋●
qīng qiū
clear autumn

凄○緊△
qī jǐn
chilly and hurrying

翠△減△
cuì jiǎn
green diminishes

休●
xiū
take a rest

水△
shuǐ
water

I can't bear to climb high looking into
the distance of haze and mist.
For fear it will deepen my homesickness and yearning.
I lament that all these years I have wandered
from place to place.
For what reason do I keep postponing my returning?
She must be at this time looking afar in earnest
from her boudoir.
How many times has she mistaken other
boats on the horizon as mine?
She may not know that at this moment
I too lean on the rails and gaze into distance with
sadness.

不△忍△
bù rěn
can't bear

望△
wàng
looking at

歸○思△
guī sī
thought of returning

嘆△
tàn
lament

何○事△
hé shì
what

想△佳○人○
xiǎng jiā rén
assuming that she

誤△幾△回○
wù jǐ huí
mistaken it several times

爭○知○我△
zhēng zhī wǒ
do you know I am

正△恁△
zhèng rèn
just like you

登○高○
dēng gāo
to climb high

故△鄉○
gù xiāng
home town

難○收●
nán shōu
hard to hold back

年○來○
nián lái
for years

苦△
kǔ
causes you unwillingly

妝○樓○
zhuāng lóu
in the boudoir

天○際△
tiān jì
on the horizon

倚△闌○干○
yǐ lán gān
leaning on rail

凝○愁●
níng chóu
gazing at distance with sadness

臨○遠△
lín yuǎn
look into distance

渺○邈△
miǎo miǎo
distant and indistinct

蹤○跡△
zōng jī
traces

淹○留●
yān liú
to stay for a long period

顒○望△
yóng wàng
watching in earnest

識△歸○舟●
shí guī zhōu
as the returning boat

處△
chǔ
where

柳永

鹤冲天

黄金榜上，偶失龙头望。明代暂遗贤，如何向？未遂风云便，争不恣狂荡。何须论得丧？才子词人，自是白衣卿相。烟花巷陌，依约丹青屏障。幸有意中人，堪寻访。且恁偎红翠，风流事，平生畅。青春都一饷。忍把浮名，换了浅斟低唱！

Liu Yong

Tune: "He Chong Tian"

On Failing the Civil Service Examination

Successful candidates have been announced
on the golden billboard.
Even in times of enlightenment, leaving out
a great talent is not unusual at all.
No use to yell foul!
Since I couldn't be the man of the hour,
I may as well live a life without restraint like a debaucher.
Why bother to mourn for my loss?
Gifted scholars or lyrists in the populace are just
as good as high-ranking officials.

柳永　**liǔ yǒng**
鶴沖天　**hè chōng tiān**

黃○金○
huáng jīn
golden

榜△上▲
bǎng shàng
billboard announcing the names of finalists

偶△失△
ǒu shī
occasionally losing

龍○頭○
lóng tóu
top candidate

望▲
wàng
hope

明○代△
míng dài
enlightened period

暫△
zàn
temporarily

遺○賢○
yí xián
talents who are left out

如○何○向▲
rú hé xiàng
what can you do

未△遂△
wèi suì
not fulfilling

風○雲○
fēng yún
wind and clouds (a man of the hour)

便△
biàn
advantages

爭○不△
zhēng bù
how about

恣△
zì
throw off restraint

狂○蕩▲
kuáng dàng
debauch

何○須△
hé xū
why need

論△
lùn
to talk about

得△喪▲
de sàng
achieving and mourning

才○子△
cái zi
a talented man

詞○人○
cí rén
a lyricist

自△是△
zì shì
naturally to be

白△衣○
bái yī
the common people

卿○相▲
qīng xiāng
with a minister's look

I can seek romance in the red-light district,
behind the indistinctly painted screens.
Fortunately I can visit someone of my heart anytime.
I can lean close to those who are dressed in
red and green.
Romantic episodes have enriched my whole life.
Youth can only last for a short while.
Why not trade away an empty name
for soft singing and a small cup of wine?

煙○花○
yān huā
smoke and flowers (red-light district)*

巷△陌△
xiàng mò
streets and lanes

依○約△
yī yuē
indistinct

丹○青○
dān qīng
painting

屏○障▲
píng zhàng
protective screen

幸△有△
xìng yǒu
fortunately to have

意△中○人○
yì zhōng rén
person of my heart

堪○尋○訪▲
kān xún fǎng
worthy of visiting

且△恁△
qiě rèn
and like this

偎○
wēi
close to

紅○翠△
hóng cuì
women in red and green* *

風○流○事△
fēng liú shì
romantic episode

平○生○
píng shēng
in all my life

暢▲
chàng
pass unimpeded

青○春○
qīng chūn
youth

都○
dōu
all

一△餉△
yī xiǎng
a short provision

忍△把△
rěn bǎ
can bear to let

浮○名○
fú míng
an empty name

換△了△
huàn le
in exchange for

淺△斟○
qiǎn zhēn
filling a small cup of wine

低○唱△
dī chàng
singing softly

* Refers to where the brothels are located.
** Refers to prostitutes.

多情自古伤离别。

Since ancient times, parting is the price
lovers must pay for giving their hearts and minds.

— Liu Yong

Zhang Xian (990–1078)

张先

Zhang Xian, also known as Zi Ye (子野), was born in present-day Hu Zhou, Zhejiang province. He lived a long and healthy life by the standard of his time. He died at the age of eighty-nine.

Zhang was often called by the name of Zhang San Ying, or Three Shadows, because several of his famous quotations all had something to do with "ying" or shadow. Like Liu Yong, he was a pioneer in the development of the long form of *ci* poetry. The themes of his *ci* largely reflect the life of those who held official titles in the government: typically romantic love and the physical and mental states of beautiful lady.

He led a comfortable life through old age. At eighty, he was especially noted for his marriage to a young lady of only eighteen. For this unusual marriage, he wrote a poem to amuse himself. His friend Su Shi, a much better-known lyric poet and some forty years his junior, could not help writing a doggerel poem to make fun of him. In the poem, Su teased him with his famous line about a pear flowery tree lying on top of a flowering crab apple (一樹梨花壓海棠).

It was said that Zhang and his young concubine lived together for eight years. They were the parents of two sons and two daughters. Zhang had a total of ten children. His eldest son was older than his youngest daughter by sixty years.

张先

菩萨蛮

忆郎还上层楼曲。楼前芳草年年绿。绿似去时袍。回头风袖飘。 郎袍应已旧。颜色非长久。惜恐镜中春。不如花草新。

Zhang Xian

Tune: "Pu Sa Man"

Thinking of My Beloved

Thinking of him, I climb the winding tower.
Every year the grass before me is as green as ever.
It is as green as his robe at the time of parting.
As he looked back, his sleeves kept waving.
His robe must be old by now.
Colors shall fade in due time as we know.
Be appreciative of the youthful look in the mirror.
Don't compare it with new grass and flowers.

張先　**zhāng xiān**
菩薩蠻　**pú sà mán**

○ = 平声 (*ping* or flat tone)

△ = 仄声 (*ze* or deflected tone)

● = 平声韵 (rhymed in *ping* or flat tone)

▲ = 仄声韵 (rhymed in *ze* or deflected tone)

憶△郎○
yì láng
thinking of you

樓○前○
lóu qián
in front of the tower

綠△似△
lǜ sì
as green as

回△頭○
huí tóu
looking back

郎○袍○
láng páo
his robe

顏○色△
yán sè
color

惜○恐△
xī kǒng
pity and fear

不△如○
bù rú
not as

還○上△
hái shàng
I ascend

芳○草△
fāng cǎo
fragrant grass

去△時○
qù shí
at time of leaving

風○袖△
fēng xiù
wind blew the sleeves

應△已△
yìng yǐ
should have turned

非○
fēi
can't last

鏡△中○
jìng zhōng
in mirror

花○草△
huā cǎo
flowers and grass

層○樓○曲▲
céng lóu qū
the winding tower

年○年○綠▲
nián nián lǜ
green year after year

袍●
páo
the robe

飄●
piāo
to wave

舊▲
jiù
old

長○久▲
cháng jiǔ
a long time

春●
chūn
spring (youthful appearance)

新●
xīn
new

张先

菩萨蛮

哀筝一弄湘江曲，声声写尽湘波绿。纤指十三弦，细将幽恨传。　当筵秋水慢，玉柱斜飞雁。弹到断肠时，春山眉黛低。

Zhang Xian

Tune: "Pu Sa Man"

Playing the Song of Xiang River

With the sorrowful *zheng**, she plays
the Song of Xiang River.
Each sound vividly depicts the waves
of the river's green color.
Her slender fingers touch skillfully
the *zheng's* thirteen strings.
Her hidden bitterness is conveyed
with her heartfelt feelings.

In the banquet, she gazes at something
with her beautiful eyes.
The pins look like the wild geese
flying slantwise.
When she plays to the point of heartbreaking,
her eyebrows look like
spring mountains dwindling.

**Zheng* is a plucked stringed instrument similar to the zither.

張先　　zhāng xiān
菩薩蠻　pú sà mán

哀○箏○ *āi zhēng* sadly sounding zheng	一△弄△ *yī nòng* to pluck; to play	湘○江○曲▲ *xiāng jiāng qū* Song of Xiang River
聲○聲○ *shēng shēng* each sound	寫△盡△ *xiě jìn* fully write about	湘○波○綠▲ *xiāng bō lǜ* green waves of Xiang River
纖○指△ *xiān zhǐ* slender fingers	十△三○ *shí sān* thirteen	弦● *xián* strings
細△將○ *xì jiāng* tenderly to let	幽○恨△ *yōu hèn* hidden bitterness	傳● *chuán* convey
當○筵○ *dāng yán* in the banquet	秋○水△ *qiū shuǐ* autumn water (eyes)	慢▲ *màn* slow (gaze)
玉△柱△ *yù zhù* jade posts	斜○飛○ *xié fēi* flying sideway	雁▲ *yàn* wild geese
彈○到△ *tán dào* play at the point of	斷△腸○ *duàn cháng* heartbreaking	時● *shí* time
春○山○ *chūn shān* spring mountain	眉○黛△ *méi dài* eyes	低● *dī* lower

张先

天仙子

水调数声持酒听，午醉醒来愁未醒。送春春去几时回。临晚镜，伤流景。往事后期空记省。　沙上并禽池上暝。云破月来花弄影。重重帘幕密遮灯，风不定，人初静。明日落红应满径。

Zhang Xian

Tune: "Tian Xian Zi"

Parting of Spring

Holding a cup of wine, I listen
briefly to the Water Melody.
Melancholy remains after waking up
from afternoon tipsiness.
Spring is gone but when will it return?
Looking at the mirror at dusk,
I feel sad that time has passed so fast.
It is in vain to remember what had
happened in the recent past.

A pair of birds play on the sand
by the pond at nightfall
As clouds break away, the moon comes through.
Flowers suddenly make shadows in moonlight.
Layers of curtains shielded the lamplight.
The wind still blows outside;
my mind begins to calm down.
Alas, tomorrow fallen flowers
will all be on the road and around.

張先　　**zhāng xiān**
天仙子　**tiān xiān zi**

水△調△ *shuǐ diào* Water Melody	數△聲○ *shù shēng* sounds a few times	持○酒△聽▲ *chí jiǔ tīng* listen with wine cup
午△醉△ *wǔ zuì* afternoon nap	醒△來○ *xǐng lái* awaken	愁○未△醒▲ *chóu wèi xǐng* sorrow not yet awaken
送△春○ *sòng chūn* seeing spring off	春○去△ *chūn qù* gone is spring	幾△時○回○ *jǐ shí huí* when will return
臨○晚△鏡▲ *lín wǎn jìng* look at mirror at dusk	傷○流○景▲ *shāng liú jǐng* feel sad about time passed	
往△事△ *wǎng shì* past events	後△期○ *hòu qī* meeting afterward	空○記△省▲ *kōng jì shěng* be remembered in vain
沙○上△ *shā shàng* on the sand	并△禽○ *bìng qín* a pair of birds	池○上△暝▲ *chí shàng míng* getting dark by the pond
雲○破△ *yún pò* clouds break away	月△來○ *yuè lái* moon arrives	花○弄△影▲ *huā nòng yǐng* flowers make shadows
重○重○ *chóng chóng* layer upon layer	簾○幕△ *lián mù* curtains	密△遮○燈○ *mì zhē dēng* shield the lamp tightly
風○不△定▲ *fēng bù dìng* wind unsettled (outside)	人○初○靜▲ *rén chū jìng* I begin to calm down	
明○日△ *míng rì* tomorrow	落△紅○ *luò hóng* fallen flowers	應○滿△徑▲ *yìng mǎn jìng* must be all over the path

张先

诉衷情

花前月下暂相逢。苦恨阻从容。何况酒醒梦断，花谢月朦胧。花不尽，月无穷。两心同。此时愿作，杨柳千丝，绊惹春风。

Zhang Xian

Tune: "Su Zhong Qing"

Brief Encounter

We encounter briefly under moonlight
in front of the flowers.
I regret not to take time
to know more about each other.
Dream was broken after sobering up from wine.
Flowers wither in misty moonlight.
Flowers will reappear.
The moon will always be there.
I wish that our two hearts will follow the same path.
I only wish now to become thousands
of willow branches.
With them I would tie up the spring breeze.

張先　zhāng xiān
訴衷情　sù zhōng qíng

花〇前〇
huā qián
in front of flowers

月△下△
yuè xià
under the moon

暫△相〇逢●
zàn xiāng féng
meet for a short while

苦△恨△
kǔ hèn
bitter about

阻△
zǔ
being prevented

從〇容●
cóng róng
unhurried

何〇況△
hé kuàng
especially

酒△醒△
jiǔ xǐng
sobering from wine

夢△斷△
mèng duàn
dream broken

花〇謝△
huā xiè
flowers withered

月△
yuè
moon

朦〇朧●
méng lóng
unclear

花〇
huā
flowers

不△盡△
bù jìn
bloom year after year

月△
yuè
moon

無〇窮●
wú qióng
without end

兩△心〇
liǎng xīn
both hearts

同●
tóng
the same

此△時〇
cǐ shí
at this time

願△作△
yuàn zuò
willing to be

楊〇柳△千〇絲〇
yáng liǔ qiān sī
willow's thousand slender branches

絆△惹△
bàn rě
to tie up

春〇風●
chūn fēng
spring wind

张先

千秋岁

数声鶗鴂，又报芳菲歇。惜春更把残红折。雨轻风色暴，梅子青时节。永丰柳，无人尽日花飞雪。莫把幺弦拨，怨极弦能说。 天不老，情难绝。心似双丝网，中有千千结。一过也，东窗未白凝残月。

Zhang Xian

Tune:" Qian Qiu Sui"

Feeling Sad at Late Spring

Crying a few times, the cuckoo announce
that flowers are on the decline.
As spring is about to depart, I break a twig
of tarnished flowers.
The wind is strong, though the rain is light.
It is now the green-plum time.
Around Yong Feng, nobody wants to see
the falling petals flying like snow the whole day.
Don't pluck the smallest string,
for it can convey the sad feelings.
As heaven will not get old,
love is hard to stop its flow.

張先　**zhāng xiān**
千秋歲　**qiān qiū suì**

數△聲〇
shù shēng
a few sounds of

鵜〇鴂〇
tí jué
cuckoo

又△報△
yòu bào
to announce again

芳〇菲〇
fāng fēi
fragrance and beauty

歇▲
xiē
come to an end

惜△春〇
xī chūn
pitying spring

更△把△
gèng bǎ
to even allow

殘〇紅〇折▲
cán hóng zhé
tarnished flowers to be cut

雨△輕〇
yǔ qīng
light rain

風〇色△
fēng sè
wind looks

暴△
bào
violent

梅〇子△
méi zi
plum

青〇
qīng
green

時〇節▲
shí jié
season

永△豐〇
yǒng fēng
Yong Feng's

柳△
liǔ
willows

無〇人〇
wú rén
no one

盡△日〇
jìn rì
the entire day

花〇飛〇雪▲
huā fēi xuě
petals like flying snow

莫△把△
mò bǎ
don't let

么〇弦〇
mō xián
the smallest string of *pípa*

撥△
bō
to pluck

怨△極△
yuàn jí
too bitter

弦〇能〇說
xián néng shuō
string can say

天〇不△老△
tiān xià lǎo
heaven doesn't get old

情〇難〇絕▲
qíng nán jué
love will be hard to die

151

My heart is like a two-thread net
with thousands of knots.
It is all gone!
By the eastern window before daybreak,
I gaze at the waning moon.

心○似△
xīn sì
the heart like

雙○絲○網△
shuāng sī wǎn
two-thread net

中○有△
zhōng yǒu
in it

千○千○結▲
qiān qiān jié
thousands of knots

一△過△也△
yī guò yě
it is gone

東○窗○
dōng chuāng
eastern window

未△白△
wèi bái
not bright yet

凝○殘○月▲
níng cán yuè
waning moon to gaze

张先

青门引

乍暖还轻冷。风雨晚来方定。庭轩寂寞近清明，残花中酒，又是去年病。楼头画角风吹醒，入夜重门静。那堪更被明月，隔墙送过秋千影。

Zhang Xian

Tune: "Qing Men Yin"

Night Thought

It is suddenly warm and cold.
Wind and rain do not settle until
night starts to unfold.
So lonesome in the courtyard.
The Tomb-Sweeping Festival is near.
I become drunk facing the tarnished flowers.
It is the same old illness as last year.
I am awakened by the wind and the sound
of a painted horn.
After the doors are closed, it is so quite at nightfall.
How can I bear to see the bright moon
bringing the shadow of the swing over the wall?

張先　**zhāng xiān**
青門引　**qīng mén yǐn**

乍△暖△
zhà nuǎn
becoming warmer

還○
huán
then

輕○冷▲
qīng lěng
slightly cold

風○雨△
fēng yǔ
wind and rain

晚△來○
wǎn lái
until evening

方○定▲
fāng dìng
begin to settle

庭○軒○
tíng xuān
courtyard

寂△寞△
jì mò
lonely

近△清○明○
jìn qīng míng
near tomb sweeping time

殘○花○
cán huā
tarnished flowers

中○酒△
zhōng jiǔ
illness due to wine

又△是△
yòu shì
again it is

去△年○
qù nián
last year's

病▲
bìng
illness

樓○頭○
lóu tóu
over the tower

畫△角△
huà jiǎo
painted horn

風○吹○醒△
fēng chuī xǐng
wind blows me to wake up

入△夜△
rù yè
at nightfall

重○門○
zhòng mén
gate upon gate

靜▲
jìng
quiet

那△堪△
nà kān
unbearable

更△被△
gèng bèi
even let

明○月△
míng yuè
bright moon

隔○牆○
gé qiáng
over the wall

送△過△
sòng guò
send through

秋○千○影▲
qiū qiān yǐng
shadow of swing

惜恐镜中春。不如花草新。

Be appreciative of the youthful look
in the mirror.
Don't compare it with new grass and flowers.

— Zhang Xian

Yan Shu (991–1055)

晏殊

Yan Shu, a very gifted and talented person, was a child prodigy. He wrote his first essay when he was only seven. At the tender age of fourteen, he impressed the emperor by passing the civil service examination held at the imperial capital. For that, he was awarded the title of *Jinshi*. His governmental service was relatively successful and smooth throughout his career. He attained the rank of prime minister and led a wealthy and comfortable life.

Yan was considered a good officer by all accounts. Concerned about the welfare of the common people, he made every effort to promote educational and cultural activities in the masses. Several famous poets and literati such as Ouyang Xiu and Feng Zhongyan were his students. His own son Yan Jidao was also a well-known and influential poet in the Song Dynasty.

Yan Shu's *ci* poems were written in short form. The style of his poetry was influenced by that of Wen Tingyun, Wei Zhuang, and Feng Yan Zhu. His poems are noted for their elegance and richness in implications. As one who was highly successful in political and social life, Feng shied away from writing poetry that was considered too personal. Most of his poems were written to reflect life in general. His famous line 无可奈何花落去，似曾相识燕归来 (Nothing I can do to stop flowers falling. Familiar swallows are now returning.) perhaps exemplifies better the kind of poetic feelings and style.

晏殊

浣溪沙

一曲新词酒一杯。去年天气旧亭台。夕阳西下几时回。无可奈何花落去，似曾相识燕归来。小园香径独徘徊。

Yan Shu

Tune: "Wan Xi Sha"

Last Year

On the same old balcony,
with a cup of wine,
I listen to a melody sung in new lyrical lines.
The weather was just like last year.
After it sets, the sun will again rise.
But will you also arrive?
Nothing I can do to stop flowers falling.
Familiar swallows are now returning.
On the flowery path of a small garden,
I am alone, lingering.

晏殊 yàn shū
浣溪沙 wǎn xī shā

○ = 平声 (*ping* or flat tone)
△ = 仄声 (*ze* or deflected tone)
● = 平声韵 (rhymed in *ping* or flat tone)
▲ = 仄声韵 (rhymed in *ze* or deflected tone)

一△曲△
yī qū
one melody of

去△年○
qù nián
last year's

夕○陽○
xī yáng
setting sun

無○可△奈△何○
wú kě nài hé
be utterly helpless

似△曾○
sì céng
look like

小△園○
xiǎo yuán
small garden

新○詞○
xīn cí
new lyric

天○氣△
tiān qì
weather

西○下△
xī xià
descends to west

花○
huā
flowers

相○識△
xiāng shí
be acquainted with

香○徑△
xiāng jìng
fragrant path

酒△一△杯●
jiǔ yī bēi
one cup of wine

舊△亭○台●
jiù tíng tái
same old balcony

幾△時○回●
jǐ shí huí
when will return

落△去△
luò qù
have fallen and gone

燕△歸○來●
yàn guī lái
returning swallows

獨△徘○徊●
dú pái huái
pace up and down alone

晏殊

浣溪沙

一向年光有限身。等闲离别易销魂。酒筵歌席莫辞频。满目山河空念远，落花风雨更伤春。不如怜取眼前人。

Yan Shu

Tune: "Wan Xi Sha"

Now Is the Time?

A year is like a moment;
a life is but a short duration.
An ordinary farewell can be
overwhelmed with emotion.
Don't turn down a drinking and singing feast
for being held too frequent.
Waiting for someone faraway to cross mountains and
streams may end up in disappointment.
I feel sad even more when fallen
flowers are assaulted by wind and rain.
Why not enjoy the good time
with the person before my eyes?

晏殊　　**yàn shū**
浣溪沙　**wǎn xī shā**

一△向△ *yī xiàng* a moment	年〇光〇 *nián guāng* a year's time	有△限△身● *yǒu xiàn shēn* limited life
等△閒〇 *děng xián* ordinary	離〇別△ *lí bié* parting	易△銷〇魂● *yì xiāo hún* easy to be emotional
酒△筵〇 *jiǔ yán* a feast	歌〇席△ *gē xí* singing performance	莫△辭〇頻● *mò cí pín* don't decline invitation for being too frequent
滿△目△ *mǎn mù* to meet the eyes everywhere	山〇河〇 *shān hé* mountains and rivers	空〇念△遠△ *kōng niàn yuǎn* in vain to think of someone faraway
落△花〇 *luò huā* fallen flowers	風〇雨△ *fēng yǔ* wind and rain	更△傷〇春● *gèng shāng chūn* feel even worse for the waning spring
不△如〇 *bù rú* may be better	憐〇取△ *lián qǔ* to show appreciation for	眼△前〇人● *yǎn qián rén* someone in front of the eyes

晏殊

清平乐

红笺小字。说尽平生意。鸿雁在云鱼在水,惆怅此情难寄。 斜阳独倚西楼,遥山恰对帘钩。人面不知何处,绿波依旧东流。

Yan Shu

Tune: "Qing Ping Le"

Love Sickness

My lifelong feelings can be summed up
in small words on a red letter paper.
But swan geese are high in the clouds, and
fish swim deep in the water.
I feel melancholy as my message
cannot be delivered.

As the sun comes down, I lean alone
at the west tower.
Standing by the curtain, I try to look afar,
but the distant mountain blocks my view.
Ah, I don't know if I will see that face again!
Only the green waves flow to the east as ever.

晏殊　　**yàn shū**
清平樂　**qīng píng lè**

紅〇箋〇
hóng jiān
red letter paper

小△字▲
xiǎo zì
small words

說△盡△
shuō jìn
tell it all

平〇生〇
píng shēng
lifelong

意▲
yì
idea

鴻〇雁△
hóng yàn
swan geese

在△雲〇
zài yún
in the clouds

魚〇在△水▲
yú zài shuǐ
fish in the water

惆〇悵△
chóu chàng
melancholy

此△情〇
cǐ qíng
this feeling of love

難〇寄▲
nán jì
hard to send

斜〇陽〇
xié yáng
setting sun

獨△倚△
dú yǐ
I lean alone

西〇樓〇
xī lóu
west side of upstairs

遙〇山〇
yáo shān
distant mountain

恰△對△
qià duì
just happens to face

簾〇鉤●
lián gōu
curtain hooks

人〇面△
rén miàn
human face

不△知〇
bù zhī
don't know

何〇處△
hé chǔ
where is

綠△波〇
lǜ bō
green waves

依〇舊△
yī jiù
as before

東〇流●
dōng liú
flow eastward

晏殊

蝶恋花

槛菊愁烟兰泣露，罗幕轻寒，燕子双飞去。
明月不谙离恨苦，斜光到晓穿朱户。
昨夜西风凋碧树，独上高楼，望尽天涯路。
欲寄彩笺兼尺素，山长水阔知何处。

Yan Shu

Tune: "Die Lian Hua"

Where to Send My Letter?

Chrysanthemums by the balustrade
look gloomy in the mist.
The dewy orchids appear in tears.
The silken curtain feels the autumn chill.
Swallows fly away in pairs.
The bright moon has no clue to parting sorrow.
Its slanting light keeps shining upon me until
dawn through the door and window.

Last night, the west wind withered up the trees.
I go up to the high tower and
look as far as I can see.
I wish to send you a letter and a poem.
But mountains are long; rivers are wide.
How do I know your whereabouts?

晏殊　yàn shū
蝶戀花　dié liàn huā

檻△菊△
jiàn jú
balustrade chrysanthemums

愁○煙○
chóu yān
worry about mist

蘭○泣△露▲
lán qì lù
orchids shed dewdrops

羅△幕△
luó mù
silken curtain

輕○寒○
qīng hán
slightly cold

燕△子△
yàn zi
swallows

雙○飛○
shuāng fēi
fly in pair

去▲
qù
go away

明○月△
míng yuè
bright moon

不△諳○
bù ān
doesn't know well

離○恨△苦▲
lí hèn kǔ
the pain of parting

斜○光○
xié guāng
slanting light

到△曉△
dào xiǎo
up until dawn

穿○朱○戶▲
chuān zhū hù
shines through decorated windows

昨△夜△
zuó yè
last night

西○風○
xī fēng
west wind

凋○碧△樹▲
diāo bì shù
causes green leaves to fall

獨△上△
dú shàng
go up alone

高○樓○
gāo lóu
high tower

望△盡△
wàng jìn
look as far as I can

天○涯○
tiān yá
remote

路▲
lù
road

欲△寄△
yù jì
I wish to send

彩△箋○
cǎi jiān
poems on paper

兼○尺△素▲
jiān chǐ sù
and letters

山○長○
shān cháng
mountains: long

水△闊△
shuǐ kuò
water: wide

知○何○處▲
zhī hé chù
don't know where

165

晏殊

木兰花

燕鸿过后莺归去。细算浮生千万绪。长于春梦几多时，散似秋云无觅处。 闻琴解佩神仙侣。挽断罗衣留不住。劝君莫作独醒人，烂醉花间应有数。

Yan Shu

Tune: "Mu Lan Hua"

Don't Be the Only Sobering Person

Swallows and swan geese are gone;
no orioles are left behind.
Moods and feelings are too many
to numerate in this life.
You came into my spring dream:
so brief and haste.
You then vanished like the autumn clouds
without a trace.

I am reminded of Wen Jun's reaction to the sound of
zither and that of removing the jade pendant
by the immortal mate.
Even though I had torn your silk sleeves apart,
you would not have chosen to stay.
I advise you not try to be the only sobering person.
For getting drunk among the flowers is your fate.

晏殊　　yàn shū
木蘭花　mù lán huā

燕△鴻○
yàn hóng
swallows and swan geese

過△後△
guò hòu
after they are gone

鶯○歸○去▲
yīng guī qù
orioles go home

細△算△
xì suàn
examine carefully

浮○生○
fú shēng
this life

千○萬△緒▲
qiān wàn xù
thousands of moods and feelings

長○於○
zhǎng yú
to grow as

春○夢△
chūn mèng
spring dream

幾△多○時○
jǐ duō shí
so brief a time

散△似△
sǎn sì
to vanish like

秋○雲○
qiū yún
autumn clouds

無○覓△處▲
wú mì chǔ
nowhere to be found

聞○琴○
wén qín
listening to plucked instrument

解△佩△
jiě pèi
remove jade pendant

神○仙○侶▲
shén xiān lǚ
immortal companion

挽△斷△
wǎn duàn
torn apart by pulling

羅○衣○
luó yī
silk dress

留○不△住▲
liú bù zhù
can't keep one to stay

勸△君○
quàn jūn
I advise you

莫△作△
mò zuò
not to be

獨△醒△人○
dú xǐng rén
the only sobering person

爛△醉△
làn zuì
be drunken

花○間○
huā jiān
among flowers

應△有△數▲
yìng yǒu shù
should know how things stand

晏殊

木兰花

绿杨芳草长亭路，年少抛人容易去。楼头残梦五更钟，花底离愁三月雨。　无情不似多情苦，一寸还成千万缕。天涯地角有穷时，只有相思无尽处。

Yan Shu

Tune: "Mu Lan Hua"

Lovesickness

The sight of green willows, grass,
and pavilions on the road can break my heart.
For a young man with ambition, leaving his
love behind isn't too hard.
The sound of the drum from the tower
tells me that it is now the wee hours.
So my dream will not last any longer.
Only the fallen flowers after an April rain
can understand.
Compared to the heartless ones, a passionate
person is far more in pain.
How can my heart be big enough to be wrapped by
thousands of thread-like sorrowful feelings?
The edges can be reached, be it earth or sky.
But lovesickness seems to have no end in sight.

晏殊 yàn shū
木蘭花 mù lán huā

綠△楊○ *lǜ yáng* green poplars	芳○草△ *fāng cǎo* fragrant grass	長○亭○路▲ *cháng tíng lù* a road with long pavilions
年○少△ *nián shǎo* young people	拋○人○ *pāo rén* leaving other behind	容○易△去▲ *róng yì qù* easy to go
樓○頭○ *lóu tóu* upstairs	殘○夢△ *cán mèng* waning dream	五△更○鐘○ *wǔ gèng zhōng* just before dawn
花○底△ *huā dǐ* under flowers	離○愁○ *lí chóu* parting sorrow	三○月△雨▲ *sān yuè yǔ* rain in the third month
無○情○ *wú qíng* lack of passion	不△似△ *bù sì* is unlike	多○情○苦▲ *duō qíng kǔ* pain of passionate love
一△寸△ *yī cùn* one inch (of heart)	還○成○ *huán chéng* can turn into	千○萬△縷▲ *qiān wàn lǚ* thousands of threads
天○涯○ *tiān yá* end of sky	地△角△ *dì jiǎo* earth's corner	有△窮○時○ *yǒu qióng shí* to have an ending point
只△有△ *zhǐ yǒu* only	相○思○ *xiāng sī* lovesickness	無○盡△處▲ *wú jìn chǔ* doesn't have an end

长于春梦几多时，散似秋云无觅处。

You came into my spring dream:
so brief and haste.
You then vanished like the autumn clouds
without a trace.

   —Yan Shu

Ouyan Xiu (1007–1073)

欧阳修

Ouyang Xiu was also called Ouyang Yongshu. He was acclaimed as "one of the greatest literary masters of the Tang and Song Dynasties."

Ouyang lost his father when he was only four years old. His literate mother taught him to write on ash with reed stems. His talents were multi-faceted, not only excelling in governmental service, but also in writing essays, *shi*, and *ci* poetry. He passed the imperial examination with the rank of *jinshi* at the age of twenty-two.

A friend of Feng Zhongyan, Su Shi, and Su's brother Su Zhe, Ouyang promoted a writing style that is relatively free from pompous and obscure expressions. He played an important role in continuing this literary tradition.

In his middle-age years, Ouyang nicknamed himself the Drunkard Lord. At the age of sixty, he called himself Liu-Yi Ju Shi (the Six-One Retired Scholar). He explained that he sought happiness in having the five things around: one bottle of wine, one zither, one chess, one thousand copies of the ancient bronze and stone inscriptions, one *wan* (ten thousand) of books, and one old man himself. According to Ouyang, with these six ones, a person can achieve true freedom.

欧阳修

蝶恋花

庭院深深深几许，杨柳堆烟，帘幕无重数。玉勒雕鞍游冶处，楼高不见章台路。 雨横风狂三月暮，门掩黄昏，无计留春住。泪眼问花花不语，乱红飞过秋千去。

Ouyan Xiu

Tune: "Die Lian Hua"

So Deep Is the Courtyard

The courtyard is so deep; so deep indeed.
The willow trees are shrouded with piles of mist.
They look like curtains with layers upon layers.
On a horse with jade strap and carved saddle,
I am heading to the fun place.
But the buildings are so tall and I can't find
the ZhangTai Street.

Wind and rain come violently at dusk in late April.
The door is closed in the evening.
I am unable to keep spring from leaving.
In tears, I ask the flowers why but without a reply.
The red petals fly disorderly over the swing.

歐陽修　ōu yáng xiū
蝶戀花　dié liàn huā

○ = 平声 (*ping* or flat tone)
△ = 仄声 (*ze* or deflected tone)
● = 平声韵 (rhymed in *ping* or flat tone)
▲ = 仄声韵 (rhymed in *ze* or deflected tone)

庭○院△
tíng yuàn
courtyard

楊○柳△
yáng liǔ
willows

簾○幕△
lián mù
curtains

玉△勒△
yù lè
jade strap

樓○高○
lóu gāo
buildings are tall

雨△橫○
yǔ héng
windy rain

門○掩△
mén yǎn
door closed

無○計△
wú jì
no way

淚△眼△
lèi yǎn
in tears

亂△紅○
luàn hóng
petals randomly

深○深○
shēn shēn
so deep

堆○煙○
duī yān
mists are piled up

無○重○數▲
wú chóng shù
uncountable

雕○鞍○
diāo ān
carved saddle

不△見△
bù jiàn
can't see

風○狂○
fēng kuáng
fierce wind

黃○昏○
huáng hūn
at dusk

留○
liú
to keep

問△花○
wèn huā
ask flowers

飛○過△
fēi guò
fly over

深○幾△許▲
shēn jǐ xǔ
so deep indeed

游○冶△處▲
yóu yě chǔ
going for an outing

章○台○路▲
zhāng tái lù
Zhang Tai Road

三○月△暮▲
sān yuè mù
late April

春○住▲
chūn zhù
spring staying

花○不△語▲
huā bù yǔ
flowers say nothing

秋○千○去▲
qiū qiān qù
the swing

欧阳修

生查子

去年元夜时,花市灯如昼。月上柳梢头,人约黄昏后。 今年元夜时,月与灯依旧。不见去年人,泪湿春衫袖。

Ouyan Xiu

Tune: "Sheng Cha Zi"

Lantern Festival

At last year's Lantern Festival,
the lanterns of the flower market
were as bright as noontime.
We promised to meet at dusk when
the moon reached the top of willows
and beamed its shining light.

At this year's Lantern Festival,
both the moon and lanterns
are just as bright.
Only you are nowhere in sight.
With my blue sleeves, I wipe
my tearful eyes.

歐陽修　ōu yáng xiū
生查子　shēng chá zi

去△年〇
qù nián
last year

花〇市△
huā shì
flower market

月△上△
yuè shàng
moon descends

人〇約△
rén yuē
people agree to meet

今〇年〇
jīn nián
this year

月△與△
yuè yǔ
moon and

不△見△
bù jiàn
don't see

淚△濕△
lèi shī
tears moisten

元〇夜△
yuán yè
Lantern Festival

燈〇
dēng
lanterns

柳△
liǔ
willow

黃〇昏〇
huáng hūn
dusk

元〇夜△
yuán yè
Lantern Festival

燈〇
dēng
lanterns

去△年〇
qù nián
last year

春〇衫〇
chūn shān
spring shirt

時〇
shí
time

如〇晝▲
rú zhòu
like noontime

梢〇頭〇
shāo tóu
the tip of a tree

後▲
hòu
after

時〇
shí
time

依〇舊▲
yī jiù
as before

人〇
rén
person

袖▲
xiù
sleeves

欧阳修

采桑子

轻舟短棹西湖好，绿水逶迤。芳草长堤。隐隐笙歌处处随。　无风水面琉璃滑，不觉船移。微动涟漪。惊起沙禽掠岸飞。

Ouyan Xiu

Tune: "Cai Sang Zi"

The West Lake

With a short oar I row my skiff.
So beautiful is the scenery at West Lake.
Green water winds its way through.
On the long bank, fragrant grasses grow.
Indistinct music and songs follow the direction I row.

The water surface is as smooth as colored glaze.
The boat is not felt moving at all.
Ripples appear whenever the water is stirred.
The seagulls are frightened to skim over the shore.

歐陽修　**ōu yáng xiū**
采桑子　**cǎi sāng zi**

輕○舟○ *qīng zhōu* skiff	短△棹△ *duǎn zhào* short oar	西○湖○好△ *xī hú hǎo* West Lake is beautiful
綠△水△ *lǜ shuǐ* green water	逶○迤● *wēi yǐ* wind its way through	
芳△草△ *fāng cǎo* fragrant grass	長○堤● *cháng dī* (grow) on the long bank	
隱△隱△ *yǐn yǐn* indistinct	笙○歌○ *shēng gē* music and songs	處△處△隨● *chǔ chù suí* follow everywhere
無○風○ *wú fēng* no wind	水△面△ *shuǐ miàn* on water surface	琉○璃○滑△ *liú lí huá* as smooth as colored glaze
不△覺△ *bù jué* don't feel	船○移● *chuán yí* boat is moving	
微○動△ *wéi dòng* slightly stir	漣○漪● *lián yī* ripples	
驚○起△ *jīng qǐ* frighten	沙○禽○ *shā qín* sand gull	掠△岸△飛● *luè àn fēi* skim over the shore

欧阳修

采桑子

群芳过后西湖好，狼籍残红。飞絮蒙蒙。垂柳阑干尽日风。　笙歌散尽游人去，始觉春空。垂下帘栊。双燕归来细雨中。

Ouyan Xiu

Tune: "Cai Sang Zi"

The West Lake Remains Beautiful

Flowers of all sorts have withered.
The West Lake is still as picturesque as ever.
Fallen flowers are scattered pile upon pile.
Catkins in the air freely drift or fly.
Against the rails, the willows hang low.
The whole day the wind blows.

No more piping and song;
the tourists have all gone.
Suddenly I feel a sense of
emptiness in my mind.
I drop the curtains and blinds.
In the drizzle, a pair of
swallows are on their returning flight.

歐陽修　ōu yáng xiū
采桑子　cǎi sāng zi

群○芳○ *qún fāng* all kinds of flowers	過△後△ *guò hòu* have withered	西○湖○好△ *xī hú hǎo* West Lake (is) still nice
狼○籍△ *láng jí* scattered	殘○紅● *cán hóng* fading red (flowers)	
飛○絮△ *fēi xù* flying catkins	朦○朦● *méng méng* indistinct	
垂○柳△ *chuí liǔ* weeping willow	闌○干○ *lán gān* rails	盡△日△風● *jìn rì fēng* windy all day
笙○歌○ *shēng gē* music and song	散△盡△ *sǎn jìn* come to an end	游○人○去△ *yóu rén qù* tourists are gone
始△覺△ *shǐ jué* starting to feel	春○空● *chūn kōng* emptiness in spring	
垂○下△ *chuí xià* lower down	簾○櫳● *lián lóng* screens and blinds	
雙△燕△ *shuāng yàn* a pair of swallows	歸○來○ *guī lái* return	細△雨△中● *xì yǔ zhōng* in the drizzle

欧阳修

浪淘沙

把酒祝东风。且共从容。垂杨紫陌洛城东。总是当时携手处，游遍芳丛。 聚散苦匆匆。此恨无穷。今年花胜去年红。可惜明年花更好，知与谁同。

Ouyan Xiu

Tune: "Lang Tao Sha"

This Year's Flowers

I toast to the east wind with a cup of wine.
Let's take it easy at such a time.
The willows-dropping road of
eastern Luo Yang is my favorite scene.
We used to come here hand in
hand for sightseeing.

Meeting and parting are always in such a hurry.
This regret will be long-lasting.
Comparing to those of last year,
this year's flowers are brighter and more red.
Next year they may be even better.
Ah, with whom will I spend time together?

歐陽修　　ōu yáng xiū
浪淘沙　　làng táo shā

把△酒△
bǎ jiǔ
holding a cup of wine

祝△
zhù
I wish well

東○風●
dōng fēng
east wind

且△
qiě
for the time being

共△
gòng
let's together

從○容●
cóng róng
be unhurried and linger on

垂○楊○
chuí yáng
dropping willow

紫△陌△
zǐ mò
purple path

洛△城○東●
luò chéng dōng
east side of Luo Yang City

總△是△
zǒng shì
all were used to be

當○時○
dāng shí
then

攜○手△處△
xié shǒu chù
where we held each other's hand

游○遍△
yóu biàn
toured all around

芳○叢●
fāng cóng
flower bushes

聚△散△
jù sǎn
gathering and parting

苦△
kǔ
be troubled by

匆○匆●
cōng cōng
haste and brief

此△恨△
cǐ hèn
this regret

無○窮●
wú qióng
without end

今○年○
jīn nián
this year

花○勝△
huā shèng
flowers better than

去△年○紅●
qù nián hóng
last year's red color

可△惜△
kě xī
it is a pity

明○年○
míng nián
next year

花○更△好△
huā gèng hǎo
flowers will even be better

知○與△
zhī yǔ
not knowing with

誰○
shéi
whom

同●
tóng
together

181

欧阳修

踏莎行

候馆梅残，溪桥柳细。草薰风暖摇征辔。离愁渐远渐无穷，迢迢不断如春水。　寸寸柔肠，盈盈粉泪。楼高莫近危栏倚。平芜尽处是春山，行人更在春山外。

Ouyan Xiu

Tune: "Ta Suo Xing"

Parting Grief

Plum flowers have withered at the inn.
By the stream bridge, the willow branches
are slender and thin.
Grass is fragrant; wind is warm.
The bridle of the horse I ride is wavering.
The further I go, the greater is my parting pain.
It is like the spring water that keeps flowing
to a faraway place without ending.

You must be feeling grief in your heart.
Your eyes are filled with tears.
The tower is very high, so don't go near
the rails for the farthermost sight.
You can only see the spring mountain
at the end of the grassland.
But I am already at the mountain's other side.

歐陽修　　ōu yáng xiū
踏莎行　　tà suō xíng

候△館△
hòu guǎn
hotel

梅〇殘〇
méi cán
plum flowers wither

溪〇橋〇
xī qiáo
brook bridge

柳△細▲
liǔ xì
willows branches small

草△薰〇
cǎo xūn
grass: fragrant

風〇暖△
fēng nuǎn
wind: warm

搖〇征〇轡▲
yáo zhēng pèi
bridle is shaking

離〇愁〇
lí chóu
parting grief

漸△遠△
jiàn yuǎn
further it goes

漸△無〇窮〇
jiàn wú qióng
longer it lasts

迢〇迢〇
tiáo tiáo
far away

不△斷△
bù duàn
without interruption

如〇春〇水▲
rú chūn shuǐ
is like spring water

寸△寸△
cùn cùn
each inch of

柔〇腸〇
róu cháng
tender intestines (heart)

盈〇盈〇
yíng yíng
be filled with

粉△淚▲
fěn lèi
tears

樓〇高〇
lóu gāo
tower is high

莫△近△
mò jìn
don't be near

危〇欄〇倚▲
wēi lán yǐ
lean on dangerous rails

平〇蕪〇
píng wú
wide open grassland

盡△處△
jìn chǔ
where it ends

是△春〇山〇
shì chūn shān
is the spring mountain

行〇人〇
xíng rén
traveler

更△在△
gèng zài
is now in a place

春〇山〇外▲
chūn shān wài
beyond spring mountain

183

欧阳修

诉衷情

清晨帘幕卷轻霜。呵手试梅妆。都缘自有离恨，故画作、远山长。思往事，惜流芳。易成伤。拟歌先敛，欲笑还颦，最断人肠。

Ouyan Xiu

Tune: "Su Zhong Qing"

Pretending

In the morning, I roll up the blind
that is stained with light frost.
I breathe on my hand before I apply
makeup in the plume-flower style.
Because I feel some parting pain,
I paint my eyebrows to represent
a mountain's length.
I think of the past, and lament
that the time has passed.
But it so easy to feel hurt.
Before singing, I first pretend to be sad.
I knit my eyebrows even though I want to smile.
This has to be my most heartbreaking time.

歐陽修　　ōu yáng xiū
訴衷情　　sù zhōng qíng

清○晨○
qīng chén
morning

簾○幕△
lián mù
curtain

捲△輕○霜●
juǎn qīng shuāng
roll up light frost

呵○手△
hē shǒu
breathe on hand

試△
shì
trying to

梅○妝●
méi zhuāng
apply a plum-flower makeup

都○緣○
dōu yuán
all because

自△有△
zì yǒu
I myself have

離○恨△
lí hèn
parting sorrow

故△
gù
therefore

畫△作△
huà zuò
paint it like

遠△山○長●
yuǎn shān cháng
the length of a distant mountain

思○往△事△
sī wǎng shì
think of the past

惜△流○芳●
xī liú fāng
lament the time passed

易△成○傷●
yì chéng shāng
easy to feel hurt

擬△歌○
nǐ gē
about to sing

先○
xiān
first

斂△
liàn
assume a serious expression

欲△笑△
yù xiào
wanting to smile

還○顰○
huán pín
but knit the brows

最△
zuì
the most

斷△
duàn
(it) breaks

人○腸●
rén cháng
one's heart

欧阳修

临江仙

柳外轻雷池上雨，雨声滴碎荷声。小楼西角断虹明。阑干倚处，待得月华生。燕子飞来窥画栋，玉钩垂下帘旌。凉波不动簟纹平。水精双枕，傍有堕钗横。

Ouyan Xiu

Tune: "Lin Jiang Xian"

Waiting

A light thunder is heard beyond the willow.
Rain starts to fall in the pool.
The sound of rain overwhelms
the drifting sound of lotus leaves.
A section of the rainbow shines upon
the chamber's west corner.
She leans on the rails
waiting for the moon to rise.

Swallows fly over and peep
behind the painted beams.
The curtain hangs down from
the jade hooks naturally.
The wave-like bamboo mat seems
flat, still, and cool.
By the side of the two crystal pillows,
a golden hairpin lies horizontally.

歐陽修　　ōu yáng xiū
臨江仙　　lín jiāng xiān

柳△外△	輕○雷○	池○上△雨△
liǔ wài	qīng léi	chí shàng yǔ
beyond the willow	light thunder	rain in the pool

雨△聲○　　滴△碎△　　荷○聲●
yǔ shēng　　dī suì　　hé shēng
sound of rain　　breaks up　　sound of lotus

小△樓○　　西○角△　　斷△虹○明●
xiǎo lóu　　xī jiǎo　　duàn hóng míng
little storied building　　west corner　　part of rainbow is bright

闌○干○　　倚△處△
lán gān　　yǐ chǔ
rails　　on which one can lean

待△得△　　月△華○　　生●
dài de　　yuè huá　　shēng
waiting for　　the moon　　to rise

燕△子△　　飛○來○　　窺○畫△棟△
yàn zi　　fēi lái　　kuī huà dòng
swallows　　fly over here　　peep behind the painted beam

玉△鉤○　　垂○下△　　簾○旌●
yù gōu　　chuí xià　　lián jīng
jade hooks　　hang down　　curtain

涼○波○　　不△動△　　簟△紋○平●
liáng bō　　bù dòng　　diàn wén píng
cold air　　without movement　　bamboo mat lies flat

水△精○　　雙○枕△
shuǐ jīng　　shuāng zhěn
crystal　　pillows in pair

傍△有△　　墮△釵○橫●
bàng yǒu　　duò chāi héng
at the side　　gold hairpin lies horizontally

欧阳修

玉楼春

别后不知君远近。触目凄凉多少闷。渐行渐远渐无书,水阔鱼沈何处问。夜深风竹敲秋韵。万叶千声皆是恨。故倚单枕梦中寻,梦又不成灯又烬。

Ouyan Xiu

Tune: "Yu Lou Chun"

Where Are You?

After we parted, I have no idea
how far you are.
Everything touching my eyes triggers
dreariness and boredom in my heart.
The further you are away, the fewer
letters I've got.
Water is wide; fish go deep.
Where can I find an answer?

The night is deep.
Bamboos rustle in the wind.
The autumn tune is in the making.
All the sounds of leaves are but regrets to me.
Leaning on a solitary pillow, I try to find
you in my dream.
But the candlelight has already turned
into ashes before I succeed in dreaming.

歐陽修　　ōu yáng xiū
玉樓春　　yù lóu chūn

別△後△
bié hòu
after parting

觸△目△
chù mù
everything in view

漸△行〇
jiàn xíng
more walking

水△闊△
shuǐ kuò
water is wide

夜△深〇
yè shēn
night is deep

萬△葉△
wàn yè
ten thousand leaves

故△欹△
gù yǐ
so to lean on

夢△又△
mèng yòu
but dream

不△知〇
bù zhī
don't know

淒〇涼〇
qī liáng
dreary

漸△遠△
jiàn yuǎn
further away

魚〇沈〇
yú shěn
fish go deep

風〇竹△
fēng zhú
wind and bamboo

千〇聲〇
qiān shēng
thousand sounds

單〇枕△
dān zhěn
single pillow

不△成〇
bù chéng
not succeed

君〇遠△近▲
jūn yuǎn jìn
how far or near you are

多〇少△悶▲
duō shǎo mèn
so bored

漸△無〇書〇
jiàn wú shū
fewer messages

何〇處△問▲
hé chǔ wèn
where can I ask

敲〇秋〇韻▲
qiāo qiū yùn
strike an autumn rhyme

皆〇是△恨▲
jiē shì hèn
all are regrets

夢△中〇尋〇
mèng zhōng xún
to find you in dream

燈〇又△燼▲
dēng yòu jìn
candle turns into ashes

欧阳修

蝶恋花

谁道闲情抛弃久。每到春来，惆怅还依旧。日日花前常病酒。不辞镜里朱颜瘦。　河畔青芜堤上柳。为问新愁，何事年年有。独立小桥风满袖。平林新月人归后。

Ou Yan Xiu

Tune: "Die Lian Hua"

Feelings of Uneasiness

Who says that feelings of uneasiness
have permanently gone?
When spring is here, the melancholy comes back.
I drink excessively in front
of the flowers every day.
I care little that the image in the mirror
shows a thinner face.

The grass by the riverside is so green.
Willows on the bank provide such a nice scene.
Why then is there new sorrow to yearly come along?
I stand by the little bridge alone,
with my sleeves filled with the wind.
After I have returned, I see the new moon
over the plain grove starting to beam.

歐陽修 ōu yáng xiū
蝶戀花 dié liàn huā

誰〇道△
shéi dào
who says

每△到△
měi dào
whenever

悃〇悵△
chóu chàng
melancholy

日△日△
rì rì
every day

不△辭〇
bù cí
care not

河〇畔△
hé pàn
riverside

為〇問△
wéi wèn
to ask why

何〇事△
hé shì
for what reason

獨△立△
dú lì
standing alone

平〇林〇
píng lín
plain grove

閒〇情〇
xián qíng
uneasy feelings

春〇來〇
chūn lái
spring comes

還〇
huán
remains

花〇前〇
huā qián
before flowers

鏡△裏△
jìng lǐ
in the mirror

青〇蕪〇
qīng wú
green glass

新〇愁〇
xīn chóu
new sorrow

年〇年〇
nián nián
every year

小△橋〇
xiǎo qiáo
little bridge

新〇月△
xīn yuè
new moon

拋〇棄△久▲
pāo qì jiǔ
have abandoned permanently

依〇舊▲
yī jiù
as ever

常〇病△酒▲
cháng bìng jiǔ
often drink excessively

朱〇顏〇瘦▲
zhū yán shòu
young face becomes thinner

堤〇上△柳▲
dī shàng liǔ
willows on bank

有▲
yǒu
it is here

風〇滿△袖▲
fēng mǎn xiù
sleeves filled with wind

人〇歸〇後▲
rén guī hòu
after the person has returned

191

欧阳修

玉楼春

樽前拟把归期说，欲语春容先惨咽。人生自是有情痴，此恨不关风与月。　离歌且莫翻新阕，一曲能教肠寸结。直须看尽洛城花，始共春风容易别。

Ouyan Xiu

Tune: "Yu Lou Chun"

Sentimental Feelings

I am about to tell you the date of leaving
in front of the wine.
Before uttering my words, my vernal face
has turned into one with teary eyes.
In life we were born naturally with sentimental feelings.
Such a grief has nothing to do with moon and wind.

Don't add a new parting song to an old one.
One song is enough to make the heart
deeply grieved and broken.
Go immediately to see all the flowers in Lou City.
It will then be easier to bid farewell to the vernal
breeze.

歐陽修　　ōu yáng xiū
玉樓春　　yù lóu chūn

樽○前○
zūn qián
in front of wine jar

擬△把△
nǐ bǎ
want to

歸○期○說▲
guī qī shuō
tell about returning date

欲△語△
yù yǔ
before speaking

春○容○
chūn róng
vernal complexion

先○慘△咽▲
xiān cǎn yàn
first sadly weep

人○生○
rén shēng
life

自△是△
zì shì
naturally

有△情○痴○
yǒu qíng chī
to have sentimental feelings

此△恨△
cǐ hèn
such a grief

不△關○
bù guān
nothing to do with

風△與△月▲
fēng yǔ yuè
wind and moon

離○歌○
lí gē
parting song

且△莫△
qiě mò
better not to

翻○新○闋▲
fān xīn què
turn to a new musical piece

一△曲△
yī qū
one song

能○教○
néng jiào
can let

腸○寸△結▲
cháng cùn jié
intestines (heart) deeply grieved

直○須○
zhí xū
should immediately

看△盡△
kàn jìn
see all

洛△城○花○
luò chéng huā
Luo City's flowers

始△共△
shǐ gòng
then

春○風○
chūn fēng
with vernal breeze

容○易△別▲
róng yì bié
easy to part

人生自是有情痴，此恨不关风与月。

In life we were born naturally
with sentimental feelings.
Such a grief has nothing to do
with moon and wind.

— Ouyang Xiu

Yan Jidao (1048–1118?)

晏几道

Yan Jidao was the seventh—also the youngest—son of Yan Shu, a famus poet and prime minister in the Song Dynasty. Jidao was eighteen years old when his father died. Although he was born into a wealthy and powerful family, he had to struggle financially as a middle-aged man.

    Several reasons accounted for the downfall of his family fortune. For one thing, he failed to manage the money prudently, and he was very generous to help others without demanding repayment. Also, he was too proud to ask his father's former colleagues and friends for help in times of need. He never wanted to compromise his moral standard for selfish and personal gains.

    Yan wrote his poems mainly in *xiaoling* or short form. The many ups and downs he went through in his life might have contributed to the breadth and dept of his poetry. In general, Jidao's poems were more personal and sentimental than those written by his father. Scholars tend to give the younger Yan a higher mark when it comes to evaluating creative ideas, genuine feelings, and uniqueness in poetic style.

    Yan was once in love with several female singers he met in his old friends' houses. Among them were Lian, Ping, Hong, and Yun, whom he identified by names in some of his poems. In the poem to the tune of *Ling Jiang Xian*, for example, he describes how he first met Xiao Ping. In the introductory session of this book, as you may recall, we gave a detailed analysis of his poem in which he conveys his feelings toward an unnamed singer and dancer.

晏几道

鹧鸪天

彩袖殷勤捧玉钟。当年拚却醉颜红。舞低杨柳楼心月，歌尽桃花扇底风。从别后，忆相逢。几回魂梦与君同。今宵剩把银釭照，犹恐相逢是梦中。

Yan Jidao

Tune: "Zhe Gu Tian"

Is This Reunion a Dream?

Her sleeves looked colorful and bright;
she politely handed me a cup of wine.
I went all out to drink in those days
for a flushed and red face.
She kept dancing until the moon shone
upon the floor of the Willow Tree Tower.
She quitted singing only after she could no longer
create a wind with her peach-blossom fan.

Since we parted,
I often remember how we first met.
Time and again, I dreamt of us being together.
Tonight, I just want to make sure
that the lamp is bright.
I am so afraid that we are reunited
in dream, not in the real life.

晏幾道　**yàn jǐ dào**
鷓鴣天　**zhè gū tiān**

○ ＝ 平声 (*ping* or flat tone)

△ ＝ 仄声 (*ze* or deflected tone)

● ＝ 平声韵 (rhymed in *ping* or flat tone)

▲ ＝ 仄声韵 (rhymed in *ze* or deflected tone)

彩△袖△
căi xiù
colorful sleeves

當○年○
dāng nián
in those days

舞△低○
wŭ dī
danced; (until moon) let droop

歌○盡△
gē jìn
sang; (until wind) exhausted

從○
cóng
since

憶△
yì
remembered

幾△回○
jĭ huí
several times

今○宵○
jīn xiāo
tonight

猶○恐△
yóu kŏng
for fear that

殷○勤○
yīn qín
very courteous

拚△卻△
pàn què
went all out

楊○柳△
yáng liŭ
willow tree (tower)

桃○花○
táo huā
peach blossom (fan)

別△後△
bié hòu
we bade farewell

相○逢●
xiāng féng
how we met

魂○夢△
hún mèng
my dreams

剩△把△
shèng bă
to make sure

相○逢○
xiāng féng
our meeting

捧△玉△鍾●
pěng yù zhōng
hold a wine cup in both hands

醉△顏○紅●
zuì yán hóng
to drink, resulting in face flushed and red

樓○心○月△
lóu xīn yuè
moon on the tower's floor

扇△底△風●
shàn dĭ fēng
wind under fan

與△君○同●
yŭ jūn tóng
were with you

銀○釭○照△
yín gōng zhào
the lamp is well lighted

是△夢△中●
shì mèng zhōng
is in the dream

晏几道

鹧鸪天

醉拍春衫惜旧香。天将离恨恼疏狂。年年陌上生秋草，日日楼中到夕阳。云渺渺，水茫茫。征人归路许多长。相思本是无凭语，莫向花笺费泪行。

Yan Jidao

Tune: "Zhe Gu Tian"

On Hearing Cuckoo's Crying at Night

Feeling tipsy, I try to dust off my spring dress,
but want to keep her old perfume there.
Heaven makes me pay with parting grief
for being unscrupulously free.
Year after year, autumn grasses on the paths
of the rice field start to wither.
Day after day, I wait for the sun to set in the tower.

Away clouds drift.
So boundless is the water.
The homeward journey is very long for a warrior,
Lovesickness is such an unreliable word to express.
So don't moisten in vain your colorful letter paper
with your tears!

晏幾道　　yàn jǐ dào
鷓鴣天　　zhè gū tiān

醉△拍△
zuì pāi
in tipsiness, I pat on

天○將○
tiān jiāng
Heaven turns into

年○年○
nián nián
year after year

日△日△
rì rì
day after day

雲○
yún
clouds

水△
shuǐ
water

征○人○
zhēng rén
a warrior

相○思○
xiāng sī
lovesickness

莫△向△
mò xiàng
don't try to use

春○衫○
chūn shān
spring clothes

離○恨△
lí hèn
parting sorrow

陌△上△
mò shàng
paths in the rice field

樓○中○
lóu zhōng
in the tower

渺△渺△
miǎo miǎo
indistinct

茫○茫○●
máng máng
boundless

歸○路△
guī lù
returning road

本△是△
běn shì
in essence is

花○箋○
huā jiān
flowery letter paper

惜△舊△香●
xī jiù xiāng
appreciate the old scent

惱△疏○狂●
nǎo shū kuáng
irritated by being unrestrained

生○秋○草△
shēng qiū cǎo
grow autumn grass

到△夕△陽●
dào xī yáng
wait for the sunset

許△多○長●
xǔ duō cháng
very long

無○憑○語△
wú píng yǔ
a word that can't be validated

費△淚△行●
fèi lèi xíng
tears to shed in vain

199

晏几道

鹧鸪天

小令樽前见玉箫。银灯一曲太妖娆。歌中醉倒谁能恨，唱罢归来酒未消。春悄悄，夜迢迢。碧云天共楚宫遥。梦魂惯得无拘检，又踏杨花过谢桥。

Yan Jidao

Tune: "Zhe Gu Tian"

Her Manner of Singing

I like to watch, with a cup of wine,
how Yu Xiao sings her song in short lyric rhyme.
So enchanting to listen her singing
in silver lamplight.
No one ever complains of getting drunk
whenever she sings.
When it is over, I still feel tipsy on returning.

Spring is very quiet.
So long is the night.
She must be living in the high palace
over the blue sky.
I get used to being unrestrained in my dream.
I step on the willow catkins and walk over
the fairy bridge once again.

晏幾道　yàn jǐ dào
鷓鴣天　zhè gū tiān

小△令△
xiǎo lìng
short melody

銀〇燈〇
yín dēng
silver lamp

歌〇中〇
gē zhōng
in the middle of singing

唱△罷△
chàng bà
after singing is over

春〇
chūn
spring

夜△
yè
night

碧△雲〇天〇
bì yún tiān
blue-clouds sky

夢△魂〇
mèng hún
in the dream

又△踏△
yòu tà
again step upon

樽〇前〇
zūn qián
in front of wine cup

一△曲△
yī qū
one song

醉△倒△
zuì dào
drunk

歸〇來〇
guī lái
return home

悄△悄△
qiǎo qiǎo
so quiet

迢〇迢●
tiáo tiáo
so long

共△
gòng
and (as far as)

慣△得△
guàn de
get used to

楊〇花〇
yáng huā
catkins

見△玉△簫●
jiàn yù xiāo
see Yu Xiao

太△妖〇嬈●
tài yāo ráo
extremely beautiful

誰〇能〇恨△
shéi néng hèn
how can one feel regret

酒△未△消●
jiǔ wèi xiāo
effect of wine remains

楚△宮〇遙●
chǔ gōng yáo
Chu Palace far away

無〇拘〇檢△
wú jū jiǎn
without restraint

過△謝△橋●
guò xiè qiáo
pass over Xie Bridge.

201

晏几道

临江仙

梦后楼台高锁，酒醒帘幕低垂。去年春恨却来时，落花人独立，微雨燕双飞。 记得小苹初见，两重心字罗衣。琵琶弦上说相思。当时明月在，曾照彩云归。

Yan Jidao

Tune: "Ling Jiang Xian"

Thinking of Xiao Ping

Awaking from my dream, I find the high tower locked.
Back from tipsiness, I notice that
the curtain hangs low.
The memory of my parting sorrow last spring
has resurfaced once again.
I stand alone as flowers are falling.
Two swallows fly together in light rain.

I remember how I met Xiao Ping the first time.
She wore a silken dress with the word
"heart" embroidered twice.
With her *pipa*, she conveyed her true feelings
by plucking the strings.
The moon is still the same moon
that escorted the beautiful cloud home.

晏幾道 yàn jǐ dào
臨江仙 lín jiāng xiān

夢△後△
mèng hòu
after the dream

酒△醒△
jiǔ xǐng
sobered after drinking

去△年〇
qù nián
last year

落△花〇
luò huā
flowers were falling

微〇雨△
wéi yǔ
in drizzle

記△得△
jì de
remember

兩△重〇
liǎng chóng
double layers

琵〇琶〇
pí pá
pipa

當〇時〇
dāng shí
at that time

曾〇照△
céng zhào
it had shined for

樓〇台〇
lóu tái
terrace

簾〇幕△
lián mù
curtains

春〇恨△
chūn hèn
spring grief

人〇
rén
person

燕△
yàn
swallows

小△蘋〇
xiǎo píng
Little Ping

心〇字△
xīn zì
the character for heart

弦〇上△
xián shàng
on the strings

明〇月△
míng yuè
bright moon

彩△雲〇
cǎi yún
clouds

高〇鎖△
gāo suǒ
locked deep

低〇垂●
dī chuí
hang low

卻△來〇時●
què lái shí
came at that time

獨△立△
dú lì
stood alone

雙〇飛●
shuāng fēi
fly in pair

初〇見△
chū jiàn
met the first time

羅〇衣●
luó yī
on the silken dress

說△相〇思●
shuō xiāng sī
talk about lovesickness

在△
zài
was there

歸●
guī
to return home

相思本是无凭语，莫向花笺费泪行。

Lovesickness is such an unreliable word to express.
So don't moisten in vain your colorful letter paper with your tears!

— Yang Jidao

Part Four

The Latter Northern Song Period

Su Shi (1037–1101)

苏 轼

Su Shi was brought up in present-day Meishan, Sichuan. He was popularly referred to as Su Dongpo, a name he gave himself because his house was situated on the eastern slope.

Su Shi was multitalented in literature, painting, and calligraphy. Along with his father Su Xun and younger brother Su Che, he was named as one of the prose masters in the Tang and Song Dynasties. In *shi* poetry, he and Ouyang Xiu are often considered as being in the same class. In *ci*, Su Shi and Xing Qiji are jointly referred to as Su-Xing.

Su Shi passed the imperial examination at the age of twenty-two. The essay he wrote as part of the examination caught the eyes of the chief examination Ouyang Xiu. Ouyang was impressed very much by Su's talent and skill as revealed in his writing. In the days ahead, Ouyang became Su's patron. Like Ouyang, Su preferred a style of poetry writing that stressed spontaneous and natural expression. In the scope of subject matter, Su was able to break away from his predecessors, who were confined to the poetics of love, parting sorrow, and feelings of hardship. Su expand his subject matter to include his reactions to the society as a whole. Some of his poems carry a philosophical favor.

As talented and well-known as Su Shi became, his political career was not very smooth. His political fortune depended largely on the people who were in power. He was put in jail for four months because one of his poems was cited by his political enemy as evidence that he deliberately ridiculed the emperor.

Su wrote about four thousand poems in various forms. The number of *ci* poems alone is over three hundred. He was without question one of the top-notch men of letters in the history of Chinese literature.

苏轼

水调歌头

丙辰中秋欢饮达旦，大醉作此篇，兼怀子由。

明月几时有，把酒问青天。不知天上宫阙，今夕是何年。我欲乘风归去，又恐琼楼玉宇，高处不胜寒。起舞弄清影，何似在人间。转朱阁，低绮户，照无眠。不应有恨，何事偏向别时圆。人有悲欢离合，月有阴晴圆缺，此事古难全。 但愿人长久，千里共婵娟。

Su Shi

Tune: "Shui Diao Ge Tou"

Mid-Autumn Moon

When did the bright moon appear for the first time?
Holding a cup of wine, I ask the blue sky:
In the celestial palace what year is it tonight?
I wish to return there by riding with the wind,
but am afraid that those beautiful buildings
up there are too high and chilly for me to be in.
Here on earth I can dance with my
own moonlit shadow whenever I like.
Where else in the universe can I
be so carefree to please my mind?

蘇軾　　sū shì
水調歌頭　shuǐ diào gē tóu

○ =　平声　(*ping* or flat tone)
△ =　仄声　(*ze* or deflected tone)
● =　平声韵　(rhymed in *ping* or flat tone)
▲ =　仄声韵　(rhymed in *ze* or deflected tone)

明○月△
míng yuè
bright moon

把△酒△
bǎ jiǔ
holding wine (cup)

不△知○
bù zhī
do not know

今○夕△
jīn xī
tonight

我△欲△
wǒ yù
I wish to

又△恐△
yòu kǒng
but fear

高○處△
gāo chǔ
on height

起△舞△
qǐ wǔ
start to dance

何○似△
hé sì
how can it be like

幾△時○
jǐ shí
when; what time

問△
wèn
ask

天○上△
tiān shàng
heaven

是△
shì
is

乘○風○
chéng fēng
ride on wind

瓊○樓○
qióng lóu
splendid building

不△勝△
bù shèng
unable to bear

弄△
nòng
playing with

在△
zài
in

有△
yǒu
to have

青○天●
qīng tiān
blue sky

宮○闕△
gōng quē
palace

何○年●
hé nián
what year

歸○去△
guī qù
to return

玉△宇△
yù yǔ
jeweled palace

寒●
hán
the chill

清○影△
qīng yǐng
clear shadow

人○間●
rén jiān
human world

The moon now shifts her beam from the red pavilion
to the lower window and door.
She then shines on this person who is
unable to fall asleep at all.
The moon is not supposed to hold grudges.
But why does she always show her round face
when parting is about to take place?

Separation and reunion, sadness and delight.
Ah, these are part of human life.
The moon may be in the full or on the wane.
Sometimes she is gloomy and sometimes
she is bright.
Imperfections do exist since ancient times.
I can only wish we will lead a long and healthy life.
But for now, let's enjoy moonlight together
over a thousand miles.

轉△
zhuǎn
it switches (light) to

低△
dī
it descends to

照△
zhào
shines upon

不△應△
bù yìng
shouldn't

何○事△
hé shì
for what reason

人△有△
rén yǒu
people have

月△有△
yuè yǒu
moon has

此△事△
cǐ shì
this thing

但△願△
dàn yuàn
can only wish

千○里△
qián lǐ
a thousand *li*

朱○閣△
zhū gé
red pavilion

綺△戶△
qǐ hù
window and door

無○眠●
wú mián
one who can't sleep

有△恨△
yǒu hèn
have regret

偏△向△
piān xiàng
must become

悲○歡○
bēi huān
sadness and joy

陰○晴○
yīn qíng
gloom and clearness

古△
gǔ
since ancient time

人○
rén
people

共△
gòng
share together

別△時○圓●
bié shí yuán
full in separation

離○合△
lí hé
separation and union

圓○缺△
yuán quē
fullness and wane

難○全●
nán quán
not perfect

長○久△
cháng jiǔ
live long

嬋○娟●
chán juān
the moon; moonlight

苏轼

念奴娇·赤壁怀古

大江东去，浪淘尽，千古风流人物。故垒西边。人道是、三国周郎赤壁。乱石崩云，惊涛拍岸。卷起千堆雪。江山如画，一时多少豪杰。遥想公瑾当年，小乔初嫁了，雄姿英发。羽扇纶巾，谈笑间、樯橹灰飞烟灭。故国神游，多情应笑我，早生华发。人生如梦，一樽还酹江月。

Su Shi

Tune: "Nian Nu Jiao"

Reflecting on the Red Cliff

Great river flows eastward.
Its waves have washed away all elegant
men and heroes of past generations.
West of the old fortress is said to be Zhou Yu's
Red Cliff at the Epoch of the Three Kingdoms.
Raveled rocks break through the clouds;
billows smite the shore.
A thousand heaps of snow breaks off.
So picturesque are the rivers and mountains.
So many great men and heroes emerged.

蘇軾　　**sū shì**
念奴嬌　**niàn nú jiāo**

大△江○ *dà jiāng* great river	東○去△ *dōng qù* goes to east	
浪△ *làng* waves	淘○盡△ *táo jìn* wash away all	
千○古△ *qiān gǔ* ancient	風○流○ *fēng liú* elegant and talented	人○物▲ *rén wù* people
故△壘△ *gù lěi* old fortress	西○邊● *xī biān* to the west	人○道△是△ *rén dào shì* people say
三○國△ *sān guó* Three Kingdoms	周○郎○ *zhōu láng* Master Zhou	赤△壁▲ *chì bì* Red Cliff
亂△石△ *luàn shí* raveled rocks	崩○雲○ *bēng yún* break the clouds	
驚○濤○ *jīng tāo* mountainous waves	拍△岸● *pāi àn* beat the shore	
捲△起△ *juǎn qǐ* roll up	千○堆○ *qiān duī* a thousand heaps of	雪▲ *xuě* snow
江○山○ *jiāng shān* rivers and mountains	如○畫△ *rú huà* like pictures	
一△時○ *yī shí* at one time	多○少△ *duō shǎo* so many	豪○杰▲ *háo jié* talented or brave people

I fancy at the time when Zhou was married to
Xiao Qiao, his young bride.
With a feather fan in his hand, and
a silken scarf on his head, he watched,
in between laughter and chats,
all enemy ships were destroyed in smoke and fire.

If they could revisit this land in spirit,
his passionate companion would have teased
me for being young and gray.
Life is like a dream.
Let me pour a bottle of wine
and salute the river moon so bright.

遙〇想△
yáo xiǎng
think long time ago

小△喬〇
xiǎo qiáo
younger sister Qiao

雄〇姿〇
xióng zī
heroic bearing

羽△扇△
yǔ shàn
feather fan

檣〇櫓△
qiáng lǔ
masts and oars

故△國△
gù guó
fatherland

多〇情〇
duō qíng
passionate (lover)

早△生△
zǎo shēng
prematurely grow

人〇生〇
rén shēng
life

一△樽△
yī zūn
a wine vessel

公〇瑾△
gōng jǐn
Zhou Gong Jin

初〇嫁△了△
chū jià le
recently married

英〇發▲
yīng fā
heroic spirit

綸〇巾〇
guān jīn
silken scarf

灰〇飛〇
huī fēi
flying ashes

神〇游〇
shén yóu
tour in spirit

應〇笑△
yìng xiào
ought to laugh at

華〇髮▲
huá fā
gray hair

如〇夢△
rú mèng
is like a dream

還〇酹△
huán lèi
also make a libation

當〇年〇
dāng nián
in those years

談〇笑△間〇
tán xiào jiān
between talking and laughter

煙〇滅▲
yān miè
destroyed in smoke

我△
wǒ
me

江〇月▲
jiāng yuè
river moon

苏 轼

江 城 子

十年生死两茫茫。不思量。自难忘。千里孤坟，
无处话凄凉。纵使相逢应不识，尘满面，鬓如霜。
夜来幽梦忽还乡。小轩窗。正梳妆。相顾无言，
惟有泪千行。料得年年肠断处，明月夜，短松冈。

Su Shi

Tune: "Jiang Cheng Zi"

In Loving Memory of My Wife

For ten years, we have been separated between
two indistinct worlds of living and death.
Try not to think about it,
but how can I forget?
Her lonely grave is several hundred miles away.
My sadness and dreariness can
find nowhere to convey.
Even if by chance we could meet,
she wouldn't have recognized me:
The dirt is all over my face;
my temples have turned into gray.

蘇軾　　sū shì
江城子　jiāng chéng zi

十△年〇
shí nián
ten years

不△
bù
don't

自△
zì
I myself

千〇里△
qiān lǐ
one thousand *li*

無〇處△
wú chù
nowhere

縱△使△
zòng shǐ
even if

塵〇滿△面△
chén mǎn miàn
dust all over face

鬢△如〇霜●
bìn rú shuāng
temples are like frost

生〇死△
shēng sǐ
life and death

思〇量●
sī liàng
think about it

難〇忘●
nán wàng
can't forget it

孤〇墳〇
gū fén
lonely grave

話△
huà
to talk about

相〇逢〇
xiāng féng
meet each other

兩△茫〇茫●
liǎng máng máng
both boundless and indistinct

淒〇涼●
qī liáng
sadness and dreariness

應〇不△識△
yìng bù shí
shouldn't have recognized

Last night, I dreamt of suddenly returning
to my hometown.
She was combing hair by
the window in a small room.
Looking at each other without a word,
our tears kept streaming down.
Year after year the place that would sadden my heart
at a night when the moon is bright
is the mount with small pines

夜△來○
yè lái
last night

小△
xiǎo
small

正△
zhèng
just

相○顧△
xiāng gù
looking at each other

惟○有△
wéi yǒu
only have

料○得△
liào de
figuring out

明○月△
míng yuè
moonlit

短△松○
duǎn sōng
small pine

幽○夢△
yōu mèng
secluded dream

軒○窗●
xuān chuāng
room with window

梳○妝●
shū zhuāng
combed hair and did makeup

無○言○
wú yán
without words

淚△
lèi
tears

年○年○
nián nián
year after year

夜△
yè
night

岡●
gāng
mount

忽△還○鄉●
hū huán xiāng
suddenly returned to hometown

千○行●
qiān háng
a thousand rows

腸○斷△處△
cháng duàn chǔ
place to break a heart

苏轼

临江仙

夜饮东坡醒复醉，归来仿佛三更。家童鼻息已雷鸣。敲门都不应，倚杖听江声。 长恨此身非我有，何时忘却营营。夜阑风静縠纹平。小舟从此逝，江海寄余生。

Su Shi

Tune: "Lin Jiang Xian"

Late at Night

At Eastern Slope I drank at night
alternating drunkenness with sobering time.
I returned home around midnight.
My maid servant snored like thunder without pause.
No one responded when I knocked at the door.
With a cane in my hand,
I listened to how the river chanted.

I often feel that this life is at odd with my will.
When will I be able to give up momentary thrill?
In the valley the night is deep and quite,
without waves and tides.
I wish to go away with a skiff,
on river or sea for the rest of my life.

蘇軾　　sū shì
臨江仙　lín jiāng xiān

夜△飲△
yè yǐn
drinking at night

歸○來○
guī lái
returning home

家○童○
jiā tóng
maid servant

敲○門○
qiāo mén
knocking at door

倚△杖△
yǐ zhàng
leaning on cane

長○恨△
cháng hèn
often regret

何○時○
hé shí
when

夜△闌○
yè lán
deep in the night

小△舟○
xiǎo zhōu
(with) a skiff

江○海△
jiāng hǎi
river and sea

東○坡○
dōng pō
Eastern Slope

仿△佛△
fǎng fó
appeared to be

鼻○息△
bí xī
breathing

都○
dōu
all the time

聽△
tīng
listen to

此△身○
cǐ shēn
this body

忘○卻△
wáng què
can (I) forget

風○靜△
fēng jìng
wind is quiet

從○此△
cóng cǐ
from now on

寄△
jì
to consign to

醒△復△醉○
xǐng fù zuì
sobered then tipsy

三○更●
sān gèng
after midnight

已△雷○鳴●
yǐ léi míng
already like thundering

不△應△
bù yìng
with no response

江○聲●
jiāng shēng
sound of river

非○我△有△
fēi wǒ yǒu
not owned by me

營○營●
yíng yíng
chasing money and fame

谷△紋○平●
gǔ wén píng
no ripples in ravine

逝△
shì
to vanish

餘○生●
yú shēng
rest of life

221

苏轼

蝶恋花

花褪残红青杏小。燕子飞时，绿水人家绕。枝上柳绵吹又少。天涯何处无芳草。　墙里秋千墙外道。墙外行人，墙里佳人笑。笑渐不闻声渐悄。多情却被无情恼。

Su Shi

Tune: "Die Lian Hua"

Separated By a Wall

Red color fades; flowers fall off.
Apricots remain green and small.
Swallows fly around residence and green water.
Blown by wind, willow catkins
on the branches have turned thin.
You can go to the sky's brim,
green grass can still be seen.

A wall separates an outside road
and a swing within.
A passerby stops walking;
a fair lady is heard laughing.
The sound of laughing gradually
becomes indistinct.
Eventually I can hear nothing.
Suddenly a feeling of tenderness
gives rise to a despondent feeling.

蘇軾　sū shì
蝶戀花　dié liàn huā

花○褪△ huā tùi flowers fall off	殘○紅○ cán hóng red color fades	青○杏△小▲ qīng xìng xiǎo green apricot small
燕△子△ yàn zi swallows	飛○時○ fēi shí when (they) fly	
綠△水△ lǜ shuǐ green water	人○家○ rén jiā residence	繞▲ rào to go around
枝○上△ zhī shàng on branches	柳△綿○ liǔ mián willow catkins	吹○又△少▲ chuī yòu shǎo blowing away with few left
天○涯○ tiān yá remote place	何○處△ hé chǔ where	無○芳○草▲ wú fāng cǎo without green grass
牆○里△ qiáng lǐ inside the wall	秋○千○ qiū qiān swing	牆○外△道▲ qiáng wài dào road is outside the wall
牆○外△ qiáng wài outside the wall	行○人○ xíng rén passersby	
牆○里△ qiáng lǐ inside the wall	佳○人○ jiā rén fair ladies	笑▲ xiào laugh
笑△ xiào laughing	漸△ Jiàn gradually	不△聞○ bù wén can't be heard
聲○ shēng sound	漸△ Jiàn gradually	悄▲ qiǎo becomes quiet
多○情○ duō qíng passionate feeling	卻△被△ què bèi taken over by	無○情○惱▲ wú qíng nǎo despondent feeling

苏 轼

贺新郎

乳燕飞华屋。悄无人、桐阴转午，晚凉新浴。手弄生绡白团扇，扇手一时似玉。渐困倚、孤眠清熟。帘外谁来推绣户，枉教人梦断瑶台曲。又却是，风敲竹。　石榴半吐红巾蹙。待浮花浪蕊都尽，伴君幽独。艳一枝细看取，芳心千重似束。又恐被、秋风惊绿。若待得君来向此，花前对酒不忍触。共粉泪，两簌簌。

Su Shi

Tune: "He Xin Lang"

A Fair Lady and Pomegranate Flowers

A young swallow flies into a magnificent house.
So quiet with no one in sight.
From the shade of the parasol, it is now afternoon.
After a bath in the cool of evening,
she feels refreshed.
She plays with her hands a silken white round fan.
Both the fan and her hands look like jade:
smooth and white.
Gradually feeling tired, she falls asleep soundly,
leaning slantwise.
Outside the curtain, who comes to knock
at the embroidered door?
Her sweet dream of a fairyland
is interrupted in vain.
It turns out to be the sound of bamboos
that are blown by the wind.

蘇軾　　sū shì
賀新郎　hè xīn láng

乳△燕△
rǔ yàn
young swallow

飛〇
fēi
flies

華〇屋▲
huá wū
magnificent house

悄△無〇人〇
qiǎo wú rén
quiet and nobody

桐〇陰〇
tóng yīn
shade of parasol

轉△午△
zhuǎn wǔ
switches to afternoon

晚△涼〇
wǎn liáng
evening cool

新〇浴▲
xīn yù
just taken a bath

手△弄△
shǒu nòng
playing with hands

生〇綃〇
shēng xiāo
raw silk

白△團〇扇△
bái tuán shàn
white round fan

扇△手△
shàn shǒu
fan and hand

一△時〇
yī shí
momentarily

似△玉▲
sì yù
like jade

漸△困△倚△
jiàn kùn yǐ
gradually tired and lean on

孤〇眠〇
gū mián
lie down alone

清〇熟▲
qīng shóu
fall asleep soundly

簾〇外△
lián wài
outside the curtain

誰〇來〇
shéi lái
who has come

推〇繡△戶△
tuī xiù hù
to push embroidered door

枉△教△人〇
wǎng jiào rén
in vain; for nothing

夢△斷△
mèng duàn
interrupt a dream

瑤〇台〇曲▲
yáo tái qū
secluded jade terrace

又△卻△是△
yòu què shì
it turns out to be

風〇
fēng
wind

敲〇竹▲
qiāo zhú
knocking bamboo

225

A pomegranate flower opens its lips.
It looks like a red handkerchief pressed in strips
Wait until after those showy and wanton
flowers no longer shine,
I will accompany you by your side.
With a beautiful branch in your hand,
examine it carefully from all sides.
The heart of a flower is bound by a thousand
layers of stripes.
But be mindful of the autumn wind,
for it will blow the petals away and
frighten the green.
If I can wait for you to come, in
front of the flower, together we will drink.
But how can I bear to see the scene:
Both shedding their tears,
falling down like two streams.

石△榴○
shí liú
pomegranate

半△吐△
bàn tǔ
half open

紅○巾○蹙▲
hóng jīn cù
like a wrinkled red kerchief

待△浮○花○
dài fú huā
wait for showy flowers

浪△蕊△
làng ruǐ
romantic pistils or stamen

都△盡△
dōu jìn
are over

伴△君○
bàn jūn
keep your company

幽○獨▲
yōu dú
alone in solitude

艷△一△枝○
yàn yī zhī
a beautiful branch

細△
xì
carefully

看○取△
kàn qǔ
examine it

芳○心○
fāng xīn
heart of a young lady

千○重○
qiān chóng
a thousand layers

似△束▲
sì shù
as if being bound up

又△恐△被△
yòu kǒng bèi
but be afraid

秋○風○
qiū fēng
autumn wind

驚○綠▲
jīng lǜ
scares the green

若△待△得△
ruò dài de
if it can wait for

君○
jūn
you

來○向△此○
lái xiàng cǐ
to come here

花○前○
huā qián
in front of flowers

對△酒△
duì jiǔ
drink with each other

不△忍△觸▲
bù rěn chù
can't help but feel bad

共○粉△淚△
gòng fěn lèi
drop tears with flowers

兩△簌△簌▲
liǎng sù sù
both streaming down

苏轼

卜算子·黄州定慧院寓居作

缺月挂疏桐，漏断人初静。谁见幽人独往来，缥缈孤鸿影。惊起却回头，有恨无人省。拣尽寒枝不肯栖，寂寞沙洲冷。

Su Shi

Tune: "Bu suan Zi"

Residing at Dinghui Abbey

A crescent moon hangs behind a spare parasol tree,
The water clock stops dripping;
people are quiet and gone to bed.
Who can see a secluded man walking
alone back and forth?
Or is this the dimly discernible shadow
of a swan goose?

Startled, but it turns back its head.
It has grudges no one can detect.
Looking over all the cold branches,
on none it is willing to perch.
It has chosen the cold and lonely
sand bar instead.

蘇軾　　sū shì
卜算子　bǔ suàn zi

缺△月△ *quē yuè* crescent moon	掛△ *guà* to hang	疏○桐○ *shū tóng* thin parasol
漏△斷△ *lòu duàn* watch clock stops	人○ *rén* people	初○靜▲ *chū jìng* begin to turn quiet
誰△見△ *shéi jiàn* who see	幽○人○ *yōu rén* a secluded man	獨△往△來○ *dú wǎng lái* walking back and forth alone
縹△緲△ *piāo miǎo* dimly discernible	孤○鴻○ *gū hóng* a lone swan goose	影▲ *yǐng* shadow
驚○起△ *jīng qǐ* startled, and get up	卻△ *què* but	回○頭○ *huí tóu* turn back
有△恨△ *yǒu hèn* having grudges	無○人○ *wú rén* no one	省▲ *shěng* detect
揀△盡△ *jiǎn jìn* to select all over	寒○枝○ *hán zhī* cold branches	不△肯△棲○ *bù kěn qī* unwilling to perch
寂△寞△ *jì mò* lonely	沙○洲○ *shā zhōu* sand bar	冷▲ *lěng* cold

苏轼

江城子

老夫聊发少年狂。左牵黄。右擎苍。锦帽貂裘，
千骑卷平冈。欲报倾城随太守，亲射虎，看孙郎。
酒酣胸胆尚开张。鬓微霜。又何妨。持节云中，
何日遣冯唐。会挽雕弓如满月，西北望，射天狼。

Su Shi

Tune: "Jiang Cheng Zi"

Hunting

This old man feels an urge to display
youthful behavior without restraint.
My left hand leads a yellow hound;
on my right arm is sitting a gray falcon.
Wearing embroidered hat and marten coat,
I direct a thousand horsemen sweeping
across the wide open mount.
To reward people of the entire town
for coming out to watch the magistrate,
I will personally shoot the tiger like
Sun Quan did at the time of Three Kingdoms.

蘇軾 sū shì
江城子 jiāng chéng zi

老△夫○
lǎo fū
this old man

聊○發△
liáo fā
feel the urge to display

少△年○狂●
shào nián kuáng
young man's unrestrained behavior

左△牽○黃●
zuǒ qiān huáng
pull a yellow (dog) with left hand

右△擎○蒼●
yòu qíng cāng
lift up a gray (falcon) on right hand

錦△帽△
jǐn mào
embroidered hat

貂○裘○
diāo qiú
marten coat

千○騎△
qiān qí
thousand mounted horses and men

卷△
juǎn
sweep off

平○岡●
píng gāng
open mount

欲△報△
yù bào
to reward

傾○城○
qīng chéng
whole city

隨○太△守△
suí tài shǒu
for following the magistrate

親○射△虎△
qīn shè hǔ
I myself will shoot the tiger

看△孫○郎●
kàn sūn láng
like Sun Quan (of the Three Kingdoms)

231

With a few drinks, my courage is sky high.
Who cares that my temples are slightly frosted white?
When will I serve as an imperial envoy
to Yun Zhong like Feng Tang?
Toward the northwest, I will draw my
carved bow like a full moon and shoot
the wolves from the sky.

酒△酣○
jiǔ hān
elation from wine

鬢△微○霜●
bìn wéi shuāng
temples with mild frost

持○節△
chí jié
serve as a diplomatic envoy

何○日△
hé rì
when will

會△挽△
huì wǎn
will pull

西○北△望△
xī běi wàng
look toward northwest

胸○膽△
xiōng dǎn
chest and gall (courage)

又△何○妨●
yòu hé fáng
no problem

雲○中○
yún zhōng
Yun Zhong

遣△馮○唐●
qiǎn féng táng
send Feng Tang (as an envoy)

雕○弓○
diāo gōng
painted bow

射△天○狼●
shè tiān láng
shoot the enemy wolves

尚△開○張●
shàng kāi zhāng
still open up

如○滿△月△
rú mǎn yuè
like a full moon

233

苏轼

定风波

莫听穿林打叶声。何妨吟啸且徐行。竹杖芒鞋轻胜马，谁怕，一蓑烟雨任平生。　料峭春风吹酒醒，微冷，山头斜照却相迎。回首向来萧瑟处，归去，也无风雨也无晴。

Su Shi

Tune: "Ding Feng Bo"

Wind and Rain

Going across the woods, don't listen
to the leaves-beating sound.
You might as well chant or whistle
as you walk around.
A horse is not as light as straw sandals
and a bamboo cane.
Don't be afraid of getting used to a life, wearing
straw cloak in mist and rain.

Cold spring wind can keep you
sobered up after a few drinks.
It is a bit chilly.
But the slanting sun greets me over the hill.
On my return, I reflect on all those
dreary scenes I have seen.
I feel that it is neither sunny
nor windy with rain.

蘇軾　sū shì
定風波　dìng fēng bō

莫△聽△ *mò tīng* don't listen	穿○林○ *chuān lín* woods-blowing	打△葉△聲● *dǎ yè shēng* leaves-beating sounds
何△妨○ *hé fang* might as well	吟○嘯△ *yín xiào* chant and whistle	且△徐○行● *qiě xú xíng* and walk slowly
竹△杖△ *zhú zhàng* a bamboo cane	芒○鞋○ *máng xié* sandals	輕○勝△馬△ *qīng shèng mǎ* lighter than horse
誰○怕△ *shéi pà* who is afraid		
一△蓑○ *yī suō* a straw rain cape	煙○雨△ *yān yǔ* mist and rain	任△平○生● *rèn píng shēng* let it be like that in life
料△峭△ *liào qiào* chilly	春○風○ *chūn fēng* spring wind	吹○酒△醒△ *chuī jiǔ xǐng* awaken from being tipsy
微○冷△ *wéi lěng* a bit cold		
山○頭○ *shān tóu* hilltop	斜○照△ *xié zhào* slanting light	卻△相○迎● *què xiāng yíng* on the other hand greets me
回○首△ *huí shǒu* looking back	向△來○ *xiàng lái* always	蕭○瑟△處△ *xiāo sè chù* bleak and desolate place
歸○去△ *guī qù* return home		
也△無○ *yě wú* also no	風○雨△ *fēng yǔ* wind and rain	也△無○晴● *yě wú qíng* no sunny day also

苏轼

水龙吟

似花还似非花，也无人惜从教坠。抛家傍路，思量却是，无情有思。萦损柔肠，困酣娇眼，欲开还闭。 梦随风万里。寻郎去处，又还被莺呼起。不恨此花飞尽，恨西园、落红难缀。晓来雨过，遗踪何在，一池萍碎。春色三分，二分尘土，一分流水。 细看来，不是杨花，点点是离人泪。

Su Shi

Tune: "Shui Long Yin"

Willow Catkins

Looking like flowers, but seemingly not flowers.
No one cares if they fall on the ground.
Abandoning their home, they linger by the roadside.
Appearing to be heartless, they do have
a sentimental side.
Their eyes are half-open and half-closed like
someone who is heartbroken, preoccupied, and tired.
In her dream, she rides on the wind to find
her love over several thousand miles.
But her sweet dream is awaken by the orioles.

蘇軾　　**sū shì**
水龍吟　**shuǐ lóng yín**

似△花〇
sì huā
looks like flower

還〇似△
huán sì
but even more like

非〇花〇
fēi huā
not a flower

也△無〇人〇
yě wú rén
and nobody

惜△
xī
pity for

從〇教△墜▲
cóng jiào zhuì
let them fall

拋〇家〇
pāo jiā
abandon home

傍△路△
bàng lù
be close to road

思〇量〇
sī liáng
considering

卻△是△
què shì
but is

無〇情〇有△思▲
wú qíng yǒu sī
thinking without feeling

縈〇損△
yíng sǔn
linger and hurt

柔〇腸〇
róu cháng
tender intestines

困△酣〇
kùn hān
tired with drinking

嬌〇眼△
jiāo yǎn
lovable eyes

欲△開〇
yù kāi
wish to open

還〇閉▲
huán bì
but be closed

夢△
mèng
dream

隨〇風〇
suí fēng
with wind

萬△里▲
wàn lǐ
ten thousand *li*

尋〇郎〇
xún láng
locating lover

去△處△
qù chù
whereabouts

又△還〇
yòu huán
but still let

被△鶯〇
bèi yīng
oriole

呼〇起▲
hū qǐ
call out

She hates not the willow catkins that are flown away.
But grieve over the red flowers, fallen
and cannot be restored in shape.
Rain is over, dawn has arrived.
Where can their traces be found?
I see the drifting duckweed
floating on the pond.
Of spring's three colors,
two have returned to dust, and the other
is gone with the flowing water.
Look at them carefully, they are not willow catkins,
but the teardrops of the one who is about to part.

不△恨△
bù hèn
not hating

恨△西○園○
hèn xī yuán
hating western garden

曉△來○
xiǎo lái
morning arrives

遺○蹤○
yí zōng
traces

一△池○
yī chí
a pond of

春○色△
chūn sè
spring color

二△分○
èr fēn
two parts

一△分○
yī fēn
one part

細△看○來○
xì kàn lái
look carefully

點△點△
diǎn diǎn
drop by drop

此△花○
cǐ huā
this flower

落△紅△
luò hóng
fallen red petals

雨△過△
yǔ guò
rain stops

何○在△
hé zài
where to find

萍○碎▲
píng suì
drifting duckweed

三○分○
sān fēn
(consists of) three parts

塵○土△
chén tǔ
dust

流○水▲
liú shuǐ
flowing water

不△是△
bú shì
(they are) not

是△
shì
to be

飛○盡△
fēi jìn
flying all out

難○綴▲
nán zhuì
hard to mend

楊○花○
yáng huā
willow catkins

離○人○淚▲
lí rén lèi
tears of person about to part

苏轼

永遇乐

明月如霜,好风如水,清景无限。曲港跳鱼,圆荷泻露,寂寞无人见。紞如三鼓,铿然一叶,黯黯梦云惊断。夜茫茫,重寻无处,觉来小园行遍。天涯倦客,山中归路,望断故园心眼。燕子楼空,佳人何在,空锁楼中燕。古今如梦,何曾梦觉,但有旧欢新怨。异时对,黄楼夜景。为余浩叹。

Su Shi

Tune: "Yong Yu Le"

Dreaming of Someone at Pavilion of Swallows

The moon is like frost: white and bright.
The wind is like water: cool and nice.
The night scene is clear and endless.
In the winding harbor, you can see the jumping fish.
Dewdrops rush down from lotus's round leaves.
In solitude, no one can be seen.
The time is now three drum beats.
One can hear the sound of a single falling leaf.
In gloominess, my dream is suddenly interrupted.
The night is boundless and deep.
I get up and search everywhere in the garden,
but I can find no traces.

蘇軾　　sū shì
永遇樂　yǒng yù lè

明○月△	如○	霜○
míng yuè	rú	shuāng
bright moon	is like	frost

好△風○	如○	水△
hǎo fēng	rú	shuǐ
nice wind	is like	water

清○景△	無○	限▲
qīng jǐng	wú	xiàn
clear scene	without	end

曲○港△	跳○	魚○
qū gǎng	tiào	yú
winding harbor	jump	fish

圓○荷○	瀉△	露△
yuán hé	xiè	lù
round lotus leaves	rush down	dewdrops

寂△寞△	無○人○	見▲
jì mò	wú rén	jiàn
lonely	nobody	see

紞△如○	三○鼓△	
dǎn rú	sān gǔ	
like beating	three drums	

鏗○然○	一△葉△	
kēng rán	yī yè	
loud and clear	one leaf	

黯△黯△	夢○雲○	驚○斷▲
àn àn	mèng yún	jīng duàn
gloomy	dream	interrupted in fear

夜△茫○茫○	重○尋○	無○處△
yè máng máng	zhòng xún	wú chù
boundless night	search again	nowhere can be found

覺△來○	小△園○	行○遍▲
jué lái	xiǎo yuán	xíng biàn
awaken	little garden	walking every spot

A tired traveler in the remote corner of the world,
I am in the mountain, on my way home.
So homesick, I am eager to return to my old hometown.
The Pavilion of Swallow is empty.
Where can I find the fair lady?
Only the swallows are locked within.
Events of past and present are like a dream.
Has anyone waken up from dreaming?
What's left are but old pleasures
and new sorrowful feelings.
At some future time when others come to see
the scenery of the Yellow Tower at night,
would they heave for me a deep sign!

天〇涯〇
tiān yá
the end of the world

倦△客△
juàn kè
tired traveler

山〇中〇
shān zhōng
in the mountain

歸〇路△
guī lù
returning path

望△斷△
wàng duàn
looking all the way at

故〇園〇
gù yuán
hometown

心〇眼▲
xīn yǎn
mind; intention

燕△子△樓〇
yàn zi lóu
Swallow Pavilion

空〇
kōng
is empty

佳〇人〇
jiā rén
fair lady

何〇在△
hé zài
where is she

空〇鎖△
kōng suǒ
locked in vain

樓〇中〇
lóu zhōng
in the pavilion

燕▲
yàn
swallow

古△今〇
gǔ jīn
past and present

如〇夢△
rú mèng
like dream

何〇曾〇
hé céng
to have not been

夢△覺△
mèng jué
awaken from dream

但△有△
dàn yǒu
but have

舊△歡〇
jiù huān
old pleasures

新〇怨▲
xīn yuàn
new complaints

異△時〇對△
yì shí duì
facing at different time

黃〇樓〇
huáng lóu
Yellow Tower

夜△景▲
yè jǐng
night scene

為△余〇
wéi yú
for me

浩△嘆▲
hào tàn
sign deeply

苏轼

西江月

照野弥弥浅浪，横空隐隐层霄。障泥未解玉骢骄。我欲醉眠芳草。可惜一溪风月，莫教踏碎琼瑶。解鞍欹枕绿杨桥。杜宇一声春晓。

Su Shi

Tune: "Xi Jiang Yue"

A Spring Night

In the field, the moon shines
upon the wavelets to the brim.
Across the sky, clouds appear intermittently
clear and indistinct.
With the mudguard still in place, my white
horse gets excited.
I wish to sleep on the fragrant grass after some wine.

Along the stream, what a lovely and
pleasant moonlit night!
How can I let my horse tread on such a jade-like
scenes.
Unsaddled, I happily pillow
my head on the bridge by the willows.
The song of a cuckoo brings
me back to the spring daybreak from my dream.

蘇軾　　**sū shì**
西江月　**xī jiāng yuè**

照△野△ *zhào yě* shining field	彌○彌○ *mí mí* full of	淺△浪△ *qiǎn làng* wavelet
橫○空○ *héng kōng* across the sky	隱△隱△ *yǐn yǐn* indistinct	層○霄● *céng xiāo* layer of clouds
障△泥○ *zhàng ní* mudguard for a horse	未△解△ *wèi jiě* not yet released	玉△驄○驕● *yù cōng jiāo* white horse is restless
我△欲△ *wǒ yù* I wish to	醉△眠○ *zuì mián* sleep in tipsiness	芳○草▲ *fāng cǎo* (on) green grass
可△惜△ *kě xī* need to appreciate	一△溪○ *yī xī* a stream of	風○月△ *fēng yuè* wind and moon
莫△教○ *mò jiāo* don't let (it)	踏△碎△ *tà suì* tread	瓊○瑤● *qióng yáo* fine jade
解△鞍○ *jiě ān* unsaddle a horse	欹○枕△ *yī zhěn* happily pillow my head on	綠△楊○橋● *lù yáng qiáo* green willow bridge
杜△宇△ *dù yǔ* cuckoo	一△聲○ *yī shēng* one sound	春○曉▲ *chūn xiǎo* spring daybreak

苏轼

西江月

玉骨那愁瘴雾，冰肌自有仙风。海仙时遣探芳丛，倒挂绿毛幺凤。 素面常嫌粉涴，洗妆不褪唇红。高情已逐晓云空，不与梨花同梦。

Su Shi

Tune: "Xi Jiang Yue"

Plum Flower

Her intrinsic qualities can ward off unhealthy mist.
Her graceful appearance reveals
the elegance of a fairy.
The sea fairy often sends a messenger
to visit the fragrant grove.
A colorful little bird with green feathers
is seen in upside-down pose.

Her natural face loathes the stain of powder.
Washing her toilette won't diminish her lip's red color.
My heart is already gone emptied in the sky,
chasing the morning cloud.
How can it be with the pear flowers
in the same dream now?

蘇軾　**sū shì**
西江月　**xī jiāng yuè**

玉△骨△
yù gú
jade-like bone

冰○肌○
bīng jī
ice-clear flesh

海△仙○
hǎi xiān
sea fairy

倒△挂△
dào guà
in upside-town pose

素△面△
sù miàn
natural face

洗△妝○
xǐ zhuāng
washing after makeup

高○情○
gāo qíng
noble affection

不△與△
bù yǔ
can't be with

那△愁○
nà chóu
won't worry

自△有△
zì yǒu
it itself to have

時○遣△
shí qiǎn
often sends a messenger

綠△毛○
lǜ máo
green feathers

常○嫌○
cháng xián
often loathes

不△褪△
bù tuì
does not diminish

已△逐△
yǐ zhú
is already chasing

梨○花○
lí huā
pear flowers

瘴△霧△
zhàng wù
miasmal mist

仙○風●
xiān fēng
a fairy's graceful bearing

探△芳○叢●
tàn fāng cóng
to find out in the fragrant grove

么○鳳▲
yāo fèng
little colorful bird

粉△涴△
fěn wò
powder's stain

唇○紅●
chún hóng
lip's red color

曉△雲○空●
xiǎo yún kōng
morning clouds to become emptied

同○夢▲
tóng mèng
in the same dream

苏轼

西江月

世事一场大梦，人生几度新凉？夜来风叶已鸣廊，看取眉头鬓上。　酒贱常愁客少，月明多被云妨。中秋谁与共孤光，把盏凄凉北望。

Su Shi

Tune: "Xi Jiang Yue"

Looking Up Northward

World affairs are but a big dream.
In life, how many times
can we enjoy the midautumn scene?
The rustling sound of leaves and wind
can be heard in the corridor at night.
Take a look at my temples and
brows of my eyes.

Few guests would want to come
when I can only offer cheap wine.
Clouds often come to obstruct
when the moon is bright.
With whom in midautumn can
I share one single light?
I look at the north side
with a sad feeling in my mind.

蘇軾　**sū shì**
西江月　**xī jiāng yuè**

世△事△
shì shì
world affairs

人○生○
rén shēng
human life

夜△來○
yè lái
at night

看△取△
kàn qǔ
take a look at

酒△賤△
jiǔ jiàn
cheap wine

月△明○
yuè míng
moon bright

中○秋○
zhōng qiū
midautumn

把△盞△
bǎ zhǎn
holding a small cup

一△場○
yī cháng
one show of

幾△度△
jǐ dù
several times of

風○葉△
fēng yè
wind and leaves

眉○頭○
méi tóu
eyebrows

常○愁○
cháng chóu
often worry about

多○被△
duō bèi
often let

誰○與△共△
shéi yǔ gòng
with whom together

凄○然○
qī rán
in sadness

大△夢△
dà mèng
big dream

新○涼●
xīn liáng
new cold

已△鳴○廊●
yǐ míng láng
already make sounds in the corridor

鬢△上▲
bìn shàng
on the temples

客△少△
kè shǎo
fewer guests

雲○妨●
yún fáng
clouds to obstruct

孤○光●
gū guāng
single light

北△望▲
běi wàng
look at the north

苏轼

鹧鸪天

林断山明竹隐墙。乱蝉衰草小池塘。翻空白鸟时时见，照水红蕖细细香。村舍外，古城旁。杖藜徐步转斜阳。殷勤昨夜三更雨，又得浮生一日凉。

Su Shi

Tune: "Zhe Gu Tian"

Another Day

Bright mountains appear at the end of the woods.
The wall is concealed by the bamboos.
Grasses wither around the little pond.
Cicadas chirp in unpleasant sound.
White birds can be seen all the time,
flying up and down in the sky.
With images reflecting in the water,
the pink lotus flowers emit fragrance
that is very mild.

Outside the village;
By the ancient wall.
Holding a pigweed staff, I take a leisure walk at twilight.
It rained continuously after midnight last night.
I have thus earned another cool day
in this floating life.

蘇軾　sū shì
鷓鴣天　zhè gū tiān

林〇斷△ *lín duàn* at the end of woods	山〇明〇 *shān míng* bright mountains	竹△隱△牆● *zhú yǐn qiáng* bamboos conceal the wall
亂△蟬〇 *luàn chán* cicadas chirp	衰〇草△ *shuāi cǎo* withering grass	小△池〇塘● *xiǎo chí táng* a little pond
翻〇空〇 *fān kòng* flying up and down	白△鳥△ *bái niǎo* white birds	時〇時〇見△ *shí shí jiàn* can be seen all the time
照△水△ *zhào shuǐ* reflecting on water	紅〇蕖〇 *hóng qú* pink lotus flowers	細△細△香● *xì xì xiāng* light fragrance
村〇舍△外△ *cūn shě wài* outside the village	古△城〇旁● *gǔ chéng páng* by the ancient wall	
杖△藜〇 *zhàng lí* pigweed staff	徐〇步△ *xú bù* leisure walk	轉△斜〇陽● *zhuǎn xié yáng* toward sunset
殷〇勤〇 *yīn qín* with enthusiasm	昨△夜△ *zuó yè* last night	三〇更〇雨△ *sān gēng yǔ* after midnight
又△得△ *yòu de* got another	浮〇生〇 *fú shēng* floating life	一△日△涼● *yī rì liáng* one cool day

但愿人长久，千里共婵娟。

I can only wish we will lead a long and healthy life.
But for now, let's enjoy moonlight together over a thousand miles.

— Su Shi

Li Zhiyi (1038?–1117)

李之仪

Li Zhiyi was a native of present-day Shandong province. He was also known as Duanshu (端叔) and Guxi Jushi (姑溪居士), a title he gave himself.

Li worked for the great poet Su Shi when Su lived in Ding Zhou. Su once mentioned that he liked Li's poems so much that he did not quit reading them until midnight. Li's poetry, particularly those written in the long form, was influenced by Liu Yong, a style that Su Shi did not appraise highly. His short form is similar to that of Qing Guan in style.

While Su Shi believed that *ci* is a form of *shi*, Li argued that *ci* has its unique style and that it should not be subsumed under the same category. *Ci*, according to Li, differs from *shi* not only in diction, but also in feeling tone and musical rhythm. To reflect life realistically, he felt that it is necessary to describe the situations (feelings, scenes, thoughts, etc.) in detail (鋪敘) and expansion (展衍), something cannot always be done in *shi* poetry.

He defined a good *ci* poem as one that the poetic idea and feelings will continue to linger even though one has finished reading the poem. A case in point is the last sentence in his poem to the tune of *Xie Chi Chun* in which one may continue to question why the writer wishes to share his sorrow with the frontcourt willow (且將此恨，分付庭前柳).

As shown by the two poems included in this book, Li liked to write his poetry in ordinary language with a natural and smooth rhythm.

李之仪

卜算子

我住长江头，君住长江尾。日日思君不见君，共饮长江水。 此水几时休，此恨何时已。只愿君心似我心，定不负相思意。

Li Zhiyi

Tune: "Bu Suan Zi"

I Live By the River's Head

I live by the Long River's head,
you its end.
I miss you day after day.
as you are far away.
From this very river,
we both drink the same water.
When will the river cease to flow?
When will my grief no longer grow?
I can only wish that your heart is like mine.
Then our mutual love will never die.

李之儀　　**lǐ zhī yí**
卜算子　　**bǔ suàn zi**

○ = 平声 (*ping* or flat tone)
△ = 仄声 (*ze* or deflected tone)
● = 平声韵 (rhymed in *ping* or flat tone)
▲ = 仄声韵 (rhymed in *ze* or deflected tone)

我△住△ *wǒ zhù* I live in	長○江○ *cháng jiāng* Long River	頭○ *tóu* head
君○住△ *jūn zhù* you live in	長○江○ *cháng jiāng* Long River	尾▲ *wěi* tail
日△日△ *rì rì* day after day	思○君○ *sī jūn* thinking of you	不△見△君○ *bù jiàn jūn* unable to see you
共○飲△ *gòng yǐn* together drink	長○江○ *cháng jiāng* Long River	水▲ *shuǐ* water
此△水△ *cǐ shuǐ* this water	幾△時○ *jǐ shí* when will	休○ *xiū* stop (flowing)
此△恨△ *cǐ hèn* this grief	何○時○ *hé shí* when will	已▲ *Yǐ* cease
只△愿△ *zhī yuàn* only wish	君○心○ *jūn xīn* your heart	似△我△心△ *sì wǒ xīn* is like my heart
定△ *dìng* certainly	不△負△ *bù fù* will live up to	相○思○意▲ *xiāng sī yì* idea of loving each other

李之仪

谢池春

残寒销尽，疏雨过、清明后。花径敛余红，风沼萦新皱。乳燕穿庭户，飞絮沾襟袖。正佳时，仍晚昼。著人滋味，真个浓如酒。　频移带眼，空只恁、厌厌瘦。不见又思量，见了还依旧。为问频相见，何似长相守。天不老，人未偶。且将此恨，分付庭前柳。

Li Zhiyi

Tune: "Xie Chi Chun"

Seeing Each Other

Gone is the weakening cold.
Light rains come and go.
Tomb-Sweeping Day has passed.
Withered flowers are buried in the flowery path.
Breeze strikes the pond to make wrinkles.
Little swallows fly in and out the door or windows.
Flying petals stain my sleeves.
I enjoy the time from noon till night.
The rich flavor is felt like tasting good wine.

李之儀　　lǐ zhī yí
謝池春　　xiè chí chūn

殘〇寒〇
cán hán
remaining cold

銷〇盡△
xiāo jìn
used up

疏〇雨△過△
shū yǔ guò
some light rain fell

清〇明〇
qīng míng
Tomb-Sweeping Day

後▲
hòu
after

花〇徑△
huā jìng
flowery path

斂△
liàn
to collect

餘〇紅〇
yú hóng
withered red flowers

風〇沼△
fēng zhǎo
breeze over pond

縈〇
yíng
wind around

新〇皺▲
xīn zhòu
new wrinkles

乳△燕△
rǔ yàn
little swallows

穿〇
chuān
fly through

庭〇戶△
tíng hù
window and door

飛〇絮△
fēi xù
flying petals

沾〇
zhān
to stain

襟〇袖▲
jīn xiù
sleeves of clothes

正△佳〇時〇
zhèng jiā shí
at such nice occasion

仍〇
réng
still

晚△晝▲
wǎn zhòu
from afternoon to night

著△人〇
zháo rén
to make one feel

滋〇味△
zī wèi
flavor

真〇個△
zhēn gè
it really is

濃〇如〇
nóng rú
as rich as

酒▲
jiǔ
wine

I repeatedly move my belt from hole to hole.
I helplessly watch my body weight to stay low.
Not seeing her increases my pining.
After seeing her, we again end up parting.
Let me ask: if we can't break this chain,
why can't we be together from morning to evening?
Heaven can't get old, it will stay.
But I have yet got my mate.
Alas, I may as well share my sorrow
with the frontcourt willow?

頻○移○
pín yí
frequently shift

帶△眼△
dài yǎn
belt's little holes

空○只△恁△
kōng zhī rèn
only in vain to see

厭△厭△
yàn yàn
disgusted

瘦▲
shòu
thin

不△見△
bù jiàn
not seeing

又△
yòu
then will

思○量○
sī liàng
think a lot

見△了△
jiàn le
after seeing

還○
huán
still

依○舊▲
yī jiù
same as before

為○問△
wéi wèn
for that I ask

頻○
pín
frequently

相○見△
xiāng jiàn
see each other

何○似△
hé sì
why not like

長○
zhǎng
permanently

相○守▲
xiāng shǒu
spend time together

天○不△老△
tiān bù lǎo
heaven will not get old

人○未△
rén wèi
person not yet have

偶▲
ǒu
a mate

且△將○
qiě jiāng
let me take

此△恨△
cǐ hèn
this grief

分○付△
fēn fù
to share with

庭○前○
tíng qián
front of courtyard

柳▲
liǔ
willows

259

只愿君心似我心，定不负相思意。

I can only wish that your heart is like mine.
Then our mutual love will never die.

— Li Zhiyi

Huang Ting Jian (1045–1105)

黄庭坚

Huang Tingjian was born in present-day Xiu Shui, Jianxi. He passed the imperial examination with the title of *jinshi* when he was twenty-two years old. Huang was influenced by his literary father Huanf Che (黄庶) and his uncle Li Chang (李常) in the pursuit of literature and art. He started to read the Five Classics at the age of five. By seven, he showed his precocious talent in poetry by writing "Shepherd Boy" in the form of *jueju* or truncated regulated verse. His uncle was immensely impressed by his talent.

Huang's father died when he was only fifteen years old. Li Chang then became his guardian. Through his uncle's connection, he later came to know several important individuals whom Huang admired. He was especially influenced by his mentor, the great poet Su Shi. Huang was one of the so-called Four Scholars Under Su Shi (苏门四学士), a title reserved for Su's students with literary distinction. The other three scholars were Qin Guan, Zhang Lai, and Zhao Buzhi.

Huang's political career was not very smooth because he offended several officials who advocated radical changes. Besides poetry, Huang was also widely known for his techniques and skills as a calligrapher.

Huang was considered the founder of the School of Jianxi, a group of poets who believed that good poetry should be refined, elegant, and enriched by the use of allusions.

黄庭坚

清平乐

春归何处。寂寞无行路。若有人知春去处。唤取归来同住。春无踪迹谁知，除非问取黄鹂。百啭无人能解，因风飞过蔷薇。

Huang Tingjian

Tune: "Qing Ping Le"

Where Did Spring Go?

Where did spring go?
Loaded with loneliness, there is
no room to walk on the road.
If someone does know her whereabouts,
ask her to return and live with me.
But without a trace, how would one know?
Maybe you can ask the oriole.
Who can understand what it is warbling about?
With the wind, it flies over the roses.

黃庭堅　　**huáng tíng jiān**
清平樂　　**qīng píng lè**

春○歸○
chūn guī
spring returns

何○處▲
hé chǔ
where

寂△寞△
jì mò
loneliness

無○
wú
no

行○路▲
xíng lù
walking road

若△有△
ruò yǒu
if there is

人○知○
rén zhī
someone knows

春○去△處▲
chūn qù chù
where did spring go

喚△取△
huàn qǔ
ask (it)

歸○來○
guī lái
to return

同○住▲
tóng zhù
to live with

春○無○
chūn wú
spring without

蹤○跡△
zōng jī
a trace

誰○知○
shéi zhī
who knows

除○非○
chú fēi
unless

問△取△
wèn qǔ
ask

黃○鸝●
huáng lí
oriole

百△囀△
bǎi zhuǎn
hundred warbles

無○人○
wú rén
no one

能○解△
néng jiě
can understand

因○風○
yīn fēng
because of wind

飛○過△
fēi guò
to fly over

薔○薇●
qiáng wéi
roses

黄庭坚

鹧鸪天

黄菊枝头生晓寒。人生莫放酒杯干。风前横笛斜吹雨，醉里簪花倒著冠。　身健在，且加餐。舞裙歌板尽清欢。黄花白发相牵挽，付与时人冷眼看。

Huang Tingjian

Tune: "Zhe Gu Tian"

Be Myself

Yellow chrysanthemums withstand
the cold on the twig.
Don't put down the cup without wine in this life.
I play the horizontal flute in slanting rain
against the wind.
In tipsiness, I stick a flower into my hair,
then turn my cap from front to rear.

I am still fit physically;
I enjoy eating plentifully.
Dancing in a skirt, I enjoy the pure pleasure of beating
the block while singing
My white hair and the yellow flower
support each other.
I don't care how other people look
at me with their critical eyes either.

黃庭堅　huáng tíng jiān
鷓鴣天　zhè gū tiān

黃○菊△ huáng jú yellow chrysanthemum	枝○頭○ zhī tóu on the twig	生○曉△寒● shēng xiǎo hán come with morning chill
人○生○ rén shēng in life	莫△放△ mò fàng don't put it there	酒△杯○乾● jiǔ bēi gān dried wine cup
風○前○ fēng qián in front of wind	橫○笛△ héng dí holding a horizontal flute	斜○吹○雨△ xié chuī yǔ blow slantwise in rain
醉△裏△ zuì lǐ in tipsiness	簪○花○ zān huā to wear a flower	倒△著△冠● dào zháo guàn turn the hat around
身○健△在△ shēn jiàn zài still in good health	且△加○餐● qiě jiā cān can eat a lot	
舞△裙○ wǔ qún in dancing skirt	歌○板△ gē bǎn beating block in singing	盡△清○歡● jìn qīng huān to enjoy pure pleasure until exhaustion
黃○花○ huáng huā yellow flowers	白△髮△ bái fā white hair	相○牽○挽△ xiāng qiān wǎn to hold back from falling
付△與△ fù yǔ let	時○人○ shí rén people of today	冷○眼△看● lěng yǎn kàn to look at with critical eyes

黄庭坚

虞美人

天涯也有江南信。梅破知春近。夜阑风细得香迟。不道晓来开遍向南枝。玉台弄粉花应妒。飘到眉心住。平生个里愿怀深。去国十年老尽少年心。

Huang Tingjian

Tune: "Yu Mei Ren"

Seeing Plum Flowers in the South

Deep in the south, I get the same
message as in Jiang Nan.
When plums appear to burst,
I know spring is near.
In light breeze at midnight
fragrance is slow to spread.
At dawn, branches facing
the south are already blooming.
When she touches up with powder
in the beautiful terrace, it is hard for the flowers
not to feel jealous.
They drift and fall on the middle of her brow.
Recently I feel deep in my heart even more so.
Away from home, my youthful spirit
in the last ten years has really grown old.

黃庭堅　**huáng tíng jiān**
虞美人　**yú měi rén**

天〇涯〇
tiān yá
at sky's edge

梅〇破△
méi pò
plum bursting into bloom

夜△闌〇
yè lán
midnight

不△道△
bù dào
not knowing

向△南〇
xiàng nán
facing south

玉△台〇
yù tái
beautiful terrace

飄〇到△
piāo dào
drift to

平〇生〇
píng shēng
my entire life

去△國△
qù guó
away from the palace

少△年〇
shào nián
a youngster's

也△有△
yě yǒu
there is also

知〇
zhī
to know

風〇細△
fēng xì
breeze

曉△來〇
xiǎo lái
at dawn

枝●
zhī
branches

弄△粉△
nòng fěn
touch up with powder

眉〇心〇
méi xīn
middle of eyebrow

個△裏△
gè lǐ
inside me

十△年〇
shí nián
ten years

心●
xīn
heart

江〇南〇信▲
jiāng nán xìn
message like River South

春〇近▲
chūn jìn
spring is near

得△香〇遲●
de xiāng chí
fragrance comes late

開〇遍△
kāi biàn
already in bloom

花〇應〇妒▲
huā yìng dù
flowers should be envious

住▲
zhù
to stay there

願△懷〇深●
yuàn huái shēn
wishes are deep in my heart

老△盡△
lǎo jìn
grows old

黄庭坚

水调歌头

瑶草一何碧，春入武陵溪。溪上桃花无数，花上有黄鹂。我欲穿花寻路，直入白云深处，浩气展虹霓。只恐花深里，红露湿人衣。坐玉石，敲玉枕，拂金微。谪仙何处，无人伴我白螺杯。我为灵芝仙草，不为朱唇丹脸，长啸亦何为。醉舞下山去，明月逐人归。

Huang Tingjian

Tune: "Shui Diao Ge Tou"

Peach Blossom

The beautiful herb is as lovable
as a piece of greenish jade.
In spring I walk into the Wuling Stream.
On the shore, peach blossoms are too
numerous to be seen.
An oriole sits on a flowery branch happily singing.
I wish to find my way through the flowers
into the deep white clouds.
And transform my Great Spirit into a rainbow.
But I am afraid that deep into the flowers,
red dew will moisten my clothes.

黃庭堅 **huáng tíng jiān**
水調歌頭 **shuǐ diào gē tóu**

瑤〇草△
yáo cǎo
medicine herb

一△何〇碧△
yī hé bì
is like a greenish jade

春〇入△
chūn rù
enter in spring

武△陵〇溪●
wǔ líng xī
Wu Ling stream

溪〇上△
xī shàng
on the shore

桃〇花〇
táo huā
peach blossom

無〇數△
wú shù
numerous

花〇上△
huā shàng
on the flowers

有△
yǒu
there are

黃〇鸝●
huáng lí
orioles

我△欲△
wǒ yù
I want to

穿〇花〇
chuān huā
go into flowers

尋〇路△
xún lù
find the way

直〇入△
zhí rù
enter right ahead

白△雲〇
bái yún
white clouds

深〇處△
shēn chù
where it is deep

浩△氣△
hào qì
Great Spirit

展△
zhǎn
to transform into

虹〇霓●
hóng ní
rainbow and reflection

只△恐△
zhī kǒng
but be afraid of

花〇
huā
flowers

深〇裏△
shēn lǐ
where they are deep

紅〇露△
hóng lù
red dew

濕△
shī
moisten

人〇衣●
rén yī
my clothes

269

I sit on a jade-like stone;
I lean on the stone pillow;
I genteelly brush my lute.
Where is Li Bai at this moment?
Nobody is here to drink with me.
I come here for the medicine herb,
not the pink face and red lips.
Why do I need to sigh with a long whistle?
In tipsiness, I dance as I descend from the mountain.
The bright moon follows me closely on my return.

坐△玉△石△
zuò yù shí
sit on jade stone

敲○玉△枕△
qī yù zhěn
lean on jade pillow

拂△金○微●
fú jīn wéi
play the lute

謫△仙○
zhé xiān
Li Bai

何○處△
hé chǔ
where is he

無○人○
wú rén
nobody

伴△我△
bàn wǒ
to keep me company

白△螺○杯●
bái luó bēi
drink with a wine cup

我△為△
wǒ wéi
I come here for

靈○芝○
líng zhī
powerful fungus

仙○草△
xiān cǎo
medicine herb

不△為△
bù wéi
not for

朱○唇○
zhū chún
red lips

丹○臉△
dān liǎn
pink face

長○嘯△
cháng xiào
long whistling

亦△
yì
also

何○為●
hé wéi
for what

醉△舞○
zuì wǔ
dance in tipsiness

下△山○
xià shān
down the hill

去△
qù
go

明○月△
míng yuè
bright moon

逐△人○
zhú rén
chase me

歸●
guī
to return

黄庭坚

定风波

万里黔中一漏天，屋居终日似乘船。及至重阳天也霁，催醉，鬼门关外蜀江前。莫笑老翁犹气岸，君看，几人黄菊上华颠？戏马台南追雨谢，池射，风流犹拍古人肩。

Huang Ting Jian

Tune: "Din Feng Bo"

Rainy Days

Ten thousand *li* away in Qian Zhong,
it rained like the sky was leaking.
Staying inside the house all the time
as if I have been on a boat ride.
On this Double Nine Festival Day,
we finally can see a blue and clear sky.
I feel the urge to drink before the Shu River
or the Devil gate outside.

Don't laugh at this old man
who still has a lot of pride.
Look, how many old men would still
insert yellow mums
into their temple hair in white?
I can still chase southward the two Xies
on the Horse-Show stage.
When it comes to rapid shooting with arrows,
I am as good as those ancient heroes.

黃庭堅　**huáng tíng jiān**
定風波　**dìng fēng bō**

萬△里△
wàn lǐ
ten thousand *li*

屋△居○
wū jū
inside the house

及△至△
jí zhì
wait for arrival

催○醉△
cuī zuì
impulse to drink

莫△笑△
mò xiào
don't laugh at

君○看△
jūn kàn
take a look

幾△人○
jǐ rén
how many people

戲△馬△台○
xì mǎ tái
Horse-Show Stage

馳○射△
chí shè
shoot swiftly

風○流○
fēng liú
elegance in style

黔○中○
qián zhōng
Qian Zhong

終○日△
zhōng rì
all day

重○陽○
chóng yáng
Double Nine Festival

鬼△門○關○外△
guǐ mén guān wài
outside Devil Gate

老△翁○
lǎo wēng
old man

黃○菊△
huáng jú
yellow mums

南○追○
nán zhuī
chase southward

猶○拍△
yóu pāi
can still pat

一△漏△天●
yī lòu tiān
a leaky sky

似△乘△船●
sì chéng chuán
like taking a boat ride

天○也△齊△
tiān yě jì
sky clear and blue

蜀△江○前●
shǔ jiāng qián
in front of Shu River

猶○氣△岸△
yóu qì àn
still has a lot of pride

上△華○顛●
shàng huá diān
insert into white hair

兩△謝△
liǎng xiè
the two Xies (refers to poets Xie Zhan and Xie Lin Yun)

古△人○肩●
gǔ rén jiān
ancient men's shoulders

273

莫笑老翁犹气岸，君看，几人黄菊上华颠。

Don't laugh at this old man
who still has a lot of pride.
Look, how many old men
would still insert yellow mums
into their temple hair in white?

— Huang Tingjian

Qin Guan (1049–1100)

秦观

Qin Guan is popularly known as Qin Shao You today. He was a native of present-day Jiansu province. His father died when he was only fifteen years old.

Qin did not pass the imperial examination for the title of *jinshi* until he was thirty-seven. He died fourteen years later.

Qin first met Su Shi at the age of twenty-seven when he was on his way to the capital for the imperial examination. Huang Tinjian's uncle Li Chang was instrumental in bringing the two together. Su was quite impressed by Qin's talent in poetry writing. In the years to come, Su played an important role in Qin's future career. Along with HuangTinjian, Zhang Lai, and Zhao Buzhi, Qin was acclaimed the honorable tile of "Four Su Scholars." Of the four, Qin impressed Su Shi the most.

Qin excelled in both *shi* and *ci* forms as well as in essay writing. However, he was better known for his work on *ci* poetry. His style was recognized by his contemporaries as elegant, beautiful, and artistic. He was also known to be very skillful in perfecting diction and rhyme. The subject matter and themes in his poetry appear quite narrow, focusing mainly on love, parting, and sorrowful feelings. His *ci* poems, particularly the *changdiao* (long form), were influenced by Liu Yong as they shared similar interests and life experiences. They both found comfort in the so-called green mansions where beautiful singing girls were often the source of their inspiration.

Nowadays the character of Qin Quan has often been depicted in Chinese soap operas as one who was married to Su Shi's sister Su Xiaomei. However, no historical records available to substantiate the claim that Su Shi even had a sister.

秦观

浣溪沙

漠漠轻寒上小楼。晓阴无赖似穷秋。淡烟流水画屏幽。 自在飞花轻似梦，无边丝雨细如愁。宝帘闲挂小银钩。

Qin Guan

Tune: "Wan Xi Sha"

One Spring Morning

I ascend the little tower amidst a
Cloudy sky and slight chill at dawn.
It is so gloomy as though
late autumn is all around.
I see on a painted screen
the thin mist and a flowing stream.

Flying flowers are as light
as those in my dream.
The endless thread-like rain
is as small as my sorrowful feelings.
Hanging down from the little silvery hooks
is the curtain decorated with precious things.

秦觀　　qín guān
浣溪沙　wǎn xī shā

○ = 平声 (*ping* or flat tone)
△ = 仄声 (*ze* or deflected tone)
● = 平声韵 (rhymed in *ping* or flat tone)
▲ = 仄声韵 (rhymed in *ze* or deflected tone)

漠△漠△
mò mò
silent; overcast

曉△陰○
xiǎo yīn
gloomy at daybreak

淡△煙○
dàn yān
thin mist

自△在△
zì zài
at ease

無○邊○
wú biān
endless

寶△簾○
bǎo lián
decorated curtain

輕○寒○
qīng hán
slight chill

無○賴△
wú lài
unwelcome

流○水△
liú shuǐ
flowing water

飛○花○
fēi huā
flying flowers

絲○雨△
sī yǔ
thread-like drizzle

閒○掛△
xián guà
hang idly

上△小△樓●
shàng xiǎo lóu
go up to little tower

似△窮○秋●
sì qióng qiū
like deep autumn

畫△屏○幽●
huà píng yōu
on secluded painted screen

輕○似△夢△
qīng sì mèng
as light as a dream

細△如○愁●
xì rú chóu
as thin as grief

小△銀○鉤●
xiǎo yín gōu
little silvery hooks

秦观

鹊桥仙

纤云弄巧，飞星传恨，银汉迢迢暗度。金凤玉露一相逢，便胜却、人间无数。 柔情似水，佳期如梦，忍顾鹊桥归路。两情若是久长时，又岂在、朝朝暮暮。

Qin Guan

Tune: "Que Qiao Xian"

Cowherd and the Weaver

Fine clouds show their artistic faces.
Blinking stars convey their grief in space.
So dim and far to go across the Milky Way.
Meeting once a year at a time of white
dew and autumn wind is far more touching
than reunion on earth numerous times.

Their feelings are water-like tender;
their special date once a year is like a dream.
On the magpie bridge, how can they bear
to turn homeward again?
If mutual love will be long and never die,
why need to be together day and night?

秦觀　　qín guān
鵲橋仙　què qiáo xiān

纖○云○ *xiān yún* fine clouds	弄△巧△ *nòng qiǎo* try to be artful	
飛○星○ *fēi xīng* flying stars	傳○恨△ *chuán hèn* convey sorrow and regret	
銀○漢△ *yín hàn* the Milky Way	迢○迢○ *tiáo tiáo* far away	暗△度▲ *àn dù* to cross in dim light
金○風○ *jīn fēng* golden (autumn) wind	玉△露△ *yù lù* jade (white) dew	一△相○逢○ *yī xiāng féng* once-a-year annual reunion
便△勝△卻△ *biàn shèng què* will surpass	人○間○ *rén jiān* human world	無○數▲ *wú shù* numerous times
柔○情○ *róu qíng* tender feelings	似△水△ *sì shuǐ* like water	
佳○期○ *jiā qī* special occasion	如○夢△ *rú mèng* like dream	
忍△顧△ *rěn gù* can (not) bear to look back	鵲○橋○ *què qiáo* Magpie Bridge	歸○路▲ *guī lù* homebound road
兩△情○ *liǎng qíng* mutual love	若△是△ *ruò shì* if (it) is	久△長○時○ *jiǔ cháng shí* long and lasting
又△豈△在△ *yòu qǐ zài* why needs to be	朝○朝○ *zhāo zhāo* every morning	暮△暮▲ *mù mù* every evening

秦观

踏莎行

雾失楼台，月迷津渡。桃源望断无寻处。可堪孤馆闭春寒，杜鹃声里斜阳暮。驿寄梅花，鱼传尺素。砌成此恨无重数。郴江幸自绕郴山，为谁流下潇湘去。

Qin Guan

Tune: "Ta Suo Xing"

At a Lonely Inn

A tower is lost in mist.
In dim moonlight, the sight
of ferry crossing is limited.
The Land of Peach Blossoms
is nowhere to be seen.
I can't bear to be shut out
from spring chill in a lonely inn.
While the slanting sun lingers,
a cuckoo cries as evening dusk sets in.

Gifts and letters through courier
station are received.
Your comforting messages
have intensified my nostalgic feelings.
The Chen River itself flows around
the Chen Mountain.
For whom it flows down
to rivers Xiao and Xiang?

秦觀　qín guān
踏莎行　tà suō xíng

霧△失△
wù shī
mist to lose

樓○台○
lóu tái
tower; balcony

月△迷○
yuè mí
moon is lost

津○渡▲
jīn dù
(at a) ferry crossing

桃○源○
táo yuán
Land of Peach Blossoms

望△斷△
wàng duàn
end of view

無○尋○處▲
wú xún chǔ
nowhere to be found

可△堪○
kě kān
can't bear

孤○館△
gū guǎn
lonely inn

閉△春○寒○
bì chūn hán
shut out in spring chill

杜△鵑○
dù juān
cuckoo

聲○里△
shēng lǐ
in its voice

斜○陽○暮▲
xié yáng mù
slanting sun turns into dusk

驛△寄△
yì jì
sent through courier station

梅○花○
méi huā
plume flowers (gifts)

魚○傳○
yú chuán
delivered by fish (post)

尺△素▲
chǐ sù
letters

砌△成○
qì chéng
built by laying

此△恨△
cǐ hèn
such regret

無○重○數▲
wú zhòng shù
immeasurable

郴○江○
chēn jiāng
Chen River

幸△自△
xìng zì
luckily itself

繞△郴○山○
rào chēn shān
shrouds around Chen Mountain

為○誰○
wéi shéi
for whom

流○下△
liú xià
flows down

瀟○湘○去▲
xiāo xiāng qù
toward rivers Xiao and Xiang

281

秦观

八六子

倚危亭。恨如芳草，萋萋铲尽还生。念柳外青骢别后，水边红袂分时，怆然暗惊。无端天与娉婷。夜月一帘幽梦，春风十里柔情。怎奈向、欢娱渐随流水，素弦声断，翠绡香减。那堪片片飞花弄晚，蒙蒙残雨笼晴。正销凝，黄鹂又啼数声。

Qin Guan

Tune: "Ba Liu Zi"

One Spring Morning

I lean on the high pavilion.
My grief is like the luxuriant glasses.
You can uproot them, but they
will come back stronger.
I remember the time before and after we parted.
With the bluish white horse, we were
by the side of the willow trees and river.
I still feel broken in my heart.

You were a beauty of grace from heaven.
We lived in our secluded dreams
in moonlight behind the curtain.
Accompanying me for ten miles were your tender
feelings in the breeze of spring.

秦觀　　qín guān
八六子　　bā liù zi

倚△
yǐ
lean on

危○亭●
wēi tíng
high pavilion

恨△
hèn
grief

如○
rú
is like

芳○草△
fāng cǎo
fragrant grass

萋○萋○
qī qī
luxuriant growth

鏟△盡△
chǎn jìn
uproot them all

還○生●
huán shēng
still grow

念△柳△外△
niàn liǔ wài
remember beside willow

青○驄○
qīng cōng
a horse with a bluish white color

別△後△
bié hòu
after parting

水△邊○
shuǐ biān
by the water

紅○袂△
hóng mèi
red sleeves (lady)

分○時○
fēn shí
time of parting

愴○然○
chuàng rán
brokenhearted

暗△驚●
àn jīng
inwardly fearful

無○端○
wú duān
for no reason

天○與△
tiān yǔ
heaven bestows upon (me)

娉○婷●
pīng tíng
graceful and charming (lady)

夜△月△
yè yuè
night moon

一△簾○
yī lián
a curtain full of

幽○夢△
yōu mèng
secluded dream

春○風○
chūn fēng
spring breeze

十△里△
shí lǐ
ten miles

柔○情●
róu qíng
tender feeling

Unfortunately, gone with the flowing
Water is our happy moment.
No more sound can be heard from the
stringed instrument.
Gone too is the fragrance from the kerchief
that is bluish and green.
How can I bear to look at the flowers
flying piece by piece in the evening?
Or the sun that is shrouded by
misty and waning rain?
Suddenly, an oriole cries a few times,
awakening me from deep thinking.

怎△奈△向△
zěn nài xiàng
but unfortunately

歡〇娛〇
huān yú
joy and happiness

漸△隨〇
jiàn suí
gradually follow

流〇水△
liú shuǐ
flowing water

素△弦〇
sù xián
plain string

聲〇斷△
shēng duàn
sound interrupted

翠△綃〇
cuì xiāo
bluish-green fabric

香〇減△
xiāng jiǎn
fragrance diminished

那△堪〇
nà kān
how can one stand

片△片△
piàn piàn
in pieces

飛〇花〇
fēi huā
flying flowers

弄△晚△
nòng wǎn
play for fun in evening

濛〇濛〇
méng méng
misty

殘〇雨△
cán yǔ
waning rain

籠〇晴●
lóng qíng
covers a clear day

正△
zhèng
just in time

銷〇凝●
xiāo níng
back from deep thought

黃〇鸝〇
huáng lí
oriole

又△啼〇
yòu tí
again cries

數△聲●
shù shēng
a few times

秦观

满庭芳

山抹微云，天连衰草，画角声断谯门。暂停征棹，聊共引离尊。多少蓬莱旧事，空回首、烟霭纷纷。斜阳外，寒鸦万点，流水绕孤村。 销魂，当此际，香囊暗解，罗带轻分。谩赢得青楼，薄幸名存。此去何时见也，襟袖上，空惹啼痕。伤情处，高城望断，灯火已黄昏。

Qin Guan

Tune: "Man Ting Fang"

Parting

Mountains wipe off thin clouds.
Withered grasses join the sky.
The painted horn blows loudly above the city gate.
Let's delay the boat journey for a while,
and together drink some soothing wine.
How many fantasy-like memories
are now recalled through clouds and mists.
In the setting sun, I see a thousand dots of crows.
Around a lonely village, water flows without pause.

秦觀　qín guān
滿庭芳　mǎn tíng fāng

山〇
shān
mountains

天〇
tiān
sky

畫△角△聲〇
huà jiǎo shēng
sound of painted horn

暫△停〇
zàn tíng
temporarily stop

聊〇
liáo
for the moment

多〇少△
duō shǎo
how many

空〇
kōng
in vain

煙〇靄△
yān ǎi
mist and clouds

斜〇陽〇外△
xié yáng wài
outside slanting sun

流〇水△
liú shuǐ
flowing water

抹△
mǒ
wipe off

連〇
lián
joins

斷△
duàn
breaks

征〇棹△
zhēng zhào
a boat on a long journey

共△引△
gòng yǐn
together draw into

蓬〇萊〇
péng lái
penglai (romantic)

回〇首△
huí shǒu
to look back

紛〇紛●
fēn fēn
in succession

寒〇鴉〇
hán yā
crows in cold

繞△
rào
wind around

微〇雲〇
wéi yún
thin clouds

衰〇草△
shuāi cǎo
withered grass

譙〇門●
qiáo mén
city gate

離〇樽●
lí zūn
wine vessel

舊△事△
jiù shì
past events

萬△點△
wàn diǎn
ten thousand points

孤〇村●
gū cūn
a lone village

Overwhelmed with emotions,
I secretly give you a sachet.
In return, you give me a section
of the silken ribbon.
I was known as a heartless person
in the green mansion.
After we part, when can we see each other?
I can't help but shedding tears on the sleeves.
Where breaks my heart
is the diminishing view of the watchtower,
as city light is about to take over.

銷〇魂●
xiāo hún
overwhelmed with emotion

當〇此△際△　　香〇囊〇　　　暗△解△
dāng cǐ jì　　*xiāng náng*　　*àn jiě*
at this moment　a sachet　　　secretly taken out

羅〇帶△　　　　輕〇分●
luó dài　　　　*qīng fēn*
a silk ribbon　　lightly separated

謾△　　　　　　贏〇得△　　　青〇樓〇
mán　　　　　*yíng de*　　　*qīng lóu*
distained　　　to have earned　green chamber
　　　　　　　　　　　　　　　(brothel)

薄△幸△　　　　名〇存●
bó xìng　　　*míng cún*
heartless　　　name reserved

此△去△　　　　何〇時〇　　　見△也△
cǐ qù　　　　*hé shí*　　　*jiàn yě*
this departure　when　　　　to see you

襟〇袖△上△　　空〇惹△　　　啼〇痕●
jīn xiù shàng　*kōng rě*　　　*tí hén*
on front sleeves　cause in vain　trace of tears

傷〇情〇處△　　高〇城〇　　　望△斷△
shāng qíng chǔ　*gāo chéng*　　*wàng duàn*
where breaks my　tall city　　　exhaust my view
heart

燈〇火△　　　　已△　　　　　黃〇昏●
dēng huǒ　　　*yǐ*　　　　　*huáng hūn*
lights　　　　　already　　　　at dusk

秦观

江城子

西城杨柳弄春柔。动离忧。泪难收。犹记多情曾为系归舟。碧野朱桥当日事，人不见，水空流。
　　韶华不为少年留。恨悠悠。几时休。飞絮落花时候一登楼。便做春江都是泪，流不尽，许多愁。

Qin Guan

Tune: "Jiang Cheng Zi"

Returning to West Town

Willows at west side of town dance in spring.
It reminds me of the last parting scene.
My tears can't be held back from falling.
I still remember which willow tied my returning boat.
It is the same bluish green field and red bridge.
Only the person is nowhere to be seen.
And the water keeps flowing in vain.

Youthful time, once gone, will not return again.
So boundless is the grief!
When will it ever come to an end?
Once more I climb the tower
when catkins fly and flowers fall.
Even if the spring river is full of tears,
they will never cease flowing
with so much sorrow to bear.

秦觀　qín guān
江城子　jiāng chéng zi

西〇城〇
xī chéng
west town

楊〇柳△
yáng liǔ
willow

弄△春〇柔●
nòng chūn róu
dance in spring breeze

動△離〇憂●
dòng lí yōu
incite parting grief

淚△難〇收●
lèi nán shōu
tears can't be held back

猶〇記△
yóu jì
still remember

多〇情〇
duō qíng
full of affection

曾〇為△
céng wéi
for (me)

繫△歸〇舟●
xì guī zhōu
tied returning boat

碧△野△
bì yě
bluish green field

朱〇橋〇
zhū qiáo
red bridge

當〇日△事△
dāng rì shì
event on that day

人〇不△見△
rén bù jiàn
person no longer seen

水△空〇流●
shuǐ kōng liú
water flows in vain

韶〇華〇
sháo huá
beautiful years

不△為△
bù wéi
will not

少△年〇留●
shào nián liú
keep it for youngsters

恨△悠〇悠●
hèn yōu yōu
boundless grief

幾△時〇休●
jǐ shí xiū
when will it stop

飛〇絮△落△花〇
fēi xù luò huā
flying catkins and fallen flowers

時〇候△
shí hòu
at the time of

一△登〇樓●
yī dēng lóu
go up to tower

便△做△
biàn zuò
even they turn into

春〇江〇
chūn jiāng
spring river

都〇是△淚△
dū shì lèi
all tears

流〇不△盡△
liú bù jìn
can't cease flowing

許△多〇愁●
xǔ duō chóu
too many sorrows

秦观

江城子

南来飞燕北归鸿。偶相逢。惨愁容。绿鬓朱颜，重见两衰翁。别後悠悠君莫问，无限事，不言中。
　　小槽春酒滴珠红。莫匆匆。满金钟。饮散落花流水、各西东。後会不知何处是，烟浪远，暮云重。

Qin Guan

Tune: "Jiag Cheng Zi"

No Need to Ask

Like a swallow from the south
and a swan back from the north,
we meet by chance.
We look worried and anxious.
Used to be youthful in appearance,
we are now two weary old men.
So distant is the past, ask not
what we have gone through.
It is better leave many things unsaid.

Let's draw some spring wine from the little trough
and let it drip like red pearls.
Don't be hurry and fill up the cups to the brim.
After we part, we will be like the fallen flowers
drifting in the water.
Who knows where we will meet again?
Mist and waves stretch very far;
evening clouds float layer upon layer.

秦觀　qín guān
江城子　jiāng chéng zi

南○來○ *nán lái* coming from south	飛○燕△ *fēi yàn* flying swallow	北△歸○鴻● *běi guī hóng* swan geese back from north
偶△相○逢● *ǒu xiāng féng* meeting by chance	慘△愁○容● *cǎn chóu róng* worried and anxious look	綠△鬢△ *lǜ bìn* green (youthful) temples
朱○顏○ *zhū yán* red complexion	重○見△ *chóng jiàn* seeing again	兩△衰○翁● *liǎng shuāi wēng* two feeble and old men
別△後△ *bié hòu* since we parted	悠○悠○ *yōu yōu* distant pass	君○莫△問△ *jūn mò wèn* don't ask me
無○限△事△ *wú xiàn shì* too many things	不△言○中● *bù yán zhōng* in unspoken words	
小△槽○ *xiǎo cáo* little trough	春○酒△ *chūn jiǔ* spring wine	滴△珠○紅● *dī zhū hóng* drops of tears drip
莫△匆○匆● *mò cōng cōng* don't rush	滿△金○鐘● *mǎn jīn zhōng* fill golden cup	
飲△散△ *yǐn sǎn* parting after the drink	落△花○流○水△ *liú shuǐ luò huā* flowers drift in water	各△西○東● *gè xī dōng* go separate way
後△會△ *hòu huì* meeting again	不△知○ *bù zhī* don't know	何○處△是△ *hé chǔ shì* where it is
煙○浪△遠△ *yān làng yuǎn* mist and waves: far	暮△雲○重● *mù yún zhòng* clouds at dusk: layer upon layer	

秦观

好事近

春路雨添花，花动一山春色。行到小溪深处，有黄鹂千百。　飞云当面化龙蛇，夭骄转空碧。醉卧古藤阴下，了不知南北。

Qin Guan

Tune: "Hao Shi Jin"

A Dream

I dream of walking on a road in spring.
Flowers suddenly appear abundantly in the rain.
The entire mountain is revitalized by
the vernal flowers.
I walk to the little brook where the water is deep.
Thousands of yellow orioles fly or sleep.

The flying clouds before me transform
themselves into dragons and snakes.
Shrinking or distending at will, they
put the emerald sky back in place.
I lie drunk under the shadow of the old vines,
not knowing I am facing the eastern or western side.

秦觀　qín guān
好事近　hǎo shì jìn

春○路△
chūn lù
spring road

花○動△
huā dòng
flowers activate

行○到△
xíng dào
walk to

有△
yǒu
there are

飛○雲○
fēi yún
flying clouds

夭△驕○
yāo jiāo
shrine and distend at will

醉△臥△
zuì wò
lying drunk

了△
liǎo
completely

雨△
yǔ
rain

一△山○
yī shān
the entire mountain

小△溪○
xiǎo xī
little brook

黃○鸝○
huáng lí
yellow orioles

當△面△
dāng miàn
in front of me

轉△
zhuǎn
change to

古△藤○
gǔ téng
old vine

不△知○
bù zhī
not knowing

添○花○
tiān huā
to add more flowers

春○色▲
chūn sè
spring color

深○處△
shēn chù
where it is deep

千○百△
qiān bǎi
in the hundreds and thousands

化△龍○蛇○
huà lóng shé
transform into dragons and snakes

空○碧▲
kōng bì
emerald sky

陰○下△
yīn xià
under shadow

南○北▲
nán běi
south and north

两情若是久长时,又岂在、朝朝暮暮。

If mutual love will be long and never die,
why need to be together day and night?

— Qin Guan

He Zhu (1052–1125)

贺铸

With blood linkage to Queen Xiaohui (孝惠皇后), He Zhu, also named He Fang Hui, was born in 1052 in present-day Henan province. His family, however, was originally from Shan Yin, present-day Shaoxing, Zhejiang province.

He was known to be a master of both the pen and the sword. Tall and strong in appearance, he was idealistic, ambitious, and chivalrous in spirit. He had in his early years aspired to follow the footsteps of several of his ancestors to be a military officer. His pride and strong sense of justice might have made it hard for him to reach his goal: a high-level officer.

A series of struggles and frustrations did provide him with the kind of life experiences that might have made a difference in the quality of his poetry.

He Zhu was well vested in the writing of both *shi* and *ci* poetry. His style was elegant and refined. The scope of his subject matter was much broader in relation to other poets before him. Some of his poems also reveal the sensitive side of his personality.

The mourning poem, for example, included in the selection reflects the genuine feelings for the death of his beloved wife. In spite of her wealthy and noble origin, she was willing to share bliss and adversity together with him. This poem is considered one of the best mourning poems ever written in both *shi* and *ci* forms.

贺铸

鹧鸪天

重过阊门万事非，同来何事不同归！梧桐半死清霜后，头白鸳鸯失伴飞。原上草，露初晞。旧栖新垄两依依。空床卧听南窗雨，谁复挑灯夜补衣。

He Zhu

Tune: "Che Gu Tian"

Mourning

Everything seems so different, passing
through the front gate.
Together we came, why must we return
on separate way?
The parasol tree is now half-dead after the frost.
The white-haired mandarin duck must fly
alone without his mate.

Grass on the plain;
dewdrops begin to dry in the sun.
How can one leave an old residence
and new grave behind!
By the southwest window, I lie
on the empty bed, listening to the rain outside.
Who again will stir the wick of the lamp
and repair the clothes at night?

賀鑄　　　*hè zhù*
鷓鴣天　　*zhè gū tiān*

○ ＝ 平声 (*ping* or flat tone)
△ ＝ 仄声 (*ze* or deflected tone)
● ＝ 平声韵 (rhymed in *ping* or flat tone)
▲ ＝ 仄声韵 (rhymed in *ze* or deflected tone)

重○過△
chóng guò
pass through again

閶○門○
chāng mén
front gate

萬△事△非●
wàn shì fēi
everything is different

同○來○
tóng lái
came together

何○事△
hé shì
why then

不△同○歸●
bù tóng guī
not return together

梧○桐○
wú tóng
parasol tree

半△死△
bàn sǐ
half died

清○霜○後△
qīng shuāng hòu
after clear frost

頭○白△
tóu bái
white-haired

鴛○鴦○
yuān yāng
mandarin duck

失△伴△飛●
shī bàn fēi
to fly alone without mate

原○上△草△
yuán shàng cǎo
grass on the plain

露△初○晞●
lù chū xī
dewdrops begin to dry in the sun

舊△棲○
jiù qī
old residence

新○壟△
xīn lǒng
new grave

兩△依○依●
liǎng yī yī
reluctant to part

空○床○
kōng chuáng
empty bed

臥△聽△
wò tīng
lie down to listen

南○窗○雨△
nán chuāng yǔ
rain from southern window

誰○復△
shéi fù
who again will

挑△燈○
tiāo dēng
stir the wick of a lamp

夜△補△衣●
yè bǔ yī
to repair clothes at night

贺铸

浣溪沙

不信芳春厌老人。老人几度送余春。惜春行乐莫辞频。巧笑艳歌皆我意，恼花颠酒拚君瞋。物情惟有醉中真。

He Zhu

Tune: "Wan Xi Sha"

Enjoy the Spring at Old Age

I don't believe that spring gets tired of old men.
Old men don't want to see spring off too often.
Do frequently seek pleasures and enjoy spring time.
Laughing and singing suit me just fine.
Don't be upset by my lovesickness
and excessive drinking.
Feelings and things can only be real in
the state of drunkenness.

賀鑄　**hè zhù**
浣溪沙　**wǎn xī shā**

不△信△
bù xìn
don't believe

芳○春○
fāng chūn
beautiful spring

厭△老△人●
yàn lǎo rén
tired of old people

老△人○
lǎo rén
old people

幾△度△
Jǐ dù
repeatedly

送△餘○春●
sòng yú chūn
see the waning spring off

惜△春○
xī chūn
appreciating spring

行○樂△
xíng lè
seeking pleasures

莫△辭○頻●
mò cí pín
don't complain of being too frequent

巧△笑△
qiǎo xiào
laughing happily

艷△歌○
yàn gē
charming song

皆○我△意△
jiē wǒ yì
all are my wishes

惱△花○
nǎo huā
irritating flowers

顛○酒△
diān jiǔ
drinking too much

拚△君○瞋●
pàn jūn chēn
all out to make you angry

物△情○
wù qíng
things and feelings

惟○有△
wéi yǒu
only be

醉△中○真●
zuì zhōng zhēn
real in drunken state

贺铸

浣溪沙

楼角初消一缕霞。淡黄杨柳暗栖鸦。玉人和月摘梅花。笑捻粉香归洞户,更垂帘幕护窗纱。东风寒似夜来些。

He Zhu

Tune: "Wan Xi Sha"

Spring Night

A wisp of rosy cloud has just vanished
at the tower's corner.
A crow perches on a willow tree
that is in light yellow color.
The fair lady plucks a plum flower
in moonlight.
She then toys in her hand the fragrant flower
while going back inside.
She even drops the curtain
to guard the window screen.
The east wind is as cold as the chill last night.

賀鑄　　**hè zhù**
浣溪沙　**wǎn xī shā**

樓○角△ *lóu jiǎo* at corner of tower	初○消○ *chū xiāo* just disappear	一△縷△霞● *yī lǚ xiá* a wisp of rosy cloud
淡△黃○ *dàn huáng* light yellow	楊○柳△ *yáng liǔ* willow	暗△棲○鴉● *àn qī yā* a crow perches in darkness
玉△人○ *yù rén* a fair lady	和○月△ *hé yuè* with the moon	摘△梅○花● *zhāi méi huā* pluck a plum flower
笑△撚△ *xiào niǎn* laughing twist with fingers	粉○香○ *fěn xiāng* the fragrant flower	歸○洞△戶△ *guī dòng hù* go back inside
更△垂○ *gèng chuí* even drop	簾○幕△ *lián mù* curtain	護△窗○紗● *hù chuāng shā* to protect the window screen
東○風○ *dōng fēng* east wind	寒○似△ *hán sì* as cold as	夜△來○些● *yè lái xiē* last night's chill

贺铸

青玉案

凌波不过横塘路。但目送、芳尘去。锦瑟年华谁与度。月桥花院，琐窗朱户。只有春知处。　飞云冉冉蘅皋暮。彩笔新题断肠句。若问闲情都几许。一川烟草，满城风絮。梅子黄时雨。

He Zhu

Tune: "Qing Yu An"

Beautiful Years

She never walks across the Heng Tang Road.
I can only follow her fragrant dust with my eyes.
Who will spend time with her during
her youthful years?
Is it by the moonlit bridge, the flower courtyard,
or in a charming house with decorated windows?
Only spring knows where she resides.

The clouds gradually rise over the swamp
overgrown with fragrant grass at dusk.
With my colorful pen, I have written
a few heartbroken lines.
If you ask me how much pop-up sorrows
in my heart, I can tell you this:
A river full of misty grasses;
a city full of flying petals,
the rain when the plum turning yellowish from green.

賀鑄　hè zhù
青玉案　qīng yù àn

凌〇波〇
líng bō
walking at ease

但△
dàn
can only

錦△瑟△
jǐn sè
beautiful

月△橋〇
yuè qiáo
moonlit bridge

只△有△
zhǐ yǒu
only

飛〇雲〇
fēi yún
flying clouds

彩△筆△
cǎi bǐ
colorful pen

若△問△
ruò wèn
if asking

一△川〇
yī chuān
one river of

梅〇子△
méi zi
plum

不△過△
bú guò
don't pass

目△送△
mù sòng
follow with eyes

年〇華〇
nián huá
youthful years

花〇院△
huā yuàn
flower courtyard

春〇
chūn
spring

冉△冉△
rǎn rǎn
gradually

新〇題〇
xīn tí
newly written

閒〇情〇
xián qíng
mild random feelings

煙〇草△
yān cǎo
misty grass

黃〇時〇
huáng shí
to turn yellowish

橫〇塘〇路▲
héng táng lù
Heng Tang Road

芳〇塵〇去▲
fāng chén qù
her fragrant dust

誰〇與△度▲
shéi yǔ dù
whom to spend time with

瑣△窗〇朱〇戶▲
suǒ chuāng zhū hù
beautiful house with decorated windows

知〇處▲
zhī chǔ
know where she lives

蘅〇皋〇暮▲
héng gāo mù
grassy swamp at dusk

斷△腸〇句▲
duàn cháng jù
sorrowful lines

都〇幾△許▲
dōu jǐ xǔ
how much

滿△城〇風〇絮▲
mǎn chéng fēng xù
a whole city of flying petals

雨▲
yǔ
rain

305

贺铸

蝶恋花

几许伤春春复暮。杨柳清阴，偏碍游丝度。天际小山桃叶步。白苹花满湔裙处。　竟日微吟长短句。帘影灯昏，心寄胡琴语。数点雨声风约住。朦胧淡月云来去。

He Zhu

Tune: "Die Lian Hua"

Peach Blossom

Even if I feel sad, spring will not be back.
The willows are so shady and dense
that they obstruct the drifting petals.
Small hills can be seen behind the
Tao Ye Ferry in the distance.
White duckweed flowers catch my eyes
by the clothes-washing site.

The whole day, I lightheartedly write
a poem of irregular lines.
I see the shadow of the curtain in dim lamplight.
To convey my feelings, I play the two-stringed violin.
The sound of raindrops is halted by the wind.
The misty moon beaming through the clouds
can be intermittently seen.

賀鑄　　hè zhù
蝶戀花　dié liàn huā

幾△許△ jǐ xǔ how often	傷○春○ shāng chūn feel sad for spring	春○復△暮▲ chūn fù mù spring is still over
楊○柳△ yáng liǔ willows	清○陰○ qīng yīn shady and dense	
偏○礙△ piān ài happen to obstruct	遊○絲○度▲ yóu sī dù drifting petals	
天○際△ tiān jì far away	小△山○ xiǎo shān little hills	桃○葉△步▲ táo yè bù is the Tao Ye Ferry
白△蘋○花○ bái píng huā white duckweed flowers	滿△ mǎn full	浣○裙○處▲ jiān qún chǔ place to wash clothes
竟△日△ jìng rì the whole day	微○吟○ wéi yín I chant a little bit	長○短△句▲ cháng duǎn jù irregular lyrical lines
簾○影△ lián yǐng shadow of curtain	燈○昏○ dēng hūn lamp is dark	
心○寄△ xīn jì want to send	胡○琴○ hú qín foreign zither	語▲ yǔ words
數△點△ shù diǎn several drops	雨△聲○ yǔ shēng sound of rain	風○約△住▲ fēng yuē zhù blocked by wind
朦○朧○ méng lóng misty	淡△月△ dàn yuè light moonlight	雲○來○去▲ yún lái qù clouds come and go

不信芳春厌老人。老人几度送余春。

I don't believe that spring gets tired of old men.
Old men don't want to see spring off too often.

— He Zhu

Zhou Bang Yan (1056–1121)

周邦彦

Zhou Bang Yan, also known as Mei Cheng and Qing Zhen Ju Shi, was born in present-day Hangzhou, Zhejiang province. He was said to be somewhat unconventional and unbridled as a young man.

Unlike some other *ci* poets of his time, Zhou assumed mainly minor roles as a regional official. His lack of accomplishments in the field of politics might have something to do with his desire to be free from partisan conflicts, a fact of life during the period in which he lived.

Zhou was recognized as one of the most influential figures in the advancement of *ci* poetry. He was credited for creating a poetic style by synthesizing major viewpoints and models in *ci* poetry. He was especially admired for his mastery of the rules of prosody and poetic diction. Besides poetry and letters, Zhou was also a talented musician. In fact, he was the first *ci* poet and musician to come along since Liu Yiong, who shared some similar life experiences in the so-called green mansion.

Although both liu Yong and Zhou Bang Yan liked the long form, they differed in the way they handled events and scenes in their poems. Liu preferred a straightfoward approach; Zhou liked twists and turns.

Some of his *ci* poems were written to tunes that were composed by Zhou himself. The themes of his *ci* poems were mainly related to romantic love and parting feelings. Scholars in general give him high marks on techniques and artistic expression. However, they also tend to view his poetic ideas as relatively shallow and unsophisticated in comparison with other poets such as Su Shi, Ouyang Xiu, and Qin Guang.

周邦彦

浣溪沙

楼上晴天碧四垂。楼前芳草接天涯。劝君莫上最高梯。新笋已成堂下竹，落花都上燕巢泥。忍听林表杜鹃啼。

Zhou Bang Yan

Tune: "Wan Xi Sha"

Don't Go Up the Highest Stair

On this clear day, the blue sky
can be seen upstairs from all sides.
Grasses in front of the tower stretch
all the way to the edge of sky.
I advise you not to climb up to the tallest stair.
New shoots outside the hall have
become the real bamboos.
Fallen petals have transformed themselves
into the swallow's nest.
Oh, how can I stand the crying sound of cuckoos!

周邦彦　**zhōu bāng yàn**
浣溪沙　**wǎn xī shā**

○ = 平声 (*píng* or flat tone)
△ = 仄声 (*zè* or deflected tone)
● = 平声韵 (rhymed in *píng* or flat tone)
▲ = 仄声韵 (rhymed in *zè* or deflected tone)

樓○上△
lóu shàng
upstairs

晴○天○
qíng tiān
clear day

碧△四△垂●
bì sì chuí
blue sky can be seen from four sides

樓○前○
lóu qián
in front of the house

芳○草△
fāng cǎo
grasses

接△天○涯●
jiē tiān yá
reach the edge of sky

勸○君○
quàn jūn
I advise you

莫△上△
mò shàng
don't go up to

最○高○梯●
zuì gāo tī
the highest stair

新○筍△
xīn sǔn
new bamboo shoots

已△成○
yǐ chéng
have already become

堂○下△竹△
táng xià zhú
bamboos in front of the hall

落△花○
luò huā
fallen petals

都○上△
dōu shàng
all go up to

燕△巢○泥●
yàn cháo ní
the dirt of swallow's nest

忍△聽○
rěn tīng
can't bear to hear

林○表△
lín biǎo
outside the woods

杜△鵑○啼●
dù juān tí
cuckoos cry

周邦彦

少年游

并刀如水，吴盐胜雪，纤手破新橙。锦幄初温，兽烟不断，相对坐调笙。 低声问向谁行宿，城上已三更。马滑霜浓，不如休去，直是少人行。

Zhou Bang Yan

Tune: "Shao Nian You"

Where Will You Stay for the Night?

Bing's knife is as clear as water.
Wu's salt is whiter than snow.
She slices the new orange with her tender hand.
Incense rises from the animal-shape burner
The brocade canopy has turned warmer.
She plays the panpipe as they
sit opposite to each other.
She asks him softly, "Where will you stay
for the night?"
From the city wall comes the sound
of three drum beats.
So thick is the frost;
the road is too slippery for the horse.
It is better for you not to go.
Few people are on the road.

周邦彦　　zhōu bāng yàn
少年游　　shào nián yóu

并△刀〇
bìng dāo
Bing's knife

如〇水△
rú shuǐ
is like water

吳〇鹽〇
wú yán
Wu's salt

勝△雪△
shèng xuě
is whiter than snow

纖△手△
qiàn shǒu
slender hands

破△
pò
breaks

新〇橙●
xīn chéng
fresh orange

錦△幄△
jǐn wò
brocade canopy

初〇溫〇
chū wēn
starts to warm up

獸△煙〇
shòu yān
incense from animal burner

不△斷△
bù duàn
not broken

相〇對△
xiāng duì
facing each other

坐△
zuò
sit

調〇笙●
diào shēng
play the panpipe

低〇聲〇問△
dī shēng wèn
asking in low voice

向〇誰〇
xiàng shéi
with whom

行〇宿△
xíng sù
stay for the night

城〇上△
chéng shàng
on the city wall

已△
yǐ
is already

三〇更●
sān gèng
three drum beats

馬△滑△
mǎ huá
horse may slip

霜〇濃〇
shuāng nóng
frost is thick

不△如〇
bù rú
had better

休〇去△
xiū qù
not to go

直〇是△
zhí shì
it simply to be

少△人〇
shǎo rén
few people

行●
xíng
walking

313

新笋已成堂下竹，落花都上燕巢泥。

New shoots outside the hall have
become the real bamboos.
Fallen petals have transformed themselves
into the swallow's nest.

— Zhou Bangyan

Part Five

The Southern Song Period

Li Qingzhao (1084–1155)

李清照

Li Qingzhao gave herself the title of Yi An Ju Shi. She was the daughter of Li Ge Fei, a well-known scholar and literati in his time. Her stepmother, also from a literary family, was an excellent essayist in her own right. Given her good upbringing, one could easily understand why she was regarded as one of the most talented female writers of all time.

Li was taught early at home and vested in literature and classics. Her name as a poet was already widely known as she was growing up.

At the age of eighteen, Li was married to Zhao Mingcheng, with whom she shared common interest in art and poetry. They also enjoyed the habit of collecting classics. In the year 1127, Zhao died in present-day Nanjing en route to assuming a new government post. From this point on, Li led a wandering life full of uncertainties and loneliness. During the darkest days of her life, she was said to be briefly married to a man by the name of Zhang Ruzhou out of necessity. However, some scholars questioned whether her second marriage and divorce ever occured.

Without question, Li was one of the best *ci* poets in the Song Dynasty. Her lyrical poems are especially resonant with the readers. This has a lot to do with her unique writing style: spontaneous, natural, skillful, and easy-to-read. She was the first to argue that *ci* poetry has its own unique style (别是一家说) and it is different from *shi* poetry.

李清照

如梦令

昨夜雨疏风骤。浓睡不消残酒。试问卷帘人，却道海棠依旧。知否。知否。应是绿肥红瘦。

Li Qingzhao

Tune: "Ru Meng Ling"

Answering My Question

Last night, the rain drizzled;
the wind hurried.
Sleeping soundly after some wine,
I woke up still with tipsy eyes.
I asked the person who rolled
up the blind.
"The same old flowery crab apple"
was the reply.
Don't you know?
Don't you know?
You should have said:
the green is thick, but the red is thin.

李清照　**lǐ qīng zhào**
如夢令　**rú mèng ling**

○ ＝　平声 (*ping* or flat tone)
△ ＝　仄声 (*ze* or deflected tone)
● ＝　平声韵 (rhymed in *ping* or flat tone)
▲ ＝　仄声韵 (rhymed in *ze* or deflected tone)

昨△夜△
zuó yè
last night

雨△疏○
yǔ shū
rain: spare

風○驟▲
fēng zòu
wind: hurrying

濃○睡△
nóng shuì
sound sleep

不△消○
bù xiāo
did not get rid of

殘△酒▲
cán jiǔ
residual wine

試△問△
shì wèn
try to ask

捲△簾○人○
juǎn lián rén
one who rolls up the blind

卻△道△
què dào
saying instead

海△棠○
hǎi táng
crab apple

依○舊▲
yī jiù
the same

知○否▲
zhī fǒu
do you know

知○否▲
zhī fǒu
do you know

應△是△
yìng shì
should have said

綠△肥○
lǜ féi
green is plump

紅○瘦▲
hóng shòu
red is thin

李清照

醉花阴

薄雾浓云愁永昼。瑞脑消金兽。佳节又重阳,玉枕纱橱,半夜凉初透。　东篱把酒黄昏後。有暗香盈袖。莫道不消魂,帘卷西风,人比黄花瘦。

Li Qingzhao

Tune: "Zui Hua Yin"

Thinner than the Yellow Flowers

Thin mist rises; dense clouds in the sky.
I feel down all the time.
Incense stops burning in the gold animal censor.
The Double Nine Festival once again has arrived.
Through the gauze curtain and pillow,
the chill penetrated at midnight.

At dusk, I watched the chrysanthemums by
the eastern fence with a cup of wine.
My sleeves were scented with mild fragrance.
Don't say that I was not emotional at that time.
I became thinner than the yellow flowers
when the west wind flapped the blind.

李清照　**lǐ qīng zhào**
醉花陰　**zuì huā yīn**

薄△霧△ bó wù thin mist	濃○雲○ nóng yún dense clouds	愁○永△晝▲ chóu yǒng zhòu feeling sad all day long
瑞△腦△ ruì nǎo incense	消○ xiāo stop burning	金○獸▲ jīn shòu in gold animal (censor)
佳○節△ jiā jié festival	又△ yòu again	重○陽○ chóng yáng Double Nine Festival
玉△枕△ yù zhěn jade pillow	紗○櫥○ shā chú gauze curtain	
半△夜△ bàn yè midnight	涼○ liáng chill	初○透▲ chū tòu first penetrates
東○籬○ dōng lí fence to the east	把△酒△ bǎ jiǔ holding wine	黃○昏○後▲ huáng hūn hòu after dusk
有○ yǒu to have	暗△香△ àn xiāng subtle scent	盈○袖▲ yíng xiù fill the sleeve
莫△道△ mò dào don't say	不△ bù not	消○魂○ xiāo hún being emotionally affected
簾○捲△ lián juǎn curtain flaps	西○風○ xī fēng west wind	
人○比△ rén bǐ comparing me to	黃○花○ huáng huā yellow flowers	瘦▲ shòu (I am) thinner

李清照

武陵春

风住尘香花已尽，日晚倦梳头。物是人非事事休。欲语泪先流。　闻说双溪春尚好，也拟泛轻舟。只恐双溪舴艋舟。载不动、许多愁。

Li Qingzhao

Tune: "Wu Ling Chun"

A Heavy Load of Grief

The wind has halted.
The dirt smells fragrance.
Flowers are not in bloom anymore.
The day is late. I am too weary
to have my hairdo made.
Scenes and objects remain;
people are different.
Everything no longer stays the same.
Before I talk, tears fall.

I heard that at Twin Brook,
spring there is still fine.
I too wish to take a boat ride.
But I am afraid that at Twin Brook,
the skiff there is very light.
How can it carry such a heavy load
of sorrows without being capsized?

李清照　　**lǐ qīng zhào**
武陵春　　**wǔ líng chūn**

風〇住△ *fēng zhù* wind has stopped	塵〇香〇 *chén xiāng* dust scented	花〇已△盡△ *huā yǐ jìn* flowers are over
日△晚△ *rì wǎn* day is late	倦△ *juàn* weary	梳〇頭● *shū tóu* to comb hair
物△是△ *wù shì* things remain	人〇非〇 *rén fēi* people different	事△事△休● *shì shì xiū* everything comes to a halt
欲△語△ *yù yǔ* wanting to say	淚△ *lèi* tears	先〇流● *xiān liú* first shed
聞〇說△ *wén shuō* I heard	雙〇溪〇 *shuāng xī* Twin Brook	春〇尚△好△ *chūn shàng hǎo* spring is still good
也△擬△ *yě nǐ* also wish	泛△ *fàn* to row	輕〇舟● *qīng zhōu* a skiff
只△恐△ *zhǐ kǒng* only fear	雙〇溪〇 *shuāng xī* Twin Brook	舴〇艋△舟● *zé měng zhōu* small boat
載△不△動△ *zài bù dòng* unable to carry	許〇多〇 *xǔ duō* a great deal of	愁● *chóu* sorrow

李清照

一剪梅

红藕香残玉簟秋。轻解罗裳，独上兰舟。云中谁寄锦书来，雁字回时，月满西楼。花自飘零水自流。一种相思，两处闲愁。此情无计可消除，才下眉头。却上心头。

Li Qingzhao

Tune: "Yi Jian Mei"

Yearning

The fragrance of pink lotus has faded.
The bamboo mat tells that autumn is here to stay.
I gently take off my silken dress
and alone go to the fragrant boat.*
Who will send me a message through the cloud?
By the time the swan geese have returned in flight,
the western tower will be in full display
under bright moonlight.

Flowers drift randomly;
water flows freely.
In two different places, we feel the same yearning.
No way to get rid of this feeling.
Soon after I have stopped knitting my eyebrows,
my heart will be loaded with even more sorrows.

* 兰舟 here may also be an elegant name for bed.

李清照　lǐ qīng zhào
一剪梅　yī jiǎn méi

紅〇藕△ hóng ǒu pink lotus	香〇殘〇 xiāng cán fragrance has faded	玉△簟△秋● yù diàn qiū bamboo mat in autumn
輕〇解△ qīng jiě gently remove	羅〇裳〇 luó cháng a skirt of thin silk	
獨△上△ dú shàng alone go up	蘭〇舟● lán zhōu fragrant boat; elegant name of bed	
雲〇中〇 yún zhōng in the clouds	誰〇寄△ shéi jì who sends	錦△書〇來〇 jǐn shū lái a brocade letter
雁△字△ yàn zì swan geese in flight	回〇時〇 huí shí time of returning	
月△滿△ yuè mǎn moon(light) all over	西〇樓● xī lóu west tower	
花〇自△ huā zì flowers freely	飄〇零〇 piāo líng drift	水△自△流● shuǐ zì liú water flows freely
一△種△ yī zhòng one kind	相〇思〇 xiāng sī mutual yearning	
兩△處△ liǎng chǔ two places	閒〇愁● xián chóu random sorrow	
此△情〇 cǐ qíng this feeling	無〇計△ wú jì no way	可△消〇除〇 kě xiāo chú to remove
才〇下△ cái xià just lower	眉〇頭● méi tóu eyebrows	卻△上△心〇頭● què shàng xīn tóu but it rises to the heart

李清照

如梦令

常记溪亭日暮。沉醉不知归路。兴尽晚回舟,误入藕花深处。争渡。争渡。惊起一滩鸥鹭。

Li Qingzhao

Tune: "Ru Meng Ling"

Returning Home on a Boat

I am often reminded of the pavilion
by the stream at sunset.
We were too tipsy to find our way back.
Having exhausted our interests,
we returned late to the boat.
By mistake we went deep into where
the lotus flowers glow.
"Let me row!"
"Let me row!"
Our noises had frightened away
all the gulls and egrets on the shoal.

李清照　　lǐ qīng zhào
如夢令　　rú mèng lìng

常〇記△
cháng jì
often remember

溪〇亭〇
xī tíng
pavilion by the stream

日△暮▲
rì mù
at sunset

沉〇醉△
chén zuì
tipsily

不△知〇
bù zhī
didn't know

歸〇路▲
guī lù
way home

興△盡△
xìng jìn
interests have faded

晚△
wǎn
late

回〇舟〇
huí zhōu
returned to boat

誤△入△
wù rù
entered by mistake

藕△花〇
ǒu huā
lotus flowers

深〇處▲
shēn chù
deep place

爭〇渡▲
zhēng dù
fighting for rowing

爭〇渡▲
zhēng dù
fighting for rowing

驚〇起△
jīng qǐ
frightened

一△灘〇
yī tān
a shoal of

鷗〇鷺▲
ōu lù
gulls and egrets

327

李清照

点绛唇

蹴罢秋千，起来慵整纤纤手。露浓花瘦。薄汗轻衣透。 见有人来，袜铲金钗溜。和羞走。倚门回首。却把青梅嗅。

Li Qingzhao

Tune: "Dian Jiang Chun"

Shyness

She got up after playing with the swing.
Feeling tired, she casually stretched
her slender hands again.
Like dewdrops keeping a delicate flower wet,
her light clothes were moistened
by her own sweat.

Sensing that someone was coming, in shyness,
she ran away with her unrestrained socks.
Her golden pin almost fell off.
She stopped running and leaned
against the door.
Turning her head, she sniffed a green plum
as if nothing had happened at all.

李清照　　lǐ qīng zhào
點絳唇　　diǎn jiàng chún

蹴△罷△
cù bà
finished trampling on

秋○千○
qiū qiān
swing

起△來○
qǐ lái
got up

慵○整△
yōng zhěng
indolently adjust

纖○纖○手▲
xiān xiān shǒu
slender hands

露△濃○
lù nóng
dew is thick

花○瘦▲
huā shòu
flower is thin

薄△汗△
bó hàn
thin sweat

輕○衣○
qīng yī
light clothes

透▲
tòu
penetrated

見△
jiàn
seeing

有△人○
yǒu rén
someone

來○
lái
came

襪△鏟△
wà chǎn
socks slipped off

金○釵○
jīn chāi
gold hairpin

溜▲
liū
fell off

和○羞○
hé xiū
with shyness

走▲
zǒu
ran

倚○門○
yǐ mén
leaning on door

回○首▲
huí shǒu
looked back

卻△把△
què bǎ
but holding

青○梅○
qīng méi
green plum

嗅▲
xiù
sniffed

李清照

点绛唇

寂寞深闺,柔肠一寸愁千缕。惜春春去。几点催花雨。倚遍栏干,只是无情绪。人何处。连天衰草。望断归路。

Li Qingzhao

Tune: "Dian Jiang Chun"

Looking into the Distance

So solitary is my inner chamber.
Each inch of my heart is wrapped
by thousands of sorrowful threads.
In spite of my plea,
spring is not coming back.
Rain can make it hard for flowers to bear.

Leaning on every spot of the railing,
I am in no mood to enjoy the scene.
Where is he now?
What I see is but endless withering grass,
reaching the sky's brim.
Looking and looking, ah, he is
still nowhere to be seen!

李清照　**lǐ qīng zhào**
點絳唇　**diǎn jiàng chún**

寂△寞△
jì mò
lonely

深〇閨〇
shēn guī
chamber

柔〇腸〇
róu cháng
tender intestine (heart)

一△寸△
yī cùn
one inch

愁〇千〇縷▲
chóu qiān lǚ
sorrow: one thousand threads

惜△春〇
xī chūn
love spring

春〇去▲
chūn qù
spring is gone

幾△點△
jǐ diǎn
several drops

催〇花〇
cuī huā
flowing-hastening

雨▲
yǔ
rain

倚〇遍△
yǐ biàn
lean on entire

欄〇干〇
lán gān
railing

只△是△
zhǐ shì
but I am in

無〇
wú
no

情〇緒▲
qíng xù
mood

人〇
rén
person

何〇處▲
hé chǔ
where is

連〇天〇
lián tiān
sky- touching

衰〇草▲
shuāi cǎo
withering grass

望△斷△
wàng duàn
view is cut off

歸〇來〇
guī lái
returning

路▲
lù
road

李清照

凤凰台上忆吹箫

香冷金猊，被翻红浪，起来慵自梳头。任宝奁尘满，日上帘钩。生怕离怀别苦，多少事、欲说还休。新来瘦，非干病酒，不是悲秋。 休休。这回去也，千万遍阳关，也则难留。念武陵人远，烟锁秦楼。惟有楼前流水，应念我、终日凝眸。凝眸处，从今又添，一段新愁。

Li Qingzhao

Tune: "Feng Huang Tai Shang Yi Chui Xiao"

Lovesickness

The incense stops burning,
the golden-lion censor turns cold.
My quilt looks like red waves.
I manage to get up, but I am
too weary to have my hairdo made.
I let dust accumulate on my dressing case.
I don't get up until the sun shines
on the curtain rod.
Lest I am consumed by
the feelings of parting and leaving,
so many things I want to convey,
but am hesitant to say.
Recently I am losing weight.
It has nothing to do with
illness or drinking.
Neither is it caused by autumn feelings.

李清照　lǐ qīng zhào
鳳凰台上憶吹簫　fèng huáng tái shàng yì chuī xiāo

香〇冷△ *xiāng lěng* incense is cold	金〇猊〇 *jīn ní* gold-lion (censer)	
被△翻〇 *bèi fān* quilt overturns	紅〇浪△ *hóng làng* red waves	
起△來〇 *qǐ lái* get up	慵〇自△ *yōng zì* I am lazy	梳〇頭● *shū tóu* to comb hair
任△ *rèn* let	寶△奩〇 *bǎo lián* jewelry case	塵〇滿△ *chén mǎn* full of dust
日△ *rì* sun	上△ *shàng* rises above	簾〇鉤● *lián gōu* curtain hook
生〇怕△ *shēng pà* for fear of	離〇懷〇 *lí huái* parting feelings	別△苦△ *bié kǔ* parting pain
多〇少△事△ *duō shǎo shì* so many things	欲△說△ *yù shuō* wanting to say	還〇休● *hái xiū* but decide not to
新〇來〇瘦△ *xīn lái shòu* recently thin	非〇干〇 *fēi gān* nothing to do with	病△酒△ *bìng jiǔ* illness or drinking
不△是△ *bú shì* Is not	悲〇秋● *bēi qiū* lamenting autumn	

333

Forget about it! Forget about it!
He was so determined to leave this time.
Even if I repeated the Yang Pass refrains
more than a thousand times,
he wouldn't have changed his mind.
Like the Wuling fisherman, he is
in a faraway place.
I am here in a house surrounded by mist.
Only the water flowing in front notices
that I am looking afar all day long.
The place whereupon my eyes fix
will add a new set of sorrow from now on.

休○休●
xiū xiū
be done with it

這△回○	去△也△	
zhè huí	*qù yě*	
this time	(his) leaving	
千○萬△	遍△	陽○關○
qiān wàn	*biàn*	*yáng guān*
thousands	times	Yang Guan tune*
也△則△	難○留●	
yě zé	*nán liú*	
still	hard to make stay	
念△	武△陵○人○**	遠△
niàn	*wǔ líng rén*	*yuǎn*
thinking of	the Wuling person*	far away
煙○	鎖△	秦○樓●
yān	*suǒ*	*qín lóu*
mist	to lock in	private living quarter
惟○有△	樓○前○	流○水△
wéi yǒu	*lóu qián*	*liú shuǐ*
there is only	front of house	flowing water
應○念△我△	終○日△	凝○眸●
yìng niàn wǒ	*zhōng rì*	*níng móu*
should notice me	whole day long	to fix my eyes on
凝○眸○處△	從○今○	又△添○
níng móu chù	*cóng jīn*	*yòu tiān*
where my eyes fix on	from now on	add another
一△段△	新○愁●	
yī duàn	*xīn chóu*	
one part of	new sorrow	

* Yang Guan was a parting tune with trice repeated refrain.
** Wuling refers to the person who found himself in the Land of Peach Blossoms, a fictitious land of peace.

李清照

声声慢

寻寻觅觅，冷冷清清，凄凄惨惨戚戚。乍暖还寒时候，最难将息。三杯两盏淡酒，怎敌他、晚来风急。 雁过也，正伤心，却是旧时相识。 满地黄花堆积。憔悴损，如今有谁堪摘。守著窗儿，独自怎生得黑。梧桐更兼细雨，到黄昏、点点滴滴。者次第，怎一个、愁字了得。

Li Qingzhao

Tune: "Sheng, Sheng Man"

Sad Feelings

For what am I looking?
For what am I seeking?
So chilly, so dreary;
so miserable, so woeful, and so sorrowful.

At a time of sudden warmth and sudden chill,
it is hard to keep my mind still.
Two or three cups of light wine
hardly can quiet the gust wind at night.
Seeing a flock of geese passing by
only breaks my heart.
For they in the past conveyed messages
to me from afar.

李清照　　lǐ qīng zhào
聲聲慢　　shēng shēng màn

尋〇尋〇 *xún xún* search and search	覓△覓△ *mì mì* seek and seek	
冷△冷△ *lěng lěng* so cold	清〇清〇 *qīng qīng* so dreary	
凄〇凄〇 *qī qī* so miserable	慘△慘△ *cǎn cǎn* so woeful	戚△戚▲ *qī qī* so sorrowful
乍△暖△ *zhà nuǎn* suddenly warn	還〇寒〇 *huán hán* and suddenly cold	時〇候△ *shí hòu* at such a time
最△難〇 *zuì nán* most difficult	將〇息▲ *jiāng xī* to calm down (the mind)	
三〇杯〇 *sān bēi* three cups	兩△盞△ *liǎng zhǎn* two small cups	淡△酒△ *dàn jiǔ* light /weak wine
怎△敵△他〇 *zěn dí tā* how can it resist	晚△來〇 *wǎn ái* arriving in the evening	風〇急▲ *fēng jí* hurried wind
雁△過△也△ *yàn guò yě* swan geese passing by	正△傷〇心〇 *zhèng shāng xīn* just break my heart	
卻△是△ *què shì* turn out to be	舊△時〇 *jiù shí* old time	相〇識▲ *xiāng shí* acquaintances

337

The ground is piled up with yellow flowers,
so pallid, hurt, and withered.
Who now cares to pick them up?
Alone by the window, how long must I
wait until it gets dark?
Drizzling rain drifts
from the parasol tree at dusk,
drip by drip, drop by drop.
To sum up my feelings
at this very moment,
how can one single word of
"sorrow"
be enough!

滿△地△
mǎn dì
everywhere

黃○花○
huáng huā
yellow flowers

堆○積▲
duī jī
pile up

憔○悴△
qiáo cuì
withered

損△
sǔn
damaged

如○今○
rú jīn
now

有△誰○
yǒu shéi
who will

堪○摘▲
kān zhāi
bear to pluck

守△著△
shǒu zhāo
watching by

窗○兒○
chuāng ér
window

獨△自△
dú zì
alone

怎△生○
zěn shēng
how to wait

得△黑▲
de hēi
until dark

梧○桐○
wú tóng
parasol tree

更△兼○
gèng jiān
with also

細△雨△
xì yǔ
drizzle

到△黃○昏○
dào huáng hūn
when dusk sets in

點△點△
diǎn diǎn
drip by drip

滴△滴▲
dī dī
drop after drop

這△次△第△
zhě cì dì
at such a moment

怎△一△個△
zěn yī gè
how can one

愁○字△
chóu zì
word of "sorrow"

了△得▲
liǎo de
be enough

只恐双溪舴艋舟。载不动、许多愁。

But I am afraid that at Twin Brook,
the skiff there is very light.
How can it carry such a heavy load
of sorrows without being capsized?

— Li Qingzhao

Yue Fei (1103–1141)

岳飞

Yue Fei was born in present-day Henan during the southern Song Dynasty. His father named him Fei (Fly) because a big bird was flying around at the exact time when he was born. Yue Fei was also called Peng Ju, which means "pushing ahead toward an objective."

Yue was raised in a poor family with little formal education. However, he studied very hard on his own and indulged himself in books about military strategies and history. At the age of eleven, he started to develop the martial skills: fighting with a sword or spear. When he was twenty years old, he joined the army as a captain.

Yue Fei was better known as a famous general and a patriot than a poet. However, his *ci* "To Recover Lost Land" written to the tune of *Man Jiang Hong* was one of the most frequently recited poems in China after his death. Today, few educated Chinese have not listened at least once to the popular music and song based on his original lyric.

Yue was promoted to higher ranks after a significant number of victories against the *jin* invaders. As a general, Yue was often frustrated as his efforts to recover the lost land were thwarted by minister Qin Huei, who put personal interest above the country. Those in power were more interested in appeasement than fighting in the battlefield.

Yue Fei, a patriot and hero, was put to death for a trumped-up charge when he was only thirty-eight years old. He wrote, just before he died, his famous quotation: "So obvious to heaven and sun; so obvious to heaven and sun" (天日昭昭，天日昭昭).

岳飞

小重山

昨夜寒蛩不住鸣。惊回千里梦,已三更。起来独自绕阶行。人悄悄,帘外月胧明。白首为功名。旧山松竹老,阻归程。欲将心事付瑶琴。知音少,弦断有谁听。

Yue Fei

Tune: "Xiao Zhong Shan"

Reflections

The crickets kept chirping last night.
When I suddenly awoke from my distant dream,
it was already past midnight.
I got up and walked around the steps.
People were quiet.
Outside the curtain, the moon appeared bright.

Seeking official titles has turned my hair white.
Growing old on the former mountain
are bamboos and pines.
Homeward journey is delayed.
I wish to convey my feelings through the lute.
But few who can understand the tune's meanings.
With a broken string, who is willing to listen?

岳飛　　**yuè fēi**
小重山　**xiǎo zhòng shān**

昨△夜△ zuó yè last night	寒○蛩○ hán qióng cold cricket	不△住△鳴● bù zhù míng kept chirping
驚○回○ jīng huí awaken suddenly	千○里△夢△ qiān lǐ mèng thousand *li* dream	已△三○更● yǐ sān gèng already after midnight
起△來○ qǐ lái got up	獨△自△ dú zì alone	繞△階○行● rào jiē xíng walking around steps
人○悄△悄△ rén qiǎo qiǎo people quiet	簾○外△ lián wài outside curtain	月△朧○明● yuè lóng míng moon was bright
白△首△ bái shǒu white hair	為△ wéi for	功○名● gōng míng official rank
舊△山○ jiù shān former mountain	松○竹△ sōng zhú pines and bamboos	老△ lǎo old
阻△ zǔ prevent	歸○程● guī chéng journey of return	
欲△將○ yù jiāng wanting to	心○事△ xīn shì what's on the mind	付△瑤○琴● fù yáo qín entrust decorated lute
知○音○ zhī yīn one who can appreciate	少△ shǎo few	
弦○斷△ xián duàn broken string	有△誰○ yǒu shéi who is there to	聽● tīng listen

岳飞

满江红

怒发冲冠，凭阑处、潇潇雨歇。抬望眼、仰天长啸，壮怀激烈。三十功名尘与土，八千里路云和月。 莫等闲白了少年头，空悲切。靖康耻，犹未雪。臣子恨，何时灭。驾长车，踏破贺兰山缺。壮志饥餐胡虏肉，笑谈渴饮匈奴血。待从头、收拾旧山河，朝天阙。

Yue Fei

Tune: "Man Jiang Hong"

To Recover Lost Land

My angry hair seems like
rushing up to the hat.
I lean on the rails where
the rushing rain has stopped
and the sky is clear.
I lift my eyes and heave a long sigh.
My ambition is soaring in my mind.
Official ranks of thirty years are but dirt and dust.
A journey of eight thousand *li* accompanied by clouds
and moon lies ahead.
Don't let youthful hair turn into white head.
Alas, time can't be brought back.

岳飛　**yuè fēi**
滿江紅　**mǎn jiāng hóng**

怒△髮△
nù fā
angry hair

衝○冠○
chōng guàn
burst into hat

憑○闌○處△
píng lán chǔ
where lean on rails

瀟○瀟○雨△
xiāo xiāo yǔ
rushing rain

歇▲
xiē
has stopped

抬○望△眼△
tái wàng yǎn
lift looking eyes

仰△天○
yǎng tiān
look up the sky

長○嘯△
cháng xiào
heave a long sigh

壯△懷○
zhuàng huái
soaring ambition

激○烈▲
jī liè
stirs up

三○十△
sān shí
thirty years

功○名○
gōng míng
official ranks

塵○與△土△
chén yǔ tǔ
dust and dirt

八△千○里△
bá qián lǐ
eight thousand li

路△
lù
road

雲○和○月▲
yún hé yuè
clouds and moon

莫△等△閒○
mò děng xián
don't let it easily

白△了△
bái le
become white

少△年○頭○
shào nián tóu
young man's head

空○悲○切▲
kōng bēi qiē
to regret in vain

The shame of Jing Kang* has yet to avenge.
When can the humiliation of being
called subjects be changed?
Let's ride on a long line of chariots.
Tread the opening of He Lan Mountain until it is flat.
When hungry, let soldiers eat the barbarian's flesh.
Let them quench their thirst by drinking
their blood during smiling chats.
Let's start all over and recover our lost land.
Then we will return to the palace in triumph.

* It refers to the two kings being captured by the invaders in the year of Jing Kang (1127).

靖△康○恥△
jìng kāng chǐ
shame of Jing Kang

猶○未△雪▲
yóu wèi xuě
not yet avenged

臣○子△恨△
chén zi hèn
humiliation being called subjects

何○時○滅▲
hé shí miè
when can erased

駕△
jià
ride on

長○車○
cháng chē
long line of chariots

踏△破△
tà pò
tread and break

賀△蘭○山○
hè lán shān
He Lan Mountain

缺▲
quē
indentation

壯△志△
zhuàng zhì
brave men

飢○餐○
jī cān
eat while hungry

胡○虜△肉△
hú lǔ ròu
barbarian's meat

笑△談○
xiào tán
happily chat

渴△飲△
kě yǐn
drink in thirst

匈○奴○血▲
xiōng nú xiě
the Huns' blood

待△從○頭○
dài cóng tóu
wait to start again

收○拾△
shōu shí
recovering

舊△山○河○
jiù shān hé
lost land

朝○
cháo
to be received by

天○闕▲
tiān quē
(the emperor) in the palace

莫等闲白了少年头，空悲切。

Don't let youthful hair turn into white head.
Alas, time can't be brought back.

—Yue Fei

Lu You (1125–1210)

陆游

Lu You, known as Lu fang Weng (Liberated Old Man), was a prolific writer as well as a hero in the Song Dynasty. Soon after he was born, the troops of Tungusic Dynasty of Jin invaded and took over the Northern Song Dynasty. His family moved to the south, where he was raised and educated.

Lu did not succeed in his first attempt for the imperial examination. In the year 1153, he was the top examinee and awarded the rank of *jinshi*. His political career was not all that smooth due, in part, to his determination to recover the lost land in the north. His insistence to fight the enemy was often at odds with other officers who were in favor of appeasement.

In the year 1144, Lu was married to his cousin Tang Wan, whom he truly loved, at the age of twenty. The marriage lasted only about three years as Lu was under pressure from his mother to divorce his wife. The ground of the divorce: Lu's mother was not pleased with Tang.

A few years later, after the forced divorce, he happened to run into his ex-wife in Shen's Garden, which is now a tourist attraction in Shaoxing, Zhejiang province. Tang Wan invited Lu for diner after the encounter. Before he left Shen's Garden, Lu wrote his famous poem, in sadness, on the wall to the tune of *Cha Tou Feng* (p. 357). Tang Wan, a poet in her own right, harmonized Lu's poem with the same tune.

Lu You's poems are unrestrained and rich in content. Many of his poems have to do with military life and his patriotism. He died at the age of eighty-six.

陆游

卜算子·咏梅

驿外断桥边，寂寞开无主。已是黄昏独自愁，更著风和雨。　无意苦争春，一任群芳妒。零落成泥碾作尘，只有香如故。

Lu You

Tune: "Bu Suan Zi"

Plum Blossom

Outside the courier station;
by a broken bridge.
Blooming in solitude with no one to adore.
Feeling sad, alone as night's curtain
is about to fall.
You also must face wind and rain.

You have no desire to claim
for blooming first in spring.
So let other beautiful flowers show
their jealousies in vain.
Even if you are withered and crushed
to become mud or dust,
your flagrance will remain.

陆游　**lù yóu**
卜算子　**bǔ suàn zi**

○ = 平声 (*ping* or flat tone)
△ = 仄声 (*ze* or deflected tone)
● = 平声韵 (rhymed in *ping* or flat tone)
▲ = 仄声韵 (rhymed in *ze* or deflected tone)

驿△外△
yì wài
outside post station

寂△寞△
jì mò
lonely

已△是△
yǐ shì
already to be

更△著△
gèng zhuó
especially must bear

无○意△
wú yì
with no intention to

一△任△
yī rèn
just let

零○落△
líng luò
withered and fallen

只△有△
zhī yǒu
only

断△桥○
duàn qiáo
broken bridge

开○
kāi
to bloom

黄○昏○
huáng hūn
at dusk

风○和○
fēng hé
wind and

苦△争○
kǔ zhēng
be fighting bitterly for

群○芳○
qún fāng
other flowers

成○泥○
chéng ní
to become mud

香○
xiāng
fragrance

边○
biān
side

无○主▲
wú zhǔ
with no one (to appreciate)

独△自△愁○
dú zì chóu
to worry all alone

雨▲
yǔ
rain

春○
chūn
(being first in) spring

妒▲
dù
to show jealousies

碾△作△尘○
niǎn zuò chén
be crushed to dust

如○故▲
rú gù
as before

陆游

诉衷情

当年万里觅封侯。匹马戍梁州。关河梦断何处，尘暗旧貂裘。　胡未灭，鬓先秋。泪空流。此生谁料，心在天山，身老沧洲。

Lu You

Tune: "Su Zhong Qing"

Wishes Not Fulfilled

Years ago I marched three thousand miles
to seek the title of feudal lord.
On a horse, I fought to defend
the area of Liang Zhou.
My dream is cut short,
not knowing where at the frontier I was.
My old marten coat, now dust-laden,
still hangs on the wall.

The northern enemy has yet to be defeated;
my temples already look like the autumn frost.
In vain, I let my tears fall.
Who could foresee that in this life
I would grow old by a river while
my mind is still obsessed with
the Heavenly Mountains as before.

陆游 **lù yóu**
訴衷情 **sù zhōng qíng**

當○年○
dāng nián
in those years

萬△里△
wàn lǐ
ten thousand li

覓△封○侯●
mì fēng hòu
seek the title of feudal lord

匹△馬△
pǐ mǎ
on a horse

戍△
shù
defended

梁○州●
liáng zhōu
Liang Zhou

關○河○
guān hé
strategic pass and river

夢△斷△
mèng duàn
woke up from dream

何○處△
hé chǔ
not knowing where

塵○暗△
chén àn
darken by dust

舊△
jiù
old

貂○裘●
diāo qiú
marten coat

胡○
hú
northern enemies

未△滅△
wèi miè
not yet defeated

鬢△
bìn
temples

先○秋●
xiān qiū
look like (frost in) autumn

淚△
lèi
tears

空○流●
kōng liú
shed in vain

此△生○
cǐ shēng
this life

誰○料△
shéi liào
who can figure out

心○在△
xīn zài
heart is in

天○山○
tiān shān
Heavenly Mountain

身○
shēn
body

老△
lǎo
to grow old

滄○洲●
cāng zhōu
by the river

陆游

鹊桥仙

茅檐人静，蓬窗灯暗，春晚连江风雨。林莺巢燕总无声，但月夜、常啼杜宇。　催成清泪，惊残孤梦，又拣深枝飞去。故山犹自不堪听，况半世、飘然羁旅。

Lu You

Tune: "Que Qiao Xian"

On Hearing Cuckoo's Crying at Night

At night in late spring,
the entire river comes with wind and rain.
Under the thatched house, all is quiet.
By the simple window is a lamp with dim light.
No sound from the orioles and swallows.
But under this moonlit night,
I constantly hear cuckoo cry.

The noise interrupts my unfinished dream.
I can't help but shedding tears in strings.
Then the cuckoo flies away deep into the branches.
I couldn't bear to hear the crying
of cuckoos on my native hill.
Being away from home for half of a lifetime,
how can I sleep or sit still?

陆游　lù yóu
鹊桥仙　què qiáo xiān

茅○檐○	人○静△	
máo yán	rén jìng	
straw eaves	people are quiet	
蓬○窗○	灯○暗△	
péng chuāng	dēng àn	
simple window	lamp is dim	
春○晚△	连○江○	风○雨▲
chūn wǎn	lián jiāng	fēng yǔ
spring night	whole river	wind and rain
林○莺○	巢○燕○	总△无○声○
lín yīng	cháo yàn	zǒng wú shēng
orioles in the woods	swallows in the nest	all are silent
但△月△夜△	常○啼○	杜△宇▲
dàn yuè yè	cháng tí	dù yǔ
but in moonlit night	often cry	cuckoos
催○成○	清○泪△	
cuī chéng	qīng lèi	
urge to shed	clear tears	
惊○残○	孤○梦△	
jīng cán	gū mèng	
frighten unfinished	solitary dream	
又△拣△	深○枝○	飞○去▲
yòu jiǎn	shēn zhī	fēi qù
then choose	deep branches	to fly away
故△山○	犹○自△	不△堪○听○
gù shān	yóu zì	bù kān tīng
native mountain	still	can't bear to hear
况△半△世△	飘○然○	羁△旅▲
kuàng bàn shì	piāo rán	jī lǚ
let alone	drift about alone	out traveling

陆游

鹊桥仙

一竿风月，一蓑烟雨，家在钓台西住。卖鱼生怕近城门，况肯到、红尘深处。　潮生理棹，潮平系缆，潮落浩歌归去。时人错把比严光，我自是、无名渔父。

Lu You

Tune: "Que Qiao Xian"

An Ordinary Fishman

In moonlight, I hold a fishing pole in the wind.
I wear a coir raincoat whenever I fish in mist and rain.
I live at the west side, close to the fishing pier.
I am even afraid of selling my fish near the city gate.
Going deep into the mundane world
is not a decision I want to make.

In high tide, I work on my scull.
In slack tide, I tie up the cordage.
In lower tide, I sing loudly on my way home.
People have mistaken me as Yan Guan.
But I am just an ordinary fisherman, so unknown.

陆游　**lù yóu**
鵲橋仙　**què qiáo xiān**

一△竿〇
yī gān
a fishing pole

風〇月△
fēng yuè
wind and moon

一△蓑〇
yī suō
a coir raincoat

煙〇雨△
yān yǔ
mist and rain

家〇在△
jiā zài
my home is at

釣△台〇
diào tái
a platform for fishing

西〇住▲
xī zhù
residence at west side

賣△魚〇
mài yú
to sell fish

生〇怕△
shēng pà
be afraid

近△城〇門〇
jìn chéng mén
to go near city gate

況△肯△到△
kuàng kěn dào
not to mention willing to go

紅〇塵〇
hóng chén
mundane world

深〇處▲
shēn chù
deep into

潮〇生〇
cháo shēng
in high tide

理△棹△
lǐ zhào
maintain the scull

潮〇平〇
cháo píng
in slack tide

繫△纜△
xì lǎn
tie the cordage

潮〇落△
cháo luò
In low tide

浩〇歌〇
hào gē
sing aloud

歸〇去▲
guī qù
return home

時〇人〇
shí rén
nowadays, people

錯△把△
cuò bǎ
mistakenly

比△嚴〇光〇
bǐ yán guāng
compare me to Yan Guang

我△自△是△
wǒ zì shì
I am only

無〇名〇
wú míng
a nobody

漁〇父▲
yú fù
fisherman

357

陆游

钗头凤

红酥手。黄滕酒。满城春色宫墙柳。东风恶。欢情薄。一怀愁绪，几年离索。错错错。　春如旧。人空瘦。泪痕红浥鲛绡透。桃花落。闲池阁。山盟虽在，锦书难托。莫莫莫。

Lu You

Tune: "Chai Tou Feng"

Where to Send My Letter?

Your pinkish and smooth hand
brought me some wine of a precious brand.
The whole city is filled with the colors of spring.
But the willows are separated by
an imperial wall from within.
The east wind is vile.
No longer can we be together having good time.
My mind is full of sorrowful thoughts.
How can one bear several years of separation by force?
Wrong, wrong, wrong!

Spring is still the same.
You and I grow thin in vain.
Your silken kerchief is soaked in red
with traces of rouged tears.
Peach flowers will fall.
The pond and pavilion will not be visited any more.
The vow between us remains true.
But how can letters get through?
No, no, no!

陸游 lù yóu
釵頭鳳 chāi tóu fèng

紅○酥○手▲
hóng sū shǒu
pinkish and smooth hands

黃○縢○酒▲
huáng téng jiǔ
gold-brand wine

滿△城○
mǎn chéng
entire city

春○色△
chūn sè
in spring colors

宮○牆○柳▲
gōng qiáng liǔ
willows inside palace wall

東○風○惡▲
dōng fēng è
east wind is vicious

歡○情○薄▲
huān qíng bó
joyful feeling is thin

一△懷○
yī huái
a bosom of

愁○緒△
chóu xù
sorrowful feelings

幾△年○
jǐ nián
several years of

離○索▲
lí suǒ
being separated in despair

錯▲錯▲錯▲
cuò cuò cuò
wrong, wrong, wrong!

春○如○舊▲
chūn rú jiù
spring is the same

人○空○瘦▲
rén kōng shòu
I grow thin in vain

淚△痕○
lèi hén
traces of tears

紅○浥△
hóng yì
moistened in red

鮫○綃○透▲
jiāo xiāo tòu
silken kerchief is penetrated

桃○花○落▲
táo huā luò
peach blossom to fall

閒○池○閣▲
xián chí gé
unattended pond and pavilion

山○盟○
shān méng
vow between lovers

雖△在△
suī zài
though still exists

錦△書○
jǐn shū
letters

難○托▲
nán tuō
hard to depend on

莫▲莫▲莫▲
mò mò mò
no, no, no!

陆游

鹧鸪天

家住苍烟落照间。丝毫尘事不相关。斟残玉瀣行穿竹，卷罢黄庭卧看山。贪啸傲，任衰残。不妨随处一开颜。元知造物心肠别，老却英雄似等闲。

Lu You

Tune: "Zhe Gu Tian"

Away from the World

Facing the setting sun, my home is
shrouded by green mist.
Trivial mundane affairs have nothing to do with me.
After I am through with my refined wine,
I take a leisure walk in the grove of bamboos.
Having finished reading a book of Taoism, I lie
down and enjoy the mountainside.

I whistle and behave freely;
I let myself grow old naturally.
Everywhere I go, I set myself free
with laughter and smiles.
I know all along the Creator has his own device.
He just wants to let heroes become useless:
growing old and decline.

陸游　　lù yóu
鷓鴣天　zhè gū tiān

家○住△	蒼○煙○	落△照△間●
jiā zhù	cāng yān	luò zhào jiān
my house is situated	in the green mist	facing the descending sun
絲○毫○	塵○事△	不△相○關●
sī háo	chén shì	bù xiāng guān
trivial	mundane affairs	don't concern me
斟○殘○	玉△瀣△	行○穿○竹△
zhēn cán	yù xiè	xíng chuān zhú
pour the remaining	elegant wine	walk through bamboo grove
卷△罷△	黃○庭○	臥△看△山●
juǎn bà	huáng tíng	wò kàn shān
after finish reading	"Huang Ting"	lie down looking at mountain
貪○	嘯△傲△	
tān	xiào ào	
to be fond of	talking and behaving freely	
任△	衰○殘●	
rèn	shuāi cán	
let (myself) become	weaken and declined	
不△妨○	隨○處△	一△開○顏●
bù fáng	suí chù	yī kāi yán
may as well	everywhere	laugh or smile
元○知○	造△物△	心○腸○別△
yuán zhī	zào wù	xīn cháng bié
know already	the Creator	has his own purpose
老△卻△	英○雄○	似△等△閒●
lǎo què	yīng xióng	sì děng xián
treating old	heroes	as if they are useless

361

陆游

鹧鸪天

家住东吴近帝乡。平生豪举少年场。十千沽酒青楼上，百万呼卢锦瑟傍。身易老，恨难忘。尊前赢得是凄凉。君归为报京华旧，一事无成两鬓霜。

Lu You

Tune: "Zhe Gu Tian"

Getting Old

I used to live near the empirical city
of the State of East Wu.
I did something gallantly in my early life.
In the green mansion I spent a lot to buy wine.
With singing girls by my side,
I gambled without limit by throwing dice.

It is easy for this body to become old.
But it is so hard to forget my regrets and sorrows.
My reward in front of the wine vessel
was but a miserable life.
Please bring a message to my old friends
in the capital city if you please:
Before I could accomplish anything,
my temples are already frosty in appearance.

陆游　**lù yóu**
鹧鸪天　**zhè gū tiān**

家○住△ *jiā zhù* my house is situated	東○吳○ *dōng wú* in eastern Wu	近△帝△鄉● *jìn dì xiāng* near the empirical city
平○生○ *píng shēng* this life	豪○舉△ *háo jǔ* gallant act	少△年○場● *shào nián cháng* was my show when young
十△千○ *shí qiān* ten thousands	沽○酒△ *gū jiǔ* spent on buying wine	青○樓○上△ *qīng lóu shàng* in the brothel
百△萬△ *bǎi wàn* one million	呼○盧○ *hū lú* gambled on throwing dice	錦△瑟△傍● *jǐn sè bàng* accompanied by singing girls
身○ *shēn* body	易△老△ *yì lǎo* easy to get old	
恨△ *hèn* regret	難○忘● *nán wàng* hard to forget	
尊○前○ *zūn qián* before wine vessel	贏○得△ *yíng de* what can be obtained	是△凄○涼● *shì qī liáng* is misery
君○歸○ *jūn guī* on your return	為○報△ *wéi bào* to thank	京○華○舊△ *jīng huá jiù* old friends in the capital
一△事△ *yī shì* (not) a thing	無○成○ *wú chéng* accomplished	兩△鬢△霜● *liǎng bìn shuāng* both temples are like frost

陆游

鹧鸪天

懒向青门学种瓜。只将渔钓送年华。双双新燕飞春岸，片片轻鸥落晚沙。歌缥渺，橹呕哑。酒如清露鲊如花。逢人问道归何处，笑指船儿此是家。

Lu You

Tune: "Zhe Gu Tian"

My Home

I am lazy to go to Blue Gate, learning how
to grow melons and squashes.
I only wish to spend my best years
with my fishing pole.
In spring, swallows fly in pairs to the shore.
Seagulls, one by one, descend to
the sandbar at nightfall.

Let my song drift in the air.
Let the sound of sculling fill my ears.
I drink wine that tastes like clear dew.
I fry salt-fish that smell like flowery scent.
Everyone I meet asks where do I reside?
"That is my home," I point to my boat
and say with a smile.

陆游 **lù yóu**
鹧鸪天 **zhè gū tiān**

懒△向△	青○門○	學△種△瓜●
lǎn xiàng	*qīng mén*	*xué zhòng guā*
lazy to go toward	Blue Gate	learn to grow squash

只△將○	漁○釣△	送△年○華●
zhī jiāng	*yú diào*	*sòng nián huá*
only want to use	fishing pole	to spend my best years

雙○雙○	新○燕△	飛○春○岸△
shuāng shuāng	*xīn yàn*	*fēi chūn àn*
pair after pair	new swallows	fly toward the spring shore

片△片△	輕○鷗○	落△晚△沙●
piàn piàn	*qīng ōu*	*luò wǎn shā*
one by one	flying seagulls	go down and rest on the evening sand

歌○	縹△渺△	
gē	*piāo miǎo*	
song	far and indistinct	

櫓△	嘔△啞●	
lǔ	*ǒu yǎ*	
an oar; a scull	making its sound	

酒△如○	清○露△	鮓△如○花●
jiǔ rú	*qīng lù*	*zhǎ rú huā*
wine is like	clear dew	salt-fish is like flower

逢○人○	問△道△	歸○何○處△
féng rén	*wèn dào*	*guī hé chǔ*
whoever meets (me)	will ask	where are you returning

笑△指△	船○兒○	此△是△家●
xiào zhǐ	*chuán ér*	*cǐ shì jiā*
smilingly point to	the boat	this is my home

陆游

秋波媚
七月十六日晚登高兴亭望长安南山

秋到边城角声哀。烽火照高台。悲歌击筑，凭高酹酒，此兴悠哉。多情谁似南山月，特地暮云开。灞桥烟柳，曲江池馆，应待人来。

Lu You

Tune: "Qiu Bo Mei"

Looking at South Mountain

Autumn is here at the frontier.
The horn sounds so sad.
Flames brighten the Happy Pavilion.
Sung with solemn fervor, songs are heightened
with percussion instruments.
Leaning on height, I drink a toast to the sky.
The spirit and morale are so unrestrained and high.

The moon over the South Mountain
is unequally compassionate.
It drives for us the evening clouds away.
By the misty willows at the Ba Bridge,
or by the pond at the guesthouse,
there must be people waiting for us
to return in earnest.

陆游　**lù yóu**
秋波媚　**qiū bō mèi**

秋○到△
qiū dào
autumn comes to

烽○火△
fēng huǒ
flames

悲○歌○
bēi gē
to sing with solemn fervor

憑○高○
píng gāo
leaning on height

此△興△
cǐ xìng
this excitement

多○情○
duō qíng
passionate

特△地△
tè dì
specially designated

灞△橋○
bà qiáo
a bridge over the Ba River

曲○江○
qū jiāng
winding river

應△待△
yìng dài
should wait for

邊○城○
biān chéng
frontier

照△
zhào
brighten

擊△筑△
jī zhù
to strike a stringed instrument

酹△酒△
lèi jiǔ
drink a toast

悠○哉●
yōu zāi
is without restrain

誰○似△
shéi sì
who can be more like

暮△雲○
mù yún
clouds at dusk

煙○柳△
yān liǔ
misty willows

池○館△
chí guǎn
guesthouse with a pond

人○來●
rén lái
someone to come

角△聲○哀●
jiǎo shēng āi
sound of horn is sad

高○台△
gāo tái
high tower (Happy Pavilion)

南○山○月△
nán shān yuè
the moon over South Mountain

開●
kāi
to open

陆游

渔家傲

东望山阴何处是。往来一万三千里。写得家书空满纸。流清泪。书回已是明年事。寄语红桥桥下水。扁舟何日寻兄弟。行遍天涯真老矣。愁无寐。鬓丝几缕茶烟里。

Lu You

Tune: "Yu Jia Ao"

Thinking of My Brother

Where is Shan Yin? I look afar toward the east.
A round trip will require me
to travel thirteen thousand *li*.
A letter mailed home with no empty space
still leaves me with a feeling of emptiness.
I can't help but shedding my tears.
Until next year, no reply is expected to receive.

Please send a message to the water
under the Red Bridge.
When will the shallow boat start
searching for my brother?
Traveling over remote places,
I am getting old indeed.
I am too sad to fall asleep.
I see a few threads of my temple hair
in the vapor-rising tea.

陸游　**lù yóu**
漁家傲　**yú jiā ào**

東〇望△ *dōng wàng* looking toward east	山〇陰〇 *shān yīn* Shan Yin	何〇處△是▲ *hé chǔ shì* where it is
往△來〇 *wǎng lái* come and go	一△萬△ *yī wàn* ten thousand	三〇千〇里▲ *sān qiān lǐ* three thousand li
寫△得△ *xiě de* finish writing	家〇書〇 *jiā shū* letter to send home	空〇滿△紙▲ *kōng mǎn zhǐ* full of words for nothing
流〇 *liú* shed	清〇淚▲ *qīng lèi* clear tears	
書〇回〇 *shū huí* return mail	已△是△ *yǐ shì* will have to be	明〇年〇事▲ *míng nián shì* a matter for next year
寄△語△ *jì yǔ* send word to the	紅〇橋〇 *hóng qiáo* Red Bridge	橋〇下△水▲ *qiáo xià shuǐ* water under the bridge
扁△舟〇 *biǎn zhōu* a shallow boat	何〇日△ *hé rì* when	尋〇兄〇弟▲ *xún xiōng dì* to find a brother
行〇遍△ *xíng biàn* traveling all over	天〇涯〇 *tiān yá* distant places	真〇老△矣▲ *zhēn lǎo yǐ* (I am) really getting old
愁〇 *chóu* with sorrow	無〇寐▲ *wú mèi* unable to fall asleep	
鬢△絲〇 *bìn sī* temple hair	幾△縷△ *jǐ lǚ* a few threads of	茶〇煙〇里▲ *chá yān lǐ* in the midst of tea and smoke

陆游

浣溪沙

懒向沙头醉玉瓶。唤君同赏小窗明。夕阳吹角最关情。忙日苦多闲日少,新愁常续旧愁生。客中无伴怕君行。

Lu You

Tune: "Wan Xi Sha"

Don't Leave Me Behind

Not in the spirit to drink near the beach and river.
Why not come and enjoy moonlight
by the window together.
The sound of a flute in sunset
best conveys our parting feelings in the heart.
Too busy in our life and too little leisure time.
Before old sorrows have gone
new ones have arrived.
With no other companion in this alien town,
I fear that you will leave me behind.

陆游　**lù yóu**
浣溪沙　**wǎn xī shā**

懒△向△ *lǎn xiàng* lazy to go to	沙○頭○ *shā tóu* beach and river	醉△玉△瓶● *zuì yù píng* drink wine in jade cup
喚△君○ *huàn jūn* invite you	同○賞△ *tóng shǎng* to enjoy together	小△窗○明● *xiǎo chuāng míng* moonlight reflecting on little window
夕△陽○ *xī yáng* sunset	吹○角△ *chuī jiǎo* flute blowing	最△關○情● *zuì guān qíng* most relate to parting feelings
忙○日△ *máng rì* busy days	苦△多○ *kǔ duō* are too many	閒○日△少△ *xián rì shǎo* leisure days are too few
新○愁○ *xīn chóu* new sorrow	常○續△ *cháng xù* often to follow	舊△愁○生● *jiù chóu shēng* old sorrows still growing
客△中○ *kè zhōng* on road in a foreign land	無○伴△ *wú bàn* without companion	怕△君○行● *pà jūn xíng* be afraid you leave

陆游

临江仙

鸠雨催成新绿，燕泥收尽残红。春光还与美人同。论心空眷眷，分袂却匆匆。 只道真情易写，那知怨句难工。水流云散各西东。半廊花院月，一帽柳桥风。

Lu You

Tune: "Lin Jiang Xian"

Spring Feelings

Pigeons can be seen.
Rains hasten the pace of new greens.
Swallows have picked up all the fallen
petals from the flower bed.
Springtime and a beautiful lady
have something in common.
Talking intimately with her will bring
up tender feeling in vain.
Parting with her will find the time hurrying.

They say it is easy to write about true affection.
But it is hard to write a line about grief to perfection.
Waters flow to the east;
clouds vanish to the west.
The courtyard moon brightens
the flowers in half of the corridor.
The wind by the bridge blows both
the willows and someone's hat.

陆游　　lù yóu
临江仙　lín jiāng xiān

鸠○雨△ jiū yǔ pigeons and rain	催○成○ cuī chéng hasten	新○绿△ xīn lǜ new green
燕△泥○ yàn ní swallows and soil	收○尽△ shōu jìn collect all	残△红● cán hóng fallen flowers
春○光○ chūn guāng springtime	还○与△ huán yǔ also	美△人○同● měi rén tóng resemble a beauty
论△心○ lùn xīn to talk heartily	空○ kōng nothing but	眷△眷△ juàn juàn remembering with tender feelings
分○袂△ fēn mèi to part	却△ què but	匆○匆● cōng cōng too hurry
只△道△ zhǐ dào only say	真○情○ zhēn qíng true affection	易△写△ yì xiě easy to write
那△知○ nà zhī but know not	怨△句△ yuàn jù bitter sentences	难○工● nán gōng hard to make perfect
水△流○ shuǐ liú water flows	云○散△ yún sǎn clouds vanish	各△西○东● gè xī dōng each go their own way
半△廊○ bàn láng half corridor	花○ huā yuàn flowers	院△月△ yuè courtyard moon
一△帽△ yī mào one hat	柳△ liǔ qiáo willows	桥○风● fēng bridge wind

只道真情易写，那知怨句难工。

They say it is easy to write
about true affection.
But it is hard to write
a line about grief to perfection.

— Lu You

Xing Qiji (1140–1207)

辛弃疾

Xing Qiji, also named Tan Fu, was born in Licheng (present-day Jinan, Shandong province). In his middle-age years, he liked to call himself Jiaxuan, which was also the name of his residence.

When Xing was born, the Jurchun had already occupied the northern part of the Song empire. As a child, Xing was encouraged by his grandfather, a former high-level officer, to enlist in the military with a goal to recover the lost land from the Jurchun. At the age of twenty-one, he participated in an uprising movement in an attempt to overturn the Jin regime. The following year, he decided to join the Southern Song Dynasty in the south.

Xing was regarded as a hero for his contributions as a military general. His political career, however, was not at all smooth as his ambition to recapture the lost land was often met with the appeasement policy of the time. For a period of eight years, he retreated in Jiang Xi, leading a leisure life.

Xing was better known as a prolific poet than a national hero. He was considered the equal of Su Shi in terms of the breadth and depth of *ci* poetry in the Song Dynasty. Together they were also referred to as the "Haofang School," a style of poetry that allowed poets to express their ideas and feelings without undue restrains and restrictions.

More than six hundred poems survived him. His poetry is noted for its wide range in topics. He especially liked to write in plain language about military life and rural life. His style is quite unique: humorous, artistic, and often philosophical.

辛弃疾

菩萨蛮·书江西造口壁

郁孤台下清江水。中间多少行人泪。西北望长安。可怜无数山。青山遮不住。毕竟东流去。江晚正愁余。山深闻鹧鸪。

Xing Qiji

Tune: "Pu Sa Man"

Written on the Wall

The Clear River lies below the Solitary Tower.
It contains the tears of so many wayfarers.
I gaze northwest toward Chang'an.
But in between here and there
numerous mountains stand.

Though blue mountains do obstruct my view,
the eastward-running current cannot stay still.
By the river at dust, I feel heavy in my heart.
The sound of a francolin deep from the hill
tears my heart apart.

辛棄疾　xīn qì jí
菩薩蠻　cǎi sāng zi

○ ＝ 平声 (*ping* or flat tone)
△ ＝ 仄声 (*ze* or deflected tone)
● ＝ 平声韵 (rhymed in *ping* or flat tone)
▲ ＝ 仄声韵 (rhymed in *ze* or deflected tone)

鬱△孤○台○
yù gū tái
Gloomy-Lonely Tower

中○間○
zhōng jiān
in between

西○北△
xī běi
northwest

可△憐○
kě líng
it's pitiful

青○山○
qīng shān
blue mountains

畢△竟△
bì jìng
after all

江○晚△
jiāng wǎn
evening by the river

山△深○
shān shēn
deep in mountain

下△
xià
under

多○少△
duō shǎo
how many

望△
wàng
look far at

無○數△
wú shù
numerous

遮○
zhē
obstruct

東○
dōng
eastward

正△
zhèng
just

聞○
wén
can hear

清○江○水▲
qīng jiāng shuǐ
the water of Clear River

行○人○淚▲
xíng rén lèi
wayfarers' tears

長○安●
cháng ān
Chang'an

山●
shān
mountains

不△住▲
bù zhù
can't be halted

流○去▲
liú qù
flows and vanishes

愁○餘●
chóu yú
feel sad

鷓△鴣●
zhè gū
the sound of partridge

377

辛弃疾

采桑子·书博山道中壁

少年不识愁滋味，爱上层楼。爱上层楼，为赋新词强说愁。　而今识尽愁滋味，欲说还休。欲说还休。却道天凉好个秋。

Xing Qiji

Tune: "Cai Sang Zi"

Making Up the Feelings of Sorrow

As a youngster, I didn't know
the sorrow of life.
Up one storey, I climbed.
Up one storey, I climbed.
I made up feelings of sorrow
to fit my new lyrical lines.

Now that I have tasted sorrows
of all kinds.
Before I talk, I halt.
Before I talk, I halt.
I say, instead,
"What a cool day in the fall!"

辛棄疾　**xīn qì jí**
采桑子　**cǎi sāng zi**

少△年〇 *shào nián* youngster	不△識△ *bù shí* didn't know	愁〇滋〇味△ *chóu zī wèi* real taste of sorrow
愛△ *ài* love to	上△ *shàng* go up to	層〇樓● *céng lóu* tower
愛△ *ài* love to	上△ *shàng* go up to	層〇樓● *céng lóu* tower
為△賦△ *wéi fù* for composing	新〇詞〇 *xīn cí* new lyrics	強〇說△愁● *qiáng shuō chóu* make up sorrow
而〇今〇 *ér jīn* now that	識△盡△ *shí jìn* (I) have experienced	愁〇滋〇味△ *chóu zī wèi* what sorrows are alike
欲△ *yù* wanting	說△ *shuō* to say	還〇休● *huán xiū* but stop
欲△ *yù* wanting	說△ *shuō* to say	還〇休● *huán xiū* but stop
卻△道△ *què dào* end up saying	天〇涼〇 *tiān liáng* it is cool	好△個△秋● *hǎo gè qiū* what a autumn day

辛弃疾

青玉案·元夕

东风夜放花千树。更吹落、星如雨。宝马雕车香满路。凤箫声动，玉壶光转，一夜鱼龙舞。蛾儿雪柳黄金缕，笑语盈盈暗香去。众里寻他千百度。蓦然回首，那人却在，灯火阑珊处。

Xing Qiji

Tune: "Qing Yu An"

Lantern Festival

A thousand trees are set to bloom at night
by the east wind.
It even blows the starry fireworks like rain.
Beautiful horses and carved carriages
fill the road with fragrance.
Phoenix flutes produce song after song.
The moon moves and beams around.
Fish and dragon lanterns dance all night long.

Her hair is decorated with snowy willows,
golden threads, and butterfly hairpins.
With laughter, she leaves behind some mild scent.
I look for her in the crowd a thousand times.
All of a sudden, I turn my head and look back,
she is right over there under the dim light.

辛棄疾　xīn qì jí
青玉案　qīng yù àn

東〇風〇 *dōng fēng* east wind	夜△放△ *yè fàng* set to bloom at night	花〇千〇樹▲ *huā qiān shù* thousand flowery trees
更△ *gèng* even	吹〇落△ *chuī luò* blows down	星〇如〇雨▲ *xīng rú yǔ* starry fireworks like rain
寶△馬△ *bǎo mǎ* beautiful horses	雕〇車〇 *diāo chē* carved carriages	香〇滿△路▲ *xiāng mǎn lù* road filled with scent
鳳△簫〇 *fèng xiāo* phoenix flutes	聲〇 *shēng* sound	動△ *dòng* vibrates
玉△壺△ *yù hú* moon	光〇 *guāng* light	轉△ *zhuǎn* turns
一△夜△ *yī yè* a whole night	魚〇龍〇 *yú long* fish and dragon	舞▲ *wǔ* to dance
蛾〇兒〇 *é ér* butterflies (hairpin)	雪△柳△ *xuě liǔ* silvery willows	黃〇金〇縷▲ *huáng jīn lǚ* golden thread
笑△語△ *xiào yǔ* talk laughingly	盈〇盈〇 *yíng yíng* ease and graceful	暗△香〇去▲ *àn xiāng qù* leave mild scent behind
眾△裏△ *zhòng lǐ* in the crowd	尋〇他〇 *xún tā* to look for her	千〇百△度▲ *qiān bǎi dù* thousand times
驀△然〇 *mò rán* suddenly	回〇首△ *huí shǒu* turn and look back	那△人〇 *nà rén* that person
卻△在△ *què zài* turn out to be	燈〇火△ *dēng huǒ* lantern light	闌〇珊〇處▲ *lán shān chǔ* where it is dim

辛弃疾

西江月·夜行黄沙道中

明月别枝惊鹊，清风半夜鸣蝉。稻花香里说丰年。听取蛙声一片。 七八个星天外，两三点雨山前。旧时茅店社林边。路转溪桥忽见。

Xing Qiji

Tune:" Xi Jiang Yue"

Walking at Night on Yellow Sand Road

The magpies on the slanting branches
are startled by the shifting moonlight.
The cicadas chirp in breeze at midnight.
The fragrance of the rice spikes
promises an abundant year.
The croaking of frogs can be
heard everywhere.

Seven or eight stars shine
up there in the sky.
Two or three drops of rain
start to come down at the mountainside.
I turn around and cross a bridge over the stream.
By a temple of the God of Earth,
I see the former thatched inn.

辛棄疾　**xīng qì jí**
西江月　**xī jiāng yuè**

明〇月△
míng yuè
bright moon

清〇風〇
qīng fēng
clear wind

稻△花〇
dào huā
spikes of the rice plants

聽〇取△
tīng qǔ
hear

七△八△個△
qī bā gè
seven or eight

兩△三〇點△
liǎng sān diǎn
two or three drops of

舊△時〇
jiù shí
old times

路△轉△
lù zhuǎn
turn to the road

別△枝〇
bié zhī
slanting branches

半△夜△
bàn yè
midnight

香〇里△
xiāng lǐ
amid fragrance

蛙〇聲〇
wā shēng
sound of frogs

星〇
xīng
stars

雨△
yǔ
rain

茅〇店△
máo diàn
a thatched store

溪〇橋〇
xī qiáo
stream bridge

驚〇鵲△
jīng què
frighten the magpies

鳴〇蟬●
míng chán
cicadas chirp

說△豐〇年●
shuō fēng nián
signal an abundant year

一△片▲
yī piàn
everywhere

天〇外△
tiān wài
up in the sky

山〇前●
shān qián
in front of the mountain

社△林〇邊●
shè lín biān
by the temple of the God of Earth

忽△見▲
hū jiàn
suddenly is in sight

辛弃疾

西江月

醉里且贪欢笑，要愁那得功夫。近来始觉古人书。
信着全无是处。 昨夜松边醉倒，问松我醉如何。
只疑松动要来扶。以手推松曰去。

Xing Qiji

Tune: "Xi Jiang Yue"

Drunkenness

Even in drunkenness, I love to be joyful.
I don't have the time to be sorrowful.
Lately I begin to question the ancient books
I have read through.
They cannot be entirely believed to be true.

I was drunk and fell down beside
a pine tree last night.
"Am I drunk?" I asked it, the pine.
But I was afraid it would move itself to help me.
I pushed it back and said, "Go away, please!"

辛棄疾　**xīng qì jí**
西江月　**xī jiāng yuè**

醉△里△	且△貪○	歡○笑△
zuì lǐ	*qiě tān*	*huān xiào*
drunken	but hate to leave	joy and laughter

要△愁○	那△得△	功○夫●
yào chóu	*nà de*	*gōng fū*
for sorrow	how can I have	time and effort

近△來○	始△覺△	古△人○書●
jìn lái	*shǐ jué*	*gǔ rén shū*
recently	start to find out	books written by the ancients

信△著△	全○無○	是△處▲
xìn zhù	*quán wú*	*shì chù*
to believe in	completely without	correct viewpoint

昨△夜△	松○邊○	醉△倒△
zuó yè	*sōng biān*	*zuì dào*
last night	beside a pine tree	fell in drunk

問△松○	我△醉△	如○何●
wèn sōng	*wǒ zuì*	*rú hé*
asked the pine	I drank	how was it

只△疑○	松○動△	要△來○扶●
zhī yí	*sōng dòng*	*yào lái fú*
only to be afraid	the pine would move	wanting to raise me up

以△手△	推○松○	曰△去▲
yǐ shǒu	*tuī sōng*	*yuē qù*
with my hand	pushed the pine	saying, "go away!"

辛弃疾

西江月·示儿曹以家事付之

万事云烟忽过，百年蒲柳先衰。而今何事最相宜。宜醉宜游宜睡。　早趁催科了纳，更量出入收支。乃翁依旧管些儿。管竹管山管水。

Xing Qiji

Tune: "Xi Jiang Yue"

Admonition to My Son

Like clouds and mist, all things
will vanish in a hurry.
My body is like a catkin willow, which
will wither before it reaches one hundred.
The most appropriate things for me to do now
are to get drunk, to travel, and to sleep.

For taxes, take care of them as soon as you are ready.
Be sure to balance the payment and receipt.
This old man will still manage to do a few things.
Like looking after the bamboo grove, the hill, and stream.

辛棄疾　**xīng qì jí**
西江月　**xī jiāng yuè**

萬△事△
wàn shì
ten thousand things

雲○煙○
yún yān
like cloud and mist

忽△過△
hū guò
gone in a hurry

百△年○
bǎi nián
one hundred years

蒲○柳△
pú liǔ
big catkin willow

先○衰●
xiān shuāi
wither first

而○今○
ér jīn
now

何○事△
hé shì
what thing

最△相○宜●
zuì xiāng yí
is most appropriate

宜○醉△
yí zuì
good to get drunk

宜○遊○
yí yóu
good to travel

宜○睡▲
yí shuì
good to sleep

早△趁△
zǎo chèn
do it early

催○科○
cuī kē
pay taxes

了△納△
liǎo nà
finish payment

更△量○
gèng liàng
weigh more carefully

出△入△
chū rù
in and out

收○支●
shōu zhī
pay and receive

乃△翁○
nǎi wēng
this old man

依○舊△
yī jiù
still will

管△些○兒●
guǎn xiē ér
take care of these things

管△竹△
guǎn zhú
take care of bamboos

管△山○
guǎn shān
take care of the hill

管△水▲
guǎn shuǐ
take care of water

辛弃疾

鹧鸪天·送人

唱彻阳关泪未干。功名馀事且加餐。浮天水送无穷树，带雨云埋一半山。今古恨，几千般。只应离合是悲欢。江头未是风波恶，别有人间行路难。

Xing Qiji

Tune: Zhe Gu Tian

Seeing a Friend Off

Tears cannot be restrained though we have
repeatedly sung the Yang Pass's third refrain.
Eating well for good health
is more important than official rank and wealth.
With endless trees on the banks,
the water will carry you under the vast sky.
The moistened clouds will
partially cover the mountainside.
From ancient to modern times,
grief has its multifarious kinds.
Parting evokes sadness;
reunion brings delight.
On river and shore, one is expected to face
wind, waves, and tides.
But nowhere is as hard to decipher
as the human mind.

辛棄疾　　xīn qì jí
鷓鴣天　　zhè gū tiān

唱△徹△ chàng chè finished singing	陽〇關〇 yáng guān Yang Pass	淚△未△乾● lèi wèi gān tears not yet dried
功〇名〇 gōng míng official rank	餘〇事△ yú shì trivial thing	且△加〇餐● qiě jiā cān but eating well is important
浮〇天〇 fú tiān floating sky	水△送△ shuǐ sòng water to (be) escorted	無〇窮〇樹△ wú qióng shù endless trees
帶△雨△ dài yǔ with rain	雲〇埋〇 yún mái clouds to bury	一△半△山● yī bàn shān half of the mountain
今〇古△ jīn gǔ ancient to modern	恨△ hèn grief	
幾△千〇 jǐ qiān several thousand	般● bān kinds	
只△應〇 zhī yìng should (not) be	離〇合△ lí hé parting and uniting	是△悲〇歡● shì bēi huān to be sadness and joyfulness
江〇頭〇 jiāng tóu river and shore	未△是△ wèi shì not (necessarily) to be	風〇波〇惡△ fēng bō è violent waves and wind
別△有△ bié yǒu there is still	人〇間〇 rén jiān in human world	行〇路△難● xíng lù nán the road is even harder

辛弃疾

鹧鸪天·代人赋

晚日寒鸦一片愁。柳塘新绿却温柔。若教眼底无离恨，不信人间有白头。肠已断，泪难收。相思重上小红楼。情知已被山遮断，频倚阑干不自由。

Xing Qiji

Tune: "Zhe Gu Tian"

Parting Sorrow: Writing for Someone

Late in the day, crow cawing intensifies my
feeling of sadness.
The freshly green willows by
the pond show their tenderness.
If parting grief could not be sensed
and felt in the heart,
there would be fewer white-headed people among us.
My heart is wrenched;
my tears cannot be stopped.
With a heavy heart I again
ascend the little red tower.
Fully aware that the image of you
is obstructed by the mountain.
But I can't help leaning on the railing
to look repeatedly into the distance.

辛棄疾　**xīn qì jí**
鷓鴣天　**zhè gū tiān**

晚△日△ *wǎn rì* late in the day	寒○鴉○ *hán yā* crow in cool weather	一△片△愁● *yī piàn chóu* sorrow everywhere
柳△塘○ *liǔ táng* willows by the pond	新○綠△ *xīn lǜ* new green	卻△溫○柔● *què wēn róu* but show tenderness
若△教○ *ruò jiào* if we let	眼△底△ *yǎn dǐ* before us	無○離○恨△ *wú lí hèn* no parting grief
不△信△ *bù xìn* don't believe	人○間○ *rén jiān* in the human world	有△白△頭● *yǒu bái tóu* there are white-headed people
腸○ *cháng* intestines (heart)	已△斷△ *yǐ duàn* have broken	
淚△ *lèi* tears	難○收● *nán shōu* can't be held back	
相○思○ *xiāng sī* lovesickness	重○上△ *zhòng shàng* mount again	小△紅○樓● *xiǎo hóng lóu* little red tower
情○知○ *qíng zhī* knowing obviously	已△被△ *yǐ bèi* (view of him) is	山○遮○斷△ *shān zhē duàn* obstructed by mountain
頻○倚△ *pín yǐ* leaning on repeatedly	闌○干○ *lán gān* railings	不△自△由● *bù zì yóu* without freedom

辛弃疾

鹧鸪天·东阳道中

扑面征尘去路遥。香篝渐觉水沉销。山无重数周遭碧，花不知名分外娇。人历历，马萧萧。旌旗又过小红桥。愁边剩有相思句，摇断吟鞭碧玉梢。

Xing Qiji

Tune: "Zhe Gu Tian"

Marching on the Road

Dust brushes my face
as we march to a distant place.
The aloeswood in the pouch begins to fade.
Mountain upon mountain, the greens
everywhere catch my eyes.
Unknown wild flowers are dazzling and bright.

So orderly the soldiers march.
So loudly the horses neigh.
With waving banners, we again pass
another small red bridge.
The only thing that occupies my mind
is to come up with some yearning lines.
I break the whip's jade-green handle by
waving it too many times.

辛棄疾　**xīn qì jí**
鷓鴣天　**zhè gū tiān**

撲△面△	征○塵○	去△路△遙●
pū miàn	*zhēng chén*	*qù lù yáo*
brush face	marching dust	road to go is far

香○篝○	漸△覺△	水△沉○銷●
xiāng gōu	*jiàn jué*	*shuǐ chén xiāo*
fragrant basket	gradually feels like	aloeswood has faded

山○	無○重○數△	周○遭○碧△
shān	*wú zhòng shù*	*zhōu zāo bì*
mountains	too numerous to count	green all around

花○	不△知○名○	分△外△嬌●
huā	*bù zhī míng*	*fèn wài jiāo*
flowers	unknown	especially charming

人○	歷△歷△	
rén	*lì lì*	
people (soldiers)	(march) so orderly	

馬△	蕭○蕭●	
mǎ	*xiāo xiāo*	
horses	whinny	

旌○旗○	又△過△	小△紅○橋●
jīng qí	*yòu guò*	*xiǎo hóng qiáo*
banners	again pass	little red bridge

愁○邊○	剩△有△	相○思○句△
chóu biān	*shèng yǒu*	*xiāng sī jù*
only thing to worry about	left with	lines of lovesickness

搖○斷△	吟○鞭○	碧△玉△梢●
yáo duàn	*yín biān*	*bì yù shāo*
break it by waving	chanting whip	emerald-jade end

辛弃疾

鹧鸪天

欲上高楼去避愁。愁还随我上高楼。经行几处江山改，多少亲朋尽白头。归休去，去归休。不成人总要封侯。浮云出处元无定，得似浮云也自由。

Xing Qiji

Tune: :Zhe Gu Tian"

Sorrows

I wish to avoid sorrow by climbing the high tower.
But sorrow still follows me as closely as ever.
Whenever I revisit familiar places,
I am alarmed by the changes in scenery.
So many of my relatives and friends
are now with white hair.
Go home and retire.
Go home and enjoy life.
Not everyone needs official rank and ties.
No one knows the origin of the floating clouds.
But I won't mind being as free as the clouds in the sky.

辛棄疾　　xīn qì jí
鷓鴣天　　zhè gū tiān

欲△上△
yù shàng
wanting to ascend

高○樓○
gāo lóu
high tower

去△避△愁●
qù bì chóu
to avoid sorrow

愁○還○
chóu huán
sorrow still

隨○我△
suí wǒ
follows me

上△高○樓●
shàng gāo lóu
going up to the high tower

經○行○
jīng xíng
walking through

幾△處△
jǐ chǔ
several places

江○山○改△
jiāng shān gǎi
landscapes have changed

多○少△
duō shǎo
how many

親○朋○
qīn péng
relatives and friends

盡△白△頭●
jìn bái tóu
all have become white-headed

歸○
guī
go back

休○去△
xiū qù
to retire

去△
qù
go

歸○休●
guī xiū
back and retire

不△成○
bù chéng
not necessarily

人○總△
rén zǒng
every person ought to

要△封○侯●
yào fēng hóu
achieve some official rank

浮○雲○
fú yún
floating clouds

出△處△
chū chù
where they are from

原○無○定△
yuán wú dìng
no certainty

得△似△
de sì
if one can be like

浮○雲○
fú yún
floating clouds

也△自△由●
yě zì yóu
will enjoy freedom

辛弃疾

踏莎行

庚戌中秋后二夕带湖篆冈小酌

夜月楼台，秋香院宇。笑吟吟地人来去。是谁秋到便凄凉，当年宋玉悲如许。　随分杯盘，等闲歌舞。问他有甚堪悲处。思量却也有悲时，重阳节近多风雨。

Xing Qiji

Tune: "Ta Suo Xing"

Autumn Feelings

Moon shines upon the tower and terrace at night.
Autumn's fragrance can be felt
both outside and inside.
People come and go smilingly.
Who greets autumn's arrival with so much misery?
Song Yu is known for expressing
his autumn feelings in his time.

He can drink and eat as he wishes.
He can sing and dance as he likes.
What causes him to feel so dreary and why?
On second thought, there is indeed a time to feel sad.
As the Double Nine Festival approaches,
frequent wind and rain can be really bad.

辛棄疾　　　xīng qì jí
踏莎行　　　tà suō xíng

夜△月△
yè yuè
night moon

樓○台○
lóu tái
tower and terrace

秋○香○
qiū xiāng
autumn fragrance

院△宇▲
yuàn yǔ
courtyard and house

笑△吟○吟○地△
xiào yín yín dì
smilingly

人○
rén
people

來○去▲
lái qù
come and go

是△誰○
shì shéi
who is the one

秋○到△
qiū dào
when autumn arrives

便△凄△涼○
biàn qī liáng
be in a dreary mood

當○年○
dāng nián
in those years

宋△玉△
sòng yù
Song Yu

悲○如○許▲
bēi rú xǔ
was so sad

隨○分△
suí fèn
as one wishes

杯○盤○
bēi pán
cup and dishes
(drink and eat)

等△閒○
děng xián
at anytime

歌○舞▲
gē wǔ
can sing and dance

問△他○
wèn tā
ask him

有△甚△
yǒu shèn
is there anything

堪○悲○處▲
kān bēi chǔ
to make one sorrowful

思○量○
sī liàng
to think carefully

卻△也△有△
què yě yǒu
there is indeed

悲○時○
bēi shí
time to feel sad

重○陽○節△
chóng yáng jié
Double Nine Festival

近△
jìn
approaches

多○風○雨▲
duō fēng yǔ
so many winds and rains

辛弃疾

清平乐·村居

茅檐低小。溪上青青草。醉里吴音相媚好。白发谁家翁媪。大儿锄豆溪东。中儿正织鸡笼。最喜小儿无赖，溪头卧剥莲蓬。

Xing Qiji

Tune: "Qing Ping Le"

Rural Living

With thatch eaves, the house is low and small.
The grass by the stream is green.
Growing tipsy, they affectionately flatter
each other with their southern dialect.
What family is this old couple with grey hair?
East of the stream, the eldest son works
on the bean field with a hoe.
The middle son is busy weaving
a cage for the chickens.
They love dearly the youngest son
who likes to play and having fun.
By the stream he lies down,
peeling off the lotus seedpods one by one.

辛棄疾　　**xīn qì jí**
清平樂　　**qīng píng lè**

茅〇檐〇
máo yán
straw eaves

低〇小▲
dī xiǎo
low and small

溪〇上△
xī shàng
above stream

青〇青〇
qīng qīng
green

草▲
cǎo
grass

醉△裏△
zuì lǐ
in tipsiness

吳〇音〇
wú yīn
southern ascent

相〇媚△好▲
xiāng mèi hǎo
to lovingly please each other

白△髮△
bái fā
white hair

誰〇家〇
shéi jiā
whose family

翁〇媼▲
wēng ǎo
old man and old woman

大△兒〇
dà ér
eldest son

鋤〇豆△
chú dòu
hoes the bean field

溪〇東●
xī dōng
east stream

中〇兒〇
zhōng ér
middle son

正△織△
zhèng zhī
is weaving

雞〇籠●
jī lóng
chicken cage

最△喜△
zuì xǐ
like the most

小△兒〇
xiǎo ér
youngest son

無〇賴△
wú lài
(for being) naughty

溪〇頭〇
xī tóu
head of stream

臥△剝△
wò bō
peel off

蓮〇蓬●
lián péng
seedpods of lotus

辛弃疾

清平乐·独宿博山王氏庵

绕床饥鼠。蝙蝠翻灯舞。屋上松风吹急雨。破纸窗间自语。平生塞北江南。归来华发苍颜。布被秋宵梦觉，眼前万里江山。

Xing Qiji

Tune: "Qing Ping Le"

Reflections at Night

A hungry rat searches around my bed.
About the lamp some bats flirt.
The wind blows the pines.
On top of the roof the rain strikes.
The torn window paper sounds like whispering.
I defend my country north and south my whole life.
Now I have returned with an aging look and grey hair.
Warmed by only a thin quilt, I wake up from my dream this autumn night.
A thousand *li* of rivers and mountains suddenly appear in front of my eyes.

辛棄疾　　xīn qì jí
清平樂　　qīng píng lè

繞△床○
rào chuáng
around the bed

飢○鼠▲
jī shǔ
hungry rat

蝙○蝠△
biān fú
bats

翻○燈○
fān dēng
circle the lamp

舞▲
wǔ
dance

屋△上△
wū shàng
on top of the roof

松○風○吹○
sōng fēng chuī
wind blows the pines

急△雨▲
jí yǔ
rushing rain

破△紙△
pò zhǐ
torn paper

窗○間○
chuāng jiān
between the window

自△語▲
zì yǔ
talk to itself

平○生○
píng shēng
this life

塞○北△
sāi běi
northern frontier

江○南●
jiāng nán
river south

歸○來○
guī lái
return home

華○髮△
huá fā
grey hair

蒼○顏●
cāng yán
aging complexion

布△被△
bù bèi
sheeting

秋○宵○
qiū xiāo
autumn night

夢△覺△
mèng jué
awaken from a dream

眼△前○
yǎn qián
before my eyes

萬△里△
wàn lǐ
thousand li

江○山●
jiāng shān
rivers and mountains

辛弃疾

破阵子·为陈同父赋壮语以寄

醉里挑灯看剑，梦回吹角连营。八百里分麾下炙，五十弦翻塞外声。沙场秋点兵。 马作的卢飞快，弓如霹雳弦惊。了却君王天下事，赢得生前身后名。可怜白发生。

Xing Qiji

Tune: "Po Zhen Zi"

To Chen Liang: Military Review

Drunken, I stirred the wick and looked at the sword.
I dreamt of a bugle blowing in the entire camp.
Barbecued beef was allocated
to soldiers under each command.
Sounds of stringed instruments could be heard
at this northern land.
To prepare for the battle, an autumn review of troop
was held beforehand.

Horses galloped at full speed.
The twang of bows sounds like thunder
coming to my ears.
We were instructed by the supreme ruler
to accomplish the great feat.
A fame in life and death is what I will get.
What a pity to see my grey hair.

辛棄疾　　xīn qì jí
破陣子　　pò zhèn zi

醉△里△ zuì lǐ drunk	挑○燈○ tiāo dēng stir the wick of lamp	看△劍△ kàn jiàn looked at the sword
夢△回○ mèng huí dreamed about	吹○角△ chuī jiǎo horn blowing	連○營● lián yíng in the entire camp
八△百△里△ bā bǎi lǐ eight hundred Li (cow)	分○麾○ fēn huī to be shared with each command	下△炙△ xià jiǔ for barbecuing
五△十△弦○ wǔ shí xián fifty strings (musical instruments)	翻○ fān produce	塞△外△聲● sāi wài shēng sound at frontier
沙○場○ shā cháng battleground	秋○ qiū in autumn	點△兵● diǎn bīng troop review
馬△作△ mǎ zuò horses behave	的△盧○ de lú De Lu (wild horses)	飛○快△ fēi kuài flying fast
弓○如○ gōng rú bows like	霹△靂△ pī lì thunder	弦○驚● xián jīng sharp tune of string
了△卻△ liǎo què done with	君○王○ jūn wáng supreme ruler	天○下△事△ tiān xià shì military victory
贏△得△ yíng de to have won	生○前○ shēng qián in life	身○後△名● shēn hòu míng flame after death
可△憐○ kě líng so pitiful	白△髮△ bái fā white hair	生● shēng has grown

辛弃疾

最高楼

吾拟乞归，犬子以田产未置止我，赋此骂之。

吾衰矣，须富贵何时。富贵是危机。暂忘设醴抽身去，未曾得米弃官归。穆先生，陶县令，是吾师。待葺个、园儿名佚老。更作个、亭儿名亦好。闲饮酒，醉吟诗。千年田换八百主，一人口插几张匙。便休休，更说甚，是和非。

Xing Qiji

Tune: "Zui Gao Lou"

On Wealth and Retirement: Chiding My Son

I am already old.
Wealth and high position, for how
long do I have to wait?
Wealth and high position can lead to crisis.
Master Mu left for neglecting
to serve him sweet wine.
Prefect Tao would rather give up his post
for not compensating with the deserving rice.
They both taught me a lesson in life.

辛棄疾　　　xīn qì jí
最高樓　　　zuì gāo lóu

吾〇衰〇矣△
wú shuāi yǐ
I am old now

須〇
xū
must I need

富△貴△
fù guì
wealth and high position

何〇時●
hé shí
when

富△貴△
fù guì
wealth and high position

是△
shì
is

危〇機●
wēi jī
a crisis

暫△忘〇
zàn wáng
just happen to forget

設△醴△
shè lǐ
offering sweet wine

抽〇身〇去△
chōu shēn qù
to get away

未△曾〇
wèi céng
not yet to

得△米△
de mǐ
gain rice (compensation)

棄△官〇歸●
qì guān guī
return home by giving up official position

穆△先〇生〇
mù xiān shēng
Master Mu

陶〇縣△令△
táo xiàn lìng
Prefect Tao

是△吾〇師●
shì wú shī
are my teachers

I will build a garden to be named "Free Old Folk."
And a pavilion called "Also Good."
I will drink at leisure and chant poetry
when feeling tipsy.
One-thousand-year-old farmland will change hands
eight hundred times.
How many spoons are needed for feeding
one single mouth?
Forget it! Forget it!
Not to even mention of what is right
and what is wrong!

待△茸△個△
dài qì gè
wait to repair

更△作△個△
gèng zuò gè
will even build a

閒○飲△酒△
xián yǐn jiǔ
drinking at ease

千○年○田○
qiān nián tián
one-thousand-year-old farmland

一△人○口△
yī rén kǒu
one person's mouth

便△休○休○
biàn xiū xiū
forget it, forget it

園○兒○
yuán ér
a garden

亭○兒○
tíng ér
pavilion

醉△吟○詩●
zuì yín shī
to chant poetry when feeling tipsy

換△
huàn
in exchange for

插○
chā
insert

更△說△甚△
gèng shuō shèn
not to speak of

名○佚△老△
míng yì lǎo
named Old Recluse

名○亦△好△
míng yì hǎo
to name it Also Good

八△百△主△
bā bǎi zhǔ
eight hundred owners

幾△張○匙●
jǐ zhāng chí
how many spoons

是△和○非●
shì hé fēi
right and wrong

若教眼底无离恨，不信人间有白头。

If parting grief could not be sensed
and felt in the heart,
there would be fewer white-headed
people among us.

— Xing Qiji

Jiang Kui (1152?–1221)

姜夔

Jiang Kui, also called Yao Zhang, was widely known as Baishi Daoren (White Stone Taoist). The exact year of his birth is thought to be between 1152 and 1155. Jiang was a native of Poyang, now a county in Jiangxi Province.

Jiang's father, a scholar and official, relocated his family to the Hanyang area in Hubei province. Jiang's mother died when he was only a few years old. His father was also deceased about ten years later. Jiang Kui lived with his elder sister during his growing years. He later moved to Huzhou, in Zhejiang province.

Unlike many other poets in his time, Jiang was never a title holder in public service as he, a multitalented person, failed repeatedly in the civil service examination. An excellent calligrapher, he made a living by mainly selling his artwork. Among his friends were poets Yang Wanli, Xing Qiji, and Fan Chengda. They often invited him to their homes as a guest. It was said that Jiang composed his famous "Nebulbous Fragrance" and "The Plum Blossoms"during his stay as a guest in Fan Chengda's house. Fan loved those two poems so much that he arranged the marriage between Jiang and Xiao Hong, one of the talented song girls in Fan's house. In one of his poems, Jiang allures to Xiao Hong by name.

Jiang led a wandering life in the Suzhou and Tai lake area. Like Zhou Bangyuan, he composed the music for some of the lyrics he wrote. Among the poems he composed with his own melodies were "Nebulous Fragrance" and "The Plum Blossoms."

姜夔

点绛唇

燕雁无心，太湖西畔随云去。数峰清苦。商略黄昏雨。第四桥边，拟共天随住。今何许。凭栏怀古。残柳参差舞。

Jiang Kui

Tune: "Dian Jiang Chun"

Reflections

From the west bank of Tai Lake,
the northern geese fly away freely
to the south with the clouds.
Several mountain peaks
appear deserted and anguished.
They seem to discuss how to get ready
for the rain in the evening.
By the Fourth Bridge, I wish
I could go into retreat with Tian Sui.
What has happened to the world affairs now?
Leaning on the railing, I reflect on
the events of the past.
The withering willows sway individually
from side to side.

姜夔　**jiāng kuí**
點絳唇　**diǎn jiàng chún**

燕△
yàn
swallows (northern)

雁△
yàn
wild geese

無○心○
wú xīn
not emotional

太△湖○
tài hú
Tai Lake

西○畔△
xī pàn
west bank

隨○雲○去▲
suí yún qù
gone with the clouds

數△峰○
shù fēng
several peaks

清○苦▲
qīng kǔ
deserted and anguished

商○略△
shāng luè
to discuss

黃○昏○
huáng hūn
evening

雨▲
yǔ
rain

第△四△橋○
dì sì qiáo
at the Fourth Bridge

邊○
biān
side

擬△共△
nǐ gòng
want to be with

天○隨○
tiān suí
Tian Sui (Lu Gui Mang)

住▲
zhù
live

今△
jīn
now

何○許▲
hé xǔ
how is it

憑○欄○
píng lán
lean on railing

懷○古▲
huái gǔ
reflecting on ancient events

殘○柳△
cán liǔ
withering willows

參○差○
cēn cī
unevenly

舞▲
wǔ
dance

411

姜夔

鹧鸪天

元夕有所梦

肥水东流无尽期。当初不合种相思。梦中未比丹青见，暗里忽惊山鸟啼。春未绿，鬓先丝。人间别久不成悲。谁教岁岁红莲夜，两处沉吟各自知。

Jiang Kui

Tune: "Zhe Gu Tian"

A Dream on the Night of Lantern Festival

The water of Fei to the east endlessly flows.
No seeds of love in the beginning
should have been sown.
Your image in my dream was not as clear
as in your portrait.
The crying of mountain birds caused me
to wake up in darkness with a startle.

Spring not yet green;
grey temples can be seen.
Parting grief over a long time will gradually subside.
Who let us chant poetry alone in two different places
on this Lantern Festival Night year after year?
Only you and I know.

姜夔　　jiāng kuí
鷓鴣天　zhè gū tiān

肥○水△
féi shuǐ
water of Fei

東○流○
dōng liú
flows to east

無○盡△期●
wú jìn qī
without end

當○初○
dāng chū
in the beginning

不△合△
bù hé
shouldn't have

種△相○思●
zhòng xiāng sī
planted a seed of love

夢△中○
mèng zhōng
in the dream

未△比△
wèi bǐ
(you are) not as

丹○青○見△
dān qīng jiàn
clear as (your) portrait

暗△裏△
àn lǐ
in darkness

忽○驚○
hū jīng
suddenly startled by

山○鳥△啼●
shān niǎo tí
crying of mountain birds

春○未△綠△
chūn wèi lǜ
spring not yet green

鬢△先○絲●
bìn xiān sī
temples already turned grey

人○間○
rén jiān
in the human world

別△久△
bié jiǔ
too long after parting

不△成○悲●
bù chéng bēi
no longer feel sad

誰○教△
shéi jiào
who would let

歲△歲△
suì suì
year after year

紅○蓮○夜△
hóng lián yè
on Lantern Night

兩△處△
liǎng chǔ
two places

沉○吟○
chén yín
silently chant

各△自△知●
gè zì zhī
only you and I know

413

姜夔

鹧鸪天

己酉之秋，苕溪记所见

京洛风流绝代人。因何风絮落溪津。笼鞋浅出鸦头袜，知是凌波缥缈身。红乍笑，绿长嚬。与谁同度可怜春。鸳鸯独宿何曾惯，化作西楼一缕云。

Jiang Kui

Tune: "Zhe Gu Tian"

A Beauty at Tiao Brook

You were an elegant beauty
of no equal in the capital city.
Why did you appear like
the drifting catkins at the ferry?
You wore ordinary sandals with protruding socks,
You seemed like a fairy who rose
above waves and did invisible walks.

You first opened your rouge lips with a smile.
Then kept knitting your blows without delight.
With whom did you spend the beautiful springtime?
How could a mandarin duck by itself spend a long night?
You transformed yourself into a wisp of clouds,
over the west tower, and disappeared in the sky.

姜夔 **jiāng kuí**
鷓鴣天 **zhè gū tiān**

京○洛△
jīng luò
Capital Lin An

風○流○
fēng liú
elegant and refined

絕△代△人●
jué dài rén
a beauty of no equal

因○何○
yīn hé
why

風○絮△
fēng xù
like drifting willow catkins

落△溪○津●
luò xī jīn
fall on the stream ferry

籠○鞋○
lóng xié
wearing a pair of sandals

淺△出△
qiǎn chū
slightly come out

鴉○頭○襪△
yā tóu wà
protruding socks

知○是△
zhī shì
know (immediately)

凌○波○
líng bō
rise above waves

縹△緲△身●
piāo miǎo shēn
illusionary body

紅○乍△笑△
hóng zhà xiào
red (lips): suddenly smile

綠△長○顰●
lǜ cháng pín
green (brows): often knit

與△誰○
yǔ shéi
with whom

同○度△
tóng dù
to share together

可△憐○春●
kě líng chūn
the beautiful springtime

鴛○鴦○
yuān yāng
mandarin duck

獨△宿△
dú sù
sleep alone

何○曾○慣△
hé céng guàn
how can one get used to

化△作△
huà zuò
transform into

西○樓○
xī lóu
west tower

一△縷△雲●
yī lǚ yún
a wisp of cloud

姜夔

踏莎行

自沔东来,丁未元日至金陵,江上感梦而作。

燕燕轻盈,莺莺娇软。分明又向华胥见。夜长争得薄情知,春初早被相思染。　别后书辞,别时针线。离魂暗逐郎行远。淮南皓月冷千山,冥冥归去无人管。

Jiang Kui

Tune: "Ta Suo Xing"

Seeing You in My Dream

So nimble and shapely, you walk
like a swallow;
So delicate and soft, you sound
like an oriole.
How can I miss you in my dream?
After a long night of trying to fall asleep,
you succeed in seeing your heartless lover again.
Your yearning has darkened the color of early spring.

Since we parted, I sent you poetry
to comfort your heart.
To keep me company,
I carry your gift of a needle box.
I feel as though you accompany me wherever I go.
The bright moon shines over Huan Nan.
So chilly and so many mountains are in between.
On your way home in the vastness,
who will accompany you?

姜夔 **jiāng kuí**
踏莎行 **tà suō xíng**

燕△燕△　　　輕○盈○
yàn yàn　　　qīng yíng
(like) a swallow　nimble and shapely

鶯○鶯○　　　嬌△軟▲
yīng yīng　　　jiāo ruǎn
(like) an oriole　delicate and soft

分○明○　　　又△向△　　　華○胥○見▲
fēn míng　　　yòu xiàng　　huá xū jiàn
obviously　　again toward　seeing in dream

夜△長○　　　爭○得△　　　薄△情○知○
yè cháng　　　zhēng de　　　bó qíng zhī
long night　　win over to let　the heartless lover know

春○初○　　　早△被△　　　相○思○染▲
chūn chū　　　zǎo bèi　　　xiāng sī rǎn
early spring　already to be　contaminated by longing

別△後△　　　書○辭○
bié hòu　　　shū cí
after departure　letters

別△時○　　　針○線▲
bié shí　　　zhēn xiàn
at the time of parting　thread and needle box

離○魂○　　　暗△逐△　　　郎○行○遠▲
lí hún　　　àn zhú　　　láng xíng yuǎn
soul of parting　secretly chase　as far as he goes

淮○南○　　　皓△月△　　　冷△千○山○
huái nán　　　hào yuè　　　lěng qiān shān
Huai Nan　　bright moon　chill of thousands of mountains

冥○冥○　　　歸○去△　　　無○人○管▲
míng míng　　　guī qù　　　wú rén guǎn
in darkness　return　no one cares

417

姜夔

暗香

辛亥之冬，予载雪诣石湖。止既月，授简索句，且征新声，作此两曲。石湖把玩不已，使工妓隶习之，音节谐婉，乃名之曰《暗香》《疏影》。

旧时月色。算几番照我，梅边吹笛。唤起玉人。不管清寒与攀摘。何逊而今渐老，都忘却、春风词笔。但怪得、竹外疏花，香冷入瑶席。江国，正寂寂。叹寄与路遥，夜雪初积。翠尊易泣。红萼无言耿相忆。长记曾携手处，千树压、西湖寒碧。又片片吹尽也，几时见得。

Jiang Kui

Tune: "An Xiang"

Nebulous Fragrance

The same old moonlight used to shine on me
as I blew my flute beneath a plum tree many times.
I used to wake her up from sleep.
Together we plucked a twig of blossoms,
be it cold or not.
Now that I am old, I no longer can
come up for my verse with beautiful lines.
But I can still smell the cold fragrance as we dine:
From the scattered flowers by the bamboo fence
outside.

姜夔　jiāng kuí
暗香　àn xiāng

舊△時○ *jiù shí* same old	月△色▲ *yuè sè* moon color	
算△ *suàn* to count	幾△番○ *jǐ fān* how many times	照△我△ *zhào wǒ* shines on me
梅○邊○ *méi biān* by the plum tree	吹○笛▲ *chuī dí* blow the flute	
喚△起△ *huàn qǐ* awaken	玉△人○ *yù rén* the fair lady	
不△管△ *bù guǎn* don't care about	清○寒○ *qīng hán* chilly	與△攀○摘▲ *yǔ pān zhāi* still pluck one
何○遜△ *hé xùn* He Xun	而○今○ *ér jīn* now	漸△老△ *jiàn lǎo* getting old
都○忘△卻△ *dōu wàng què* already forgot	春○風○ *chūn fēng* spring wind	詞○筆▲ *cí bǐ* fine poetic lines
但△怪△得△ *dàn guài de* can only blame	竹△外△ *zhú wài* bamboo outside	疏○花○ *shū huā* scattered flowers
香○冷△ *xiāng lěng* cold fragrance	入△ *rù* enter	瑤○席▲ *yáo xí* banquet table

It is so quiet by the riverside.
I wish to send you a message, but the road is too long.
Not to mention that snow has accumulated at night.
Looking at the silent flowers with a cup of wine,
it is hard not to shed tears from my eyes.
They evoke my memory of the old times.
I can't forget the places where we walked hand in hand.
The cold and emerald water of the west lake
seemed like embracing a thousand trees in red.
Now all the plum flowers have fallen and gone.
But when will we meet again?

江〇國△
jiāng guó
the side of river

正△
zhèng
right now

寂△寂▲
jì jì
is very quiet

嘆△
tàn
lament

寄△與△
jì yǔ
send a message

路△遙〇
lù yáo
so far away

夜△雪△
yè xuě
night snow

初〇積▲
chū jī
start to accumulate

翠△尊〇
cuì zūn
in front of wine cup

易△泣▲
yì qì
easy to shed tears

紅〇萼△
hóng è
red flowers calyxes

無〇言〇
wú yán
without words

耿△相〇憶▲
gěng xiāng yì
to indulge in memory

長〇記△
cháng jì
long remember

曾〇
céng
once

攜〇手△處△
xié shǒu chǔ
where we held hands

千〇樹△壓△
qiān shù yā
pressed by a thousand trees

西〇湖〇
xī hú
West Lake

寒〇碧▲
hán bì
look like chilly emerald

又△
yǔ
also

片△片△
piàn piàn
piece by piece

吹〇盡△也△
chuī jìn yě
all blown down

幾△時〇
jǐ shí
when

見△得▲
jiàn de
to see again

姜夔

疏影

苔枝缀玉，有翠禽小小，枝上同宿。客里相逢，篱角黄昏，无言自倚修竹。昭君不惯胡沙远，但暗忆、江南江北。想佩环、月夜归来，化作此花幽独。　犹记深宫旧事，那人正睡里，飞近蛾绿。莫似春风，不管盈盈，早与安排金屋。还教一片随波去，又却怨、玉龙哀曲。等恁时、重觅幽香，已入小窗横幅。

Jiang Kui

Tune: "Shu Ying"

The Plum Blossoms

On the jade-like and mossy branch.
the tiny kingfishers perch for the night.
Far away from home, I meet you
at the corner of a hedge at twilight.
Silently you lean on a bamboo
so slender and high.
Not used to the distant Tartar sands,
Wang Zhao Jun secretly longed for her homeland:
Yangtze River's southern and northern lands.
I fancy her return with tingling pendant in moonlight.
She transforms herself into a flower of solitary delight.

姜夔　　**jiāng kuí**
疏影　　**shū yǐng**

苔○枝○	綴△玉▲	
tái zhī	*zhuì yù*	
mossy branches	decorated with jade	

有△	翠△禽○	小△小△
yǒu	*cuì qín*	*xiǎo xiǎo*
to have	kingfishers	tiny

枝○上△	同○宿▲	
zhī shàng	*tóng sù*	
on the branch	perch together	

客△裡△	相○逢○	
kè lǐ	*xiāng féng*	
in a trip	meet each other	

籬○角△	黃○昏○	
lí jiǎo	*huáng hūn*	
corner of fence	at dusk	

無○言○	自△倚△	修○竹▲
wú yán	*zì yǐ*	*xiū zhú*
silently	lean on by herself	slender bamboo

昭○君○	不△慣△	胡○沙○遠△
zhāo jūn	*bù guàn*	*hú shā yuǎn*
Wang Zhao Jun	not used to	distant Tartar desert

但△暗△憶△	江○南○	江○北▲
dàn àn yì	*jiāng nán*	*jiāng běi*
but secretly long for	south of river	north of river

想△佩△環○	月△夜△	歸○來○
xiǎng pèi huán	*yuè yè*	*guī lái*
to fancy her	moonlight	returning

化△作△	此△花○	幽△獨▲
huà zuò	*cǐ huā*	*yōu dú*
transform into	this flower	solitary and unique

I recall the story about a princess at a palace so deep.
A petal flew on her forehead while she fell asleep.
Don't let blossoms be blown away by a spring breeze.
Protect them in a place made of golden bricks.
If you let petals be carried away by water,
don't complain of the flute's mourning song later.
Searching for fragrance then would be in vain.
For it has already become the window's painted screen.

猶○記△
yóu jì
still remember

那△人○
nà rén
that person

飛○近△
fēi jìn
flying near

莫△似△
mò sì
don't be like

不△管△
bù guǎn
disregard

早△與△
zǎo yǔ
to give early

還○教○
huán jiào
also let

又△卻△怨△
yòu què yuàn
again lament at

等△恁△時○
děng rèn shí
don't wait for another time

已△入△
yǐ rù
already enter

深○宮○
shēn gōng
deep palace court

正△
zhèng
was just

蛾○綠▲
é lǜ
green-painted brows

春○風○
chūn fēng
spring breeze

盈○盈○
yíng yíng
fullness (blossoms)

安○排○
ān pái
arrangement

一△片△
yī piàn
a petal

玉△龍○
yù lóng
Jade Dragon's

重○覓△
zhòng mì
search again

小△窗○
xiǎo chuāng
small window

舊△事△
jiù shì
old affair

睡△裡△
shuì lǐ
sleeping

金○屋▲
jīn wū
golden house

隨○波○去△
suí bō qù
drift with the waves

哀○曲▲
āi qū
mourning song

幽○香○
yōu xiāng
furtive scent

橫○幅▲
héng fú
the breadth of a picture

笼鞋浅出鸦头袜，知是凌波缥缈身。

You wore ordinary sandals with protruding socks,
You seemed like a fairy who rose
above waves and did invisible walks.

— Jiang Kui

Wu Wenying (1212–1272)

吴文英

Wu Wen Ying was a native of Siming (now Ningpo), Zhejiang province. His original family name was Weng before he was adopted by the Wu family.

Wu did not succed in passing the civil service examination. Consequently, he never pursued a career in governmental service. Although he had many friends who were wealthy and in power, he did not want to take advantage of his social connections. He was content to lead a humble but carefree life.

Wu was a prolific writer of *ci* poetry. He left behind more than 350 *ci* poems. His poetry has drawn a mixture of praises and criticism since his time. Some scholars considered his poems to be obscure, artificial, and somewhat shallow in substance. On the other hand, he was also praised for his emphasis on elegant style with smooth rhythm and diction. In general, Wu's poems have been given high mark when it comes to such things as imagination, allusions, and hidden meanings. He may be considered as a pioneer in what is now called *menglong shi,,*a style of poetey writing that appears to be misty and vague in meaning.

Wu was strongly influenced by Zhou Bang Yuan and Jiang Kui. Like Zhou and Jiang, Wu was known to have composed songs for his own lyrics.

吴文英

浣溪沙

门隔花深梦旧游。夕阳无语燕归愁。玉纤香动小帘钩。落絮无声春堕泪，行云有影月含羞。东风临夜冷於秋。

Wu Wenying

Tune: "Wan Xi Sha"

Feeling Sad in Late Spring

I dreamt of coming back once more.
Flower bushes were separated by a door.
The setting sun was speechless;
the returning swallow could not hide its sadness.
The air was filled with fragrance
as she moved the little hooks of the curtain.

Petals are silently falling.
So do teardrops of Spring.
Behind the floating clouds, the moon hides.
I can see the clouds' shadow at night.
The east wind at nightfall
is colder than the fall.

吳文英　**wú wén yīng**
浣溪沙　**wǎn xī shā**

○ = 平声 (*ping* or flat tone)
△ = 仄声 (*ze* or deflected tone)
● = 平声韵 (rhymed in *ping* or flat tone)
▲ = 仄声韵 (rhymed in *ze* or deflected tone)

門○隔△
mén gé
door separates

夕△陽○
xī yáng
setting sun

玉△纖○
yù xiān
delicate fingers

落△絮△
luò xù
falling petals

行○雲○
xíng yún
floating clouds

東○風○
dōng fēng
east wind

花○深○
huā shēn
deep flowers

無○語△
wú yǔ
without a word

香○動△
xiāng dòng
stir amid fragrance

無○聲○
wú shēng
silently

有○影△
yǒu yǐng
cast shadow

臨○夜△
lín yè
at this very night

夢△舊△游●
mèng jiù yóu
dream of past roaming

燕△歸○愁●
yàn guī chóu
swallow returns with sadness

小△簾○鉤●
xiǎo lián gōu
little curtain hooks

春○墮△淚△
chūn duò lèi
like spring shedding tears

月△含○羞●
yuè hán xiū
moon shows shyness

冷△於○秋●
lěng yú qiū
turns colder than autumn

429

吴文英

风入松

听风听雨过清明，愁草瘗花铭。楼前绿暗分携路，一丝柳，一寸柔情。料峭春寒中酒，交加晓梦啼莺。西园日日扫林亭，依旧赏新晴。黄蜂频扑秋千索，有当时、纤手香凝。惆怅双鸳不到，幽阶一夜苔生。

Wu Wenying

Tune: "Feng Ru Song"

Missing You

I spent my Tomb-Sweeping Day by listening
to the wind and rain.
I was in no mood to draft an epigraph for flowers'
burying.
In front of the house, the road where
we parted looked dense and green.
One thread of willows equals to
one inch of tender feeling.
I drown myself in wine in the chill of spring.
In my morning dream, I could vaguely
hear orioles chattering.

吴文英　**wú wén yīng**
风入松　**fēng rù sōng**

听○风○
tīng fēng
listen to wind

听○雨△
tīng yǔ
listen to rain

过△清○明●
guò qīng míng
spending the Tomb-Sweeping Day

愁○草△
chóu cǎo
no mood to draft

瘗△花○
yì huā
flowers burying

铭●
míng
epigraph

楼○前○
lóu qián
in front of storied house

绿△暗△
lǜ àn
densely green

分○携○路△
fēn xié lù
the road that we parted

一△丝○
yī sī
a thread of

柳△
liǔ
willow

一△寸△
yī cùn
one inch of

柔○情●
róu qíng
tender affection

料△峭△
liào qiào
chilly

春○寒○
chūn hán
spring cold

中○酒△
zhōng jiǔ
intoxicated

交○加○
jiāo jiā
not fully awaken

晓△梦△
xiǎo mèng
in morning dream

啼○莺●
tí yīng
oriole chattering

I sweep the west garden every day.
I still enjoy the sunny day after the rain.
But the wasps keep dashing on
the ropes of the swing.
The fragrance that your tender fingers
left behind is responsible for their returning.
I lament that you can no longer be seen.
Did the moss on the steps grown in
the night prevent you from coming?

西○園○
xī yuán
the west garden

日△日△
rì rì
daily

掃△林○亭●
sǎo lín tíng
sweep the garden pavilion

依○舊△
yī jiù
still (waiting)

賞△
shǎng
to enjoy

新○晴●
xīn qíng
sunny day after rain

黃○蜂○
huáng fēng
wasps

頻○撲△
pín pū
frequently strike

秋○千○索△
qiū qiān suǒ
the rope of swing

有△當○時○
yǒu dāng shí
back then

纖△手△
qiàn shǒu
tender hands

香○凝●
xiāng níng
fragrance left behind

惆○悵△
chóu chàng
feeling sad

雙○鴛○
shuāng yuān
a pair of shoes

不△到△
bù dào
not coming

幽○階○
yōu jiē
secluded steps

一△夜△
yī yè
over one night

苔○生●
tái shēng
to have grown moss

吴文英

点绛唇

卷尽愁云，素娥临夜新梳洗。暗尘不起。酥润凌波地。　辇路重来，仿佛灯前事。情如水，小楼熏被。春梦笙歌里。

Wu Wenying

Tune: "Dian Jiang Chun"

The Eve of Lantern Festival

The dark clouds were driven away in the sky.
The moon showed her new look after a new bath at night.
No dust rising on the ground.
The place where beautiful girls gathered
was somewhat damp and bright.

I now return to the Emperor's Road.
The images of what took place in front of the lantern resurface again.
Feelings are as tender as water.
I return to the little house and seek
comfort in my warm quilt.
I hope to hear the same music and song in spring dream.

吳文英　**wú wén yīng**
點絳唇　**diǎn jiàng chún**

捲△盡△
juǎn jìn
roll up completely

愁○雲○
chóu yún
dark clouds

素△娥○
sù é
the moon

臨○夜△
lín yè
over night

新○梳○洗▲
xīn shū xǐ
new makeup and bath

暗△塵○
àn chén
gloomy dust

不△起▲
bù qǐ
not to rise

酥○潤△
sū rùn
damp and bright

凌○波○
líng bō
beautiful girls

地▲
dì
place

輦△路△
niǎn lù
Emperor Road

重○來○
chóng lái
revisit

仿△佛△
fǎng fó
seems like

燈○前○
dēng qián
before the lantern

事▲
shì
affairs

情○
qíng
feelings

如○水△
rú shuǐ
like water

小△樓○
xiǎo lóu
little house

熏○被▲
xūn bèi
warm guilt

春○夢△
chūn mèng
spring dream

笙○歌○裡▲
shēng gē lǐ
in the music and song

435

吴文英

唐多令

何处合成愁。离人心上秋。纵芭蕉、不雨也飕飕。都道晚凉天气好，有明月、怕登楼。年事梦中休。花空烟水流。燕辞归、客尚淹留。垂柳不萦裙带住，漫长是、系行舟。

Wu Wenying

Tune: "Tang Duo Ling"

Parting Feelings

How to make up a word of "sorrow"?
"Autumn" above the "heart" of those who part.*
With no rain, bananas still swish in the rain.
They all say that the day is fine
when it is cool at night.
But I am afraid to climb the height
when the moon is bright.

Like fallen flowers drifting in the stream,
my years have been wasted in my dream.
Swallows have all gone.
But I am still around.
Why don't the willow twigs encircle her skirt?
They tie my boat in vain instead.

*The Chinese character for sorrow (愁) is made up of two separate words: autumn (秋) and heart (心).

吳文英　　**wú wén yīng**
唐多令　　**táng duō ling**

何○處△	合△成○	愁●
hé chǔ	*hé chéng*	*chóu*
where	to comprise	sorrow

離○人○	心○上△	秋●
lí rén	*xīn shàng*	*qiū*
person to part	above the heart	autumn

縱△芭○蕉○	不△雨△	也△颼○颼●
zòng bā jiāo	*bù yǔ*	*yě sōu sōu*
even if banana	no rain	still being blown about

都○道△	晚△涼○	天○氣△好△
dōu dào	*wǎn liáng*	*tiān qì hǎo*
all say	evening cool	weather is good

有△明○月△	怕△	登○樓●
yǒu míng yuè	*pà*	*dēng lóu*
bright moon is there	but afraid	to climb the height

年○事△	夢△中○	休●
nián shì	*mèng zhōng*	*xiū*
my years	in the dream	passed

花○空○	煙○水△	流●
huā kōng	*yān shuǐ*	*liú*
fallen flowers	like on misty water	flow

燕△辭○歸○	客△	尚△淹○留●
yàn cí guī	*kè*	*shàng yān liú*
swallows left	traveller	still stay for a long period

垂○柳△	不△縈○	裙○帶△住△
chuí liǔ	*bù yíng*	*qún dài zhù*
dropping willows	not to encircle	the skirt tightly

漫△長○是△	繫△	行○舟●
màn cháng shì	*jì*	*xíng zhōu*
instead all along	tie	my boat

落絮无声春堕泪，行云有影月含羞。

Petals are silently falling.
So do teardrops of Spring.
Behind the floating clouds, the moon hides.
I can see the clouds' shadow at night.

— Wu Wenying

References

Barnstone, T., and Chou, P. (ed.). *The Anchor Book of Chinese Poetry: From Ancient to Contemporary, the Full 3000-Year Tradition*. New York: Anchor Books, 2005.

Herdan, I. (tr.). *The Three Hundred Tang Poems*. Taiwan: The Far East Book Co., 2000.

Graham, A.C. (tr.). *Poems of the Late T'ang*. New York: New York Review Books, 1977.

Liang, S. C. (ed.). *Far East Chinese-English Dictionary*. New York: U.S. International Publishing Inc., 1996

Rexroth, K. (tr.). *One Hundred Poems From the Chinese*. New York: A New Directions Book, 1971.

Chang, Edward C. (tr.). *How to Read a Chinese Poem: A Bilingual Anthology of Tang Poetry*. North Charleston: Booksurge Publishing, 2007.

Wu, J. (ed.). *The Pinyin Chinese-English Dictionary*. Beijing: The Commercial Press, 1979.

Weinberger, E. *Nineteen Ways of Looking at Wang Wei*. Kingston: Asphodel Press, 1987.

Xu, Y. Z. (tr.). *Golden Treasury of Chinese Lyrics*. Peking University Press, 1990.

Xu, Y.Z., Loh, B.Y., and Wu, J. (tr.). *300 Tang Poems: A New Translation*. Hong Kong: The Commercial Press, 1996.

Yip, W. *Chinese Poetry: An Anthology of Major Modes and Genres*. Durham: Duke University Press, 1997.

Witter Bynner (tr.). *Three Hundred Poems of the T'ang Dynasty 618-906*. Taiwan, Taipei: Wen Xiang Book Company, 1987.

Cai, Zong-Qi (ed.). *How to Read Chinese poetry: A Guided Anthology*. New York: Columbia University Press, 2008.

陈良运主编【中国历代词学论著选】，百花洲文艺出版社，一九九八年八月第一版。

陈良运主编【中国历代诗学论著选】，百花洲文艺出版社，一九九五年九，一九九八年八月第一版。

马自毅注译【新译人间词话】，三民书局印行，一九九四年三月初版。

沙灵娜【宋词三百首全译】，贵州人民出版社，一九九一年。

王力【诗词格律十讲】，北京商务印书馆，二零零二年第一版。

余照春亭【增广诗韵集成】，台南市大孚书局有限公司，一九九九年十二月初版。

周渊龙【对韵合璧】湖南大学出版社，二零零二年十二月第一版。

萧涤非等著【唐诗鉴赏词典】，上海辞书出版社，一九八三年十二月第一版。
丁朝阳编著【新解宋词三百首】，崇文馆，二零零六年二月。
汪中注译【新译宋词三百首】，三民书局印行，一九七七年十一月初版。
王莜芸选注【宋词三百首】，大连出版社，一九九二年八月第一版。
周汝昌等著【宋词鉴赏词典】，上海辞书出版社，二零零三年八月第一版。
萧枫主编【唐诗宋词元曲】，线装书局，二零零二年一月第一版。
俞平伯著【唐宋词选释】，人民文学初版社，一九七九年十月北京初版。
冯继魁著【唐宋诗词典故趣闻】，北京燕山初版社，一九九三年七月北京第一版。
王兆鹏、黄崇浩注评【宋词三百首注评】，凤凰初版社，二零零八年十二月第一版。
唐正秋编【中国爱情诗精选】，四川出版社集团，二零零六年六月第一版。
李保民导读【周邦彦词集】，上海古籍出版社，二零一零年七月第一版。
张璟导读【欧阳修词集】，上海古籍出版社，二零一零年七月第一版。
聂安福导读【温庭筠词集、韦庄词集】，上海古籍出版社，二零一零年八月第一版。
李英健、李克主编【辛弃疾词】，万卷出版公司，二零零九年六月第一版。
杨义主编【宋词选评】，岳麓书社出版发行，二零零六年八月第一版。